Designing Surveys

A GUIDE TO DECISIONS AND PROCEDURES

Ronald Czaja
North Carolina State University

Johnny Blair
University of Maryland

Pine Forge Press
Thousand Oaks, California • London • New Delhi

For information, address:

Pine Forge Press
A Sage Publications Company
2455 Teller Road
Thousand Oaks, California 91320
(805) 499-4224
E-mail: sales@pfp.sagepub.com

SAGE Publications Ltd.
6 Bonhill Street
London EC2A 4PU
United Kingdom

SAGE Publications India Pvt. Ltd.
M-32 Market
Greater Kailash I
New Delhi, 110 048 India

Production and Typesetting: Scratchgravel Publishing Services
Production Manager: Rebecca Holland
Designer: Lisa S. Mirski
Cover Design: Paula Shuhert and Graham Metcalfe

Printed in the United States of America

96 97 98 99 10 9 8 7 6 5 4 3 2 1

Library of Congress Cataloging-in-Publication Data
Czaja, Ronald.
　　Designing surveys : a guide to decisions and procedures / Ronald Czaja, Johnny Blair.
　　　　p.　cm. — (The Pine Forge Press series in research methods and statistics)
　　Includes bibliographical references and index.
　　ISBN 0-8039-9056-1 (pbk. : alk. paper)
　　1. Surveys.　2. Sampling (Statistics)　　I. Blair, Johnny.
　II. Title.　III. Series
　HA31.2.C93　1995
　001.4'222—dc20　　　　　　　　　　　　　　94-48280
　　　　　　　　　　　　　　　　　　　　　　　　　　CIP

About the Authors

Ronald Czaja is an Associate Professor of Sociology and Anthropology at North Carolina State University. He teaches courses in both undergraduate and graduate research methodology and medical sociology. His methodological research interests focus on sampling rare populations, response effects in surveys, and the cognitive aspects of questionnaire design. From 1969 to 1990 he worked at the Survey Research Laboratory, University of Illinois at Chicago, as project coordinator, co-head of sampling, assistant director, and principal investigator.

Johnny Blair is Associate Director of the Survey Research Center, University of Maryland. He has conducted methodological research on cognitive aspects of proxy reporting, sampling for special or rare populations, and alternative methods for pretesting questionnaires. He has been a consultant on survey design to many public and private sector organizations. From 1970 to 1989 he worked in sampling and survey management at the Survey Research Laboratory, University of Illinois at Chicago.

About the Publisher

Pine Forge Press is a new educational publisher, dedicated to publishing innovative books and software throughout the social sciences. On this and any other of our publications, we welcome your comments and suggestions.

Please call or write us at:

Pine Forge Press
A Sage Publications Company
2455 Teller Road
Thousand Oaks, California 91320
(805) 499-4224
E-mail: sales@pfp.sagepub.com

Contents

Appendix C

Series Foreword

The Pine Forge Press Series in Methods and Statistics, consisting of core books in methods and statistics and a series of satellite volumes on specialized topics, allows instructors to create a customized curriculum.The authors of the core volumes are both seasoned researchers and distinguished teachers, and the more specialized texts are written by acknowledged experts in their fields. To date, the series offers the core text in research methods and three satellite volumes focusing on sampling, field methods, and survey research. To be published soon are the core text in statistics and accompanying satellite volumes on such specific topics as regression and data analysis, as well as additional supplementary volumes in research methods.

In *Designing Surveys,* Ronald Czaja and Johnny Blair offer an accurate account of how modern survey research is conducted, but with the needs and goals of a novice researcher in mind. Based on the authors' considerable experience as survey practitioners, their primer on survey design conveys not only practical guidelines but also the logical principles underlying effective technique. This volume is streamlined enough to be used in conjunction with Russell Schutt's core text, *Investigating the Social World,* in a basic social research methods course, or it can be combined with Richard Maisel and Caroline Hodges Persell's *How Sampling Works* in a course on sample survey methodology. It can also stand alone as a compact handbook for anyone who wishes to use survey research methods to answer questions about the social world.

Richard T. Campbell
Kathleen S. Crittenden
Series Editors

Preface

Few areas of the social sciences are more widely used and valued by our society than survey research. In every sphere of human activity, from the most intimate to the most public, we depend on scientifically reliable surveys to inform our judgments about what is going on and what actions we should take as individuals, businesses, communities, and nations. Although most of us will not become professional survey researchers, it is likely that we will use information from surveys or be involved in designing a survey as part of our personal or professional lives. At one time or another, in some part of our work or personal lives, even more of us will depend on the validity and reliability of survey data generated by others. This book is written both for the nonspecialist engaged in designing a survey research project for the first time and for those who may already have some knowledge and experience with surveys.

Because of its wide use throughout all sectors of society, survey research has undergone significant changes and improvements in recent times. For example, the increase in unpublished telephone numbers in the 1970s necessitated the development of various methods of random-digit dialing. In the early 1980s, personal computers led to the development of computer-assisted telephone interviewing (CATI), making it possible to conduct more rigorous and complex telephone surveys. Today, interviewers are using personal computers in face-to-face interviews, resulting in fewer errors when using longer questionnaires and a shorter time lag between data collection and the creation of a data file for analysis. Survey research has changed in nontechnological ways as well. From advances in cognitive psychology, we have improved our understanding of the question-answering process and the design of survey questions. And in the quest for more valid and reliable surveys, we now place more emphasis on combinations of such questionnaire development procedures as focus groups, expert panels, and behavior coding.

We wrote this book because we want to encourage an approach to designing and conducting surveys that combines application of these new methodologies within a careful and practical decision-making process. Unlike the approach usually found in research methods texts, the approach here describes the design and conduct of a survey as a process of closely related decision points whose goal is to make optimum use of resources that are typically very limited. In conducting a survey, the researcher does not make all critical decisions up-front and then set the "machinery" on autopilot, returning after some time to analyze the data. There are multiple stages to every survey, and within each stage, a number of activities must take place. The interrelationship among these stages and activities must be constantly managed, monitored, and evaluated to ensure that the final product is reliable and valid. This book focuses on the many decision points in the survey process and the inevitable trade-offs between scientific rigor, schedule, and resources that these decisions necessitate.

In choosing this approach, we too had to make some decisions. Our book does not focus on the entire survey process. The emphasis is on the initial stages of a survey through completion of data collection. We chose this focus because, although there are many good books on data analysis, there are few that address the many considerations and difficult decisions involved in the survey design and data collection processes. We also want to make available to the inexperienced survey researcher the important improvements in questionnaire development tools that have been absent in methods texts. We believe this approach teaches the skills that beginning researchers need to conduct survey research and also provides the additional insights they need to analyze data. As they study this text, novice researchers will learn to recognize that all data are not of equal worth. They will learn that how the data are collected, what questions are asked of respondents, and how the questions are asked affect the results in many ways that are apparent only to those who have been involved in collecting data.

We had another purpose in writing this book. We encourage beginning researchers to recognize areas where there is still a great deal that is unknown. Once they have read this book and conducted their first survey, they will realize this. We hope this approach will encourage these future researchers to think more carefully about the practice of survey research and to conduct methodological studies as part of their substantive investigations. In this way, we can advance our knowledge in both methods studies and substantive investigations.

The successful completion of this book owes a great deal to the support we received from a number of people. We wish to thank several readers who gave us their reactions to earlier drafts, including Richard Campbell, Kathleen Crittenden, Ralph Kuhn, Michael Mussagli, Amy McLaughlin, Helen Miller, Stephanie Prescott, Stanley Presser, and Jammie Price. We want to extend special thanks to Seymour Sudman for his many helpful comments, not only on this manuscript but also throughout our years of association. Thanks go to Dominic Perri for editorial comments and to Rosalind Pinkard for typing and formatting. Two other individuals must be acknowledged for their yeoman's efforts: Elizabeth Eastman, for her extensive substantive and editorial comments on numerous drafts, and Judy Cline, for her outstanding secretarial and manuscript preparation assistance.

Comments and suggestions about the contents of this book would be appreciated. We can be reached by e-mail at the following: ronc@server.sasw.ncsu.edu and johnny@cati.umd.edu.

1 An Introduction to Surveys and to This Book

It would be difficult to name another social science method that has so quickly and pervasively penetrated our society as the sample survey. In less than two generations, the notion of relying on relatively small probability samples to measure, among other things, public attitudes and behaviors has grown from a little-noted curiosity to the dominant practice. It is commonplace to look first to surveys to gauge such important national issues as preelection preference for presidential candidates, consumer confidence in the economy, the level of unemployment, the accuracy of the decennial census, the rates of occurrence of different types of crimes, or the public's knowledge about health issues such as AIDS risk behavior. In the marketplace, surveys are used to test public reactions before new products are introduced, and on the production line, to monitor the quality of that newly made merchandise. In academia, surveys provide data for social scientists testing models and hypotheses in fields as diverse as economics, sociology, and psychology. In fact, so successful has been the survey method in so many aspects of research and public policy that one must be cautious not to use a survey in inappropriate circumstances.

This science on which we place such impressive burdens is, if not exactly a toddler, no more than an adolescent, strong in some ways, inexperienced and unsure in others. In some of its various aspects, the sample survey may rely on powerful mathematical tools; in others it is dependent on empirical experience with incomplete theoretical underpinnings; and in still others it makes use of conventions and practices that have only recently risen above the level of professional folk wisdom.

If this state of affairs is perplexing to the professional practitioners of this new science, it is especially daunting for the novice or the occasional user who needs to conduct a survey or interpret the results of one.

The Practice of Survey Research

Survey research is inherently interdisciplinary. Sampling and estimation procedures require a knowledge of probability theory and statistics. Data collection involves persuasion of respondents and then, on some level, social interaction between them and interviewers. Interviews depend on language comprehension and discourse. While few professional practitioners are expert in statistical theory, psycholinguistics or sociolinguistics, and cognitive psychology, each of these disciplines speaks to some area of survey research. When one adds to these the management expertise necessary to conduct even moderate-size surveys, the enterprise seems daunting. Yet surveys, even very large and complex ones, are done all the time. And although, to the extent we can determine, they often produce usefully reliable and valid results, in many cases they do not.

When the survey enterprise is successful, it is largely because at each stage in designing and conducting surveys researchers focus on a relatively small number of key scientific principles and practical guidelines that are applied in a series of key decisions. The aim of this book is to provide practical guidance for the reader to do the same. While it will not produce the high-level expert described above, this book will be a realistic guide to the effective conduct of small-scale surveys.

Even modest-size surveys typically require considerable time, material, money, and assistance. One can find examples of surveys designed and implemented by the lone researcher, but they are the exception. Unlike some scientific or scholarly enterprises, surveys are usually a team effort of many people with diverse skills. Even if the researcher who formulates the research questions also designs the questionnaire and analyzes the data, that person will almost always use help in collecting the data and entering it into a computer file, as well as in performing numerous clerical tasks. Thus, whether the survey is an organization's endeavor or a class project, there is a division of labor, a coordination of tasks, and the incurrence of costs. Accomplishing all this with limited resources and, at the same time, maximizing the survey's quality, requires a series of decisions by the researcher.

A project guided by such a series of judicious decisions will make the best use of all its resources—not just money, materials, and labor but also time, information, and talent. It is on these decision points, which often require compromises or trade-offs, that this book focuses. We will show how the researcher, after the specification of the research questions, reconciles the ideal with the possible through all aspects of survey and questionnaire design, sampling, and data collection. To illustrate the process, we have selected actual research projects whose design and implementation issues complement each other. Each chapter highlights the decision points in these research projects and draws on other examples as well.

As we noted earlier, surveys are not appropriate in all circumstances. Therefore, before discussing some general aspects of sample surveys, we offer the following guidelines for deciding whether or not to conduct a survey in the first place. After all, if we try to use a survey in inappropriate situations, we can hardly expect success.

Surveys are based on the desire to collect information (usually by questionnaire) about a well-defined population. The questionnaire, alternatively referred to as the instrument, typically contains a series of related questions for the respondents to answer. The questions are most often, but not always, in a closed format in which a set of numbered response alternatives is specified. The resulting numerical, or quantitative, data are then entered into a data file for statistical analysis.

This thumbnail description of a survey implies several simple, but essential, conditions for the appropriate use of surveys. The target population must be clearly defined, usually in terms of a simple combination of demographic characteristics and geographic boundaries. For example, a target population might be all persons age 18 or older residing in households with telephones in Maryland. The population should be defined so that its members can be unequivocally identified. A population defined by a set of attitudes or beliefs, however, is generally a bad idea. Nor should the definition be overly restrictive, such as immigrant males age 20 to 30 who earn between $15,000 and $35,000 per year. While there are methods for surveying rare populations, they are complex and expensive. In some cases, even these methods may not suffice to survey a particularly scarce group, such as people with an extremely rare health condition. The novice researcher should be wary of entering such territory.

In addition, we must be convinced that the majority of respondents will know the information we ask them to provide. It makes little sense to ask people questions, such as the net worth of their families, that many in the targeted population, maybe most, will not be able to answer.

Finally, the goals of the analysis should generally be statistical in nature, such as to describe or model an aggregate set of population characteristics or to answer a single or related set of research questions dependent on quantitative measures.

The Uses of Surveys

Making use of sophisticated statistical methods such as multiple regression and analysis of variance, researchers can use survey data to test hypotheses and study causal relationships between variables. The pairing of survey data with advanced analytic methods has become, along with theory building and psychology experiments in laboratories, one of the foremost means of social investigation. But on the most basic level, the idea of a survey begins with the desire to know, which is to say measure, some unknown characteristic of a population. That characteristic is often a simple parameter, such as the proportion of the adult U.S. population who smoke cigarettes or own a VCR, the total number of households that employ domestic help, or the average annual household expenditure for entertainment (however we choose to define that vague term). More complex statistics can be measured as well—for example, the ratio of savings or investments to income. A survey also may be aimed at only one segment of the population, such as the elderly, households with young children, or people who own computers. It is also common for researchers to be interested in analysis of a particular subgroup in addition to the total population results. So, for example, we may want to determine the general population's perceptions of crime as well as analyze perceptions by racial group, or by city dwellers compared to suburban residents. On the other hand, we may not be interested in the general population at all but only in farmers' attitudes about the environmental effects of pesticides or in college students' average school-year expenses. Much of survey methodology, particularly sampling theory, is aimed at obtaining estimates of such population parameters in a rigorous fashion. Most of the focus of this book is the same. Yet, it is important to understand that these survey methods are equally applicable to the needs of the model builder and the describer of populations. That is, there is not one survey methodology for the hypothesis tester and another for the policy analyst seeking only to measure parameters such as those noted above. In fact, a distinguishing property of surveys is that the resulting data are often put to both descriptive and analytic uses. Government surveys, for example, tell us things like the proportion of persons with a regular place to seek health care (National Health Interview Survey) or the total number of adults who were unemployed last month (Current Population Survey). These same data are used by sociologists, economists, and others with interests much different from obtaining those simple point estimates.

Overview of the Survey Process

Though the focus of this book is on survey design and implementation, we must begin with the process of specifying the study's analysis goals. We should recognize that this step is, in fact, usually a *process* that develops in the course of the survey's development rather than a full-blown plan from the start. It is commonplace in survey books to acknowledge that we should, at the outset, have an analysis plan that answers certain questions, such as: Are we interested in obtaining only point estimates or in more complex measures as well? Which variables are key to our research; which are secondary? Are we concerned with particular subgroup estimates, or not? Exactly what analysis is planned? What will our data tables look like? If we have multiple goals, what are their priorities? Exactly what are the research questions we hope to answer?

These are all good and important questions, and some of them can be answered right away. It is also likely that some components of the analysis plan cannot be exactly specified or will change as we develop the questionnaire. During instrument development we are forced to think much more concretely about how particular questions will be used and what—exactly—they mean. We will come up against limits on questionnaire length and have to decide which questions are retained and which are dropped. So, while lip service is often paid to the need for a fully specified analysis plan early on, which is unchanged throughout the study, the reality is usually quite different.

Regardless of the subsequent uses of the data, the survey researcher must always carefully define the target population about which information is needed; obtain or develop a sampling frame that lists that population; decide on a sample design that describes precisely how population members will be selected; develop an **estimation plan**[1] for computing values of the population parameters

[1]Note: **Boldface** terms in the text are defined in the Glossary/Index.

from the sample estimates; decide on a data collection method for conducting interviews; and specify detailed data collection procedures to ensure the quality of the data in each data collection stage.

Each of these steps involves making choices between alternative methods, and each of these technical decisions is *inherently* also a decision about the expenditure of resources. The intent of this book is to provide guidance in making decisions in the context of fixed resources. These resources will sometimes be financial, but more often (especially for the first-time researcher working with colleagues who volunteer their time) will have to do with time or other nonmonetary support. Unlike a large government or business survey, in which the goal is to achieve a certain level of precision while minimizing cost, our survey model is a fixed-cost model, meaning that our goal is to obtain the best measures we can within a given "budget."

Implicit in this decision-points approach is the notion that, while there are many wrong ways to go about designing and conducting a survey, there is no one right way. Instead, there are different approaches suited to particular goals, target populations, resources, and other constraints. We hold that (for the types of goals noted above) **probability sampling,** giving every population member a known (non-zero) chance of inclusion, is always preferred over convenience sampling, which takes whatever people are most easily obtained. In choosing the survey respondents with probability samples, we have a statistical basis for making statements based on the sample, about the population. Still, the choice of available probability sample designs is wide and the consequences of that choice important. Moreover, each design requires a series of further choices about specific implementation procedures.

We try to write questionnaires that will convey to respondents a uniformly understood request for information. This task is a difficult one for which we have fewer scientific principles to follow than we do for sample design. We know what we mean a question to convey and are often baffled as to why others don't quickly know it too. As soon as we begin testing our draft instrument, unintended meanings begin to emerge. There are many ways of testing a questionnaire, which we shall describe in detail, but a large part of the benefit of testing seems to come from simply exposing the questionnaire to people not involved in its construction. Whether they are potential respondents, friends and colleagues, or survey experts, they do not know the exact intent of the question and so must depend on what it literally says, on its words and context, to infer that intent.

Researchers often underestimate the impact of context while writing individual questions, but it often becomes _pivotal_ when those items are combined in the instrument and each question can exert a subtle influence on the interpretation of those that follow. As Caron (1992) points out, "The ambiguity inherent in all natural languages invests the context of the utterance with a determining role in the construction of meanings." Nevertheless, our efforts to avoid ambiguity must not oversimplify or undermine a question's substantive intent.

In data collection, we will always be concerned with selecting an interview method appropriate to the kinds of questions we intend to ask as well as with obtaining cooperation from as many respondents as possible. But those concerns alone will not tell us whether mail, telephone, group administration, or personal visit is best for our study; nor, once that choice is made, will they guide us through the various subsequent procedures to carry out the data collection. It is in such fundamental decision making and procedural tactics that this book offers guidance.

Throughout, we also address concerns about the effects of choices between, for example, reduced list (sampling frame) coverage versus cost of the frame; the collection of more data from a small number of respondents versus less data from a larger number; bigger samples versus better cooperation rates; or inclusion of sensitive questions versus the risk of more respondent refusals to answer them. At the same time, issues of production and quality control during data collection draw considerably on our attention and resources.

One final principle underlying our approach is the counsel of Sudman (1976) to keep in mind how good a survey needs to be for the purposes at hand. While as survey researchers we strive to conduct the highest-quality project feasible, we also recognize that all surveys do not need the same levels of precision and reliability. A survey conducted by a faculty member under a grant will likely have quality imperatives that the undergraduate class project will not; and neither requires the levels of precision of a major government survey such as the current population survey (CPS) or the National Health Interview Survey (NHIS). So while we aim for excellence in every phase of the project, we must be realistic as to what is both necessary and achievable. That realization, while not easily quantifiable, will help guide many of our choices—and may even determine whether we decide to go ahead with the survey.

/Once we have decided that a survey is both appropriate for our research and within our means, we begin to specify its major requirements. First, what is the time frame? If the study is part of a one- or two-semester class, at what point do the data need to be available? If the study is for an outside sponsor, are there time constraints posed by its needs? Once the question of project schedule is answered, we are faced with a whole series of decisions about the survey's characteristics, including the necessary sample size and approximate interview length. Before we can begin designing the survey in detail, we need at least a general notion of these study conditions, and we need to determine whether they are in line with our resources.

Thus, we cannot begin too early to list the resources at our disposal and balance them against the aims of our research. In this way we continue to shape the broad outlines of our project and prepare to make the first major decision confronting us, the selection of a data collection method.

A Brief Summary of This Book

Before we discuss data collection, we describe the general stages in the development and completion of a survey in chapter 2: survey design and preliminary planning; pretesting; final survey design and planning; data collection; data coding, data-file construction and analysis. This chapter emphasizes the critical points in the survey process and the many decisions that must be made. The chapter concludes with an example of a time schedule for a national telephone survey. The major tasks and the time allocated for each are outlined.

Chapter 3 briefly describes mail, telephone, and face-to-face surveys and points out the advantages and disadvantages of each method in terms of required resources, questionnaire design, and data quality. The data collection methods are compared with regard to costs, time needed for data collection, limitations on questionnaire length and complexity, types of questions that can be asked, use of visual aids, establishment of rapport, sensitive questions, and typical cooperation rates. A number of examples from actual studies illustrate these points.

Chapter 4, which addresses questionnaire construction, begins with a simple set of characteristics that constitute a good questionnaire. Then, through numerous examples, we show how to write individual questions that balance the information desired with the ability of respondents to provide valid and reliable answers. We also provide guidelines for deciding which questions to include in the instrument. Chapter 5 continues questionnaire design with a discussion of typical questionnaires. The crucial issue of how to begin the questionnaire is given particular attention. The reader is then shown how to organize the questionnaire from its introduction, through each section, to its conclusion. Chapter 6 is a comprehensive treatment of questionnaire testing. Drawing on the most recent research in instrument design, we show readers how to use each of the major pretesting methods and how to interpret the test results.

Chapter 7 introduces sampling basics, beginning with the differences between nonprobability and probability samples. The chapter focuses on the probability sample and illustrates why it is the preferred method. Particular attention is given to the key tasks in developing and selecting probability samples, including defining the population, constructing and evaluating sample lists, and handling unexpected situations and common problems. The chapter also responds to one of the most frequently asked questions, "What sample size do I need for my survey?" A number of examples illustrate how to use census data in planning a survey and for estimating whether the number of interviews with important subgroups will be adequate for the analysis planned.

Chapter 8 provides a number of sampling examples. We describe how to select a local and a national random-digit telephone sample and how to randomly select a respondent within a sample household for interview. The chapter concludes with two examples of how to select student samples from lists.

Chapter 9 defines the major sources of survey error, or imprecision. The reader is helped to decide which potential error sources should be of most concern in a particular study, and what steps can be taken to reduce them. Errors arising from the sampling and data collection stages are given full treatment, including sampling frame problems, unit nonresponse, and item nonresponse. Effective data collection procedures are described in detailed examples. Finally, the chapter addresses the issue of budgeting and cost trade-offs.

Chapter 10 is devoted to an often neglected phase of the survey research study—the methodological report. First, the reader is shown the importance of a complete description of the survey methods. Quality profiles are defined and their major components described. Then the reader is shown, through many examples, both how to decide what issues to include in a particular study's report and what to say about them. The chapter ends with a brief guide to the major recent literature on methodology.

2 Stages of a Survey

The five general stages in the development and completion of a survey, as shown in Exhibit 2.1, are:

1. Survey design and preliminary planning
2. Pretesting
3. Final survey design and planning
4. Data collection
5. Data coding, data-file construction, analysis, and final report

In this chapter, we discuss the decisions called for at each of the five stages. The following are especially critical points in the design and implementation of a survey (see boldface boxes in Exhibit 2.1):

- *Design survey:* Key preliminary decisions about method of data collection and sampling are made.
- *Pretest:* Decisions from multiple activities are tested and evaluated.
- *Revise survey design and operations plan:* Final design decisions are made.
- *Collect data:* Data collection and quality-control procedures are carried out.

Stage 1: Survey Design and Preliminary Planning

Stage 1 involves the issues discussed in chapter 1: specification of the research problem and the research questions that the survey will address. At this stage we must decide the goals of the research and determine how best to accomplish them within the available time and resources. We first need to specify the goals of the survey.

Exhibit 2.1 **The Stages of a Survey**

Stages involved in the questionnaire + interview techniques

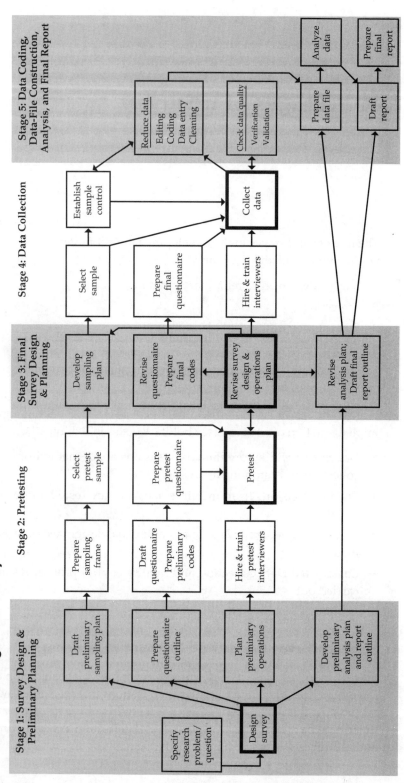

Stage 1: Survey Design & Preliminary Planning

Stage 2: Pretesting

Stage 3: Final Survey Design & Planning

Stage 4: Data Collection

Stage 5: Data Coding, Data-File Construction, Analysis, and Final Report

- Is the goal to test a hypothesis? For example,

  Females are more likely than males to believe that a woman should be allowed to have an abortion for any reason.

- Is the goal to test a causal model that suggests a series of interrelated hypotheses? For example,

  1. People with conventional values are less likely to have ever used amphetamines;

  2. People with drug-using friends are more likely to have used amphetamines; and

  3. People with conventional values are less likely to have drug-using friends.

- Is the goal to estimate the proportion of people who hold a certain belief or that engage in a specific behavior? For example,

  What proportion of the population believe that our criminal justice system is working well?

  What proportion of the population were the victims of robbery in the last year?

These three goals would typically require general population studies of adults. Other goals may not concern the general population but might relate to specific **subgroups** in the population. For example, we may be interested in knowing what dental hygienists think about changing the requirements for state licensure, what the attitudes of university faculty are about joining a union, or what proportion of a migrant worker's income is spent on health care. Another possibility is that our goal may not be concerned with individuals at all, but with organizations, groups, businesses, or governmental units. We may want to know what the annual membership rates are for specific types of organizations or the dropout rate for high school juniors and seniors for every high school or school district in a state. Specifying the goals provides the framework for the next set of decisions: Who or what is the population of interest, and what should be the method of data collection?

Making Sampling Decisions

One of the most basic sampling questions must be answered at stage 1: Who or what is the population of interest? In studies of individuals, two considerations are the eligible age of the respondents and the geographic area to which we want to generalize the results. For example, if we are doing a general population survey, should we include people 18 years and older or 21 and older, or should we include 17-year-olds? When making this decision, we need to keep the research questions in mind. If we are conducting a survey on the public's perceptions of crime on public transportation, we would want to include both respondents who use public transportation and those who do not. We should consider setting as the minimum age of eligible respondents that at which people begin regularly using the system, perhaps 16 or even 14 if we are conducting the research in areas where students use public transportation to get to and from school.

When studying groups, we must decide who in the group or organization is the most knowledgeable individual and can provide accurate information. For example, if we are interested in learning the average cost and length of a hospital stay for a specific type of surgery, we would want to survey the chief financial officer at each hospital in our sample. Sometimes determining the best person may require a phone call to the site or organization. We might also contact the head of the organization and request that he or she or a knowledgeable delegate complete the interview or the questionnaire. If we need different types of information (e.g., usual cost for cataract surgery, number of births, number of cancer patients seen) from each group, information might have to be collected from two or three different individuals within the organization. The key point is that it is important to specify or locate knowledgeable respondents—also known as informants—when seeking information about a group.

Another consideration is the geographic area we want the survey to represent. Let's continue with the example of a survey of public perceptions of crime on public transportation. In some cities, public transportation serves not only the central city but also some suburbs. However, coverage in the suburbs is usually not as extensive as it is in the central city and is often provided by a different company. We must decide how inclusive the survey should be. Should we focus only on the central city, on the entire transportation system, or on the central city and certain suburbs? There is no magic formula or rule of thumb for making that decision; it must be based on the articulation of the research questions and the available resources.

When these decisions are made, trade-offs must be considered. Consulting census data will help in determining the ramifications of expanding or contracting the age definition of eligible respondents.

Assume, for example, that we can afford 500 telephone interviews. If we use an eligible age definition of 21 and older, all 500 interviews will be conducted with people in this age group. However, if we decide to expand the definition to people 14 and older, some interviews will be conducted with people 14–20, and fewer than 500 interviews will be conducted with people 21 and older. If we learn from census data that the 14–20 age group comprises 13% of the eligible population and our survey is conducted properly, then approximately 65 interviews (13% of 500 = 65) will be conducted with respondents age 14–20, and 65 fewer interviews will be conducted with respondents 21 and older. As we will discuss later, the more interviews we conduct with a given group or subgroup, other things being equal, the more confidence we can place in the results. Thus, while the confidence in our overall survey results does not change, the confidence in the results for respondents 21 and older does change because we have fewer interviews with them. Similar trade-offs must be considered in the decision to include or exclude suburban respondents in the study universe. The logic is the same. If we have a fixed budget and decide to include some or all of the suburbs, then some of the city interviews would have to be allocated to the suburbs, resulting in less confidence in the city results. (This issue of trade-offs is discussed further in chapter 7.)

Similar decisions must be made in the study of organizations, institutions, or businesses. For example, we are interested in studying school systems, we must decide if we want to include both public and private schools. If hospitals are the population of interest, we must decide whether we are interested in only for-profit hospitals or whether we should include nonprofit hospitals. In addition, we may want to survey only hospitals with a minimum bed size or hospitals that provide specific services. We resolve these issues by examining the goals of our research and by assessing our available resources.

A second sampling question that must be addressed is the availability of a sampling frame from which to select a random sample from the study population. The **sampling frame** is the source (or sources) that includes the population of eligible people or groups. Sometimes the frame matches perfectly the population we want to study. The list or resource includes, for example, every individual or school in the population of interest. On other occasions the frame may include more than the population of interest, and we would need to screen sample members to determine whether they are eligible or not. Or, the frame may not include all of the eligible population members, and then we must decide whether it is adequate for our purpose. Here are two examples of sampling frames:

1. If we want to conduct a survey of all students enrolled at a university, we would ask the registrar's office for a list of all currently enrolled students that includes their addresses and telephone numbers. This list would be our sampling frame.

2. If we wanted to do a telephone survey of adults in North Carolina, we might go about obtaining copies of telephone directories that include, together, all areas of the state. These books would constitute our sampling frame.[1]

Telephone directories are among the most common sampling frames for general population surveys. However, using a telephone directory raises an important question—How well does the sampling frame represent the eligible population? In other words, what proportion of the eligible population does the frame include? What kinds of people may not be included on the frame? Obviously, people without telephones are excluded, as well as those with unlisted telephone numbers.

Sampling frames frequently do not include everyone in the eligible population. When the population definition and the sampling frame do not match, we need to ask the following questions: What percent of the population is missing? Who are these people? If we exclude them, how will the results for the **dependent variable**—the variable we want to explain or estimate—be affected? We are asking, in essence, how much bias we will allow in our survey. In most urban areas of the country, the percentage of households with an unlisted number is much larger than the percentage of households without telephones. Fortunately, **random-digit dialing (RDD)** techniques, which we discuss in chapter 6, allow researchers to overcome some of the bias of using a telephone directory. However, the bias from excluding nontelephone households cannot be overcome without assuming the costly task of finding them. National data indicate that about 6% of households do not have a telephone (Thornberry and Massey, 1988). On average, we would need to visit in person about seventeen households ($16.6 \times 6 \approx 100\%$) to find one without a telephone—a great expenditure of time and money. (Keep in mind that these are national figures and that the proportion for a particular area is likely to be different.)

---

[1]We will learn in chapter 6 that there is a simpler and better sampling frame for this type of telephone survey.

Most researchers who conduct surveys ignore the bias that results from excluding nontelephone households. They do so for three main reasons. First, they assume the nontelephone households will have a small or negligible effect on the final results. Since the telephone group is so much larger than the nontelephone group, the differences between them would have to be great before the results from the nontelephone group could affect the final results. Second, the cost to include nontelephone households is too great, especially since they constitute so small a percentage of the total population. Third, total sample results are of primary importance to the researcher, and subgroup results are not of major importance. In some cases, however, these assumptions are not valid, and the impact of excluding nontelephone households must be considered carefully.

The proportion of households without telephones varies by region of the country and by demographic characteristics (Thornberry and Massey, 1988). The highest incidence of households without telephones occurs in the southern United States (10.4%), in rural nonfarm areas (9.9%), in one-person households (9.9%), and in households of six or more (10.8%). Among demographic groups, the highest incidence of nontelephone households is found in African American households (15.6%), Hispanic households (4.5%–22.1%), people who are separated from spouses (18.8%), the unemployed (16%), and those living below the poverty index (27.4%). The percentage of households with telephones increases as education, family income, and age increase. Those age 65 and older have the highest telephone coverage (about 97%).

We need to ask whether it is worth trying to include nontelephone households in our survey. The answer, once again, depends on the research problem, our resources, and the location of our research. If we are interested in the opinions of the unemployed or those living below the poverty index, we will want to consider a combination of methods or a method other than a telephone survey, which would exclude one of every six unemployed persons and one of every four households below the poverty index. We should keep in mind that these are national ratios and that the numbers for any specific community may differ significantly. We also know that nontelephone households have lower incomes or are households in transition.[2] People in these types of households may hold different opinions or engage in different behaviors than people in households

---

[2]Households in transition include people who have moved recently; immigrants; the unemployed; people who are divorced, separated, or widowed; and so forth.

with telephones, depending on the variables under study. We should always consult census data or other available data about our survey area to help in planning the research. (See chapters 7 and 8.)

Designing the Questionnaire

The types of information we need to collect from respondents and how best to elicit that information are two key decisions that must be made early in the survey-design phase. We need to know whether we will be asking many **open-ended questions** ("What is the most difficult problem facing families today?"), mostly **closed-ended questions** ("Do you approve or disapprove of abortion?"), or both. In the former category of questions, the respondents answer in their own words. In the latter, respondents choose from a list of provided responses. We should also consider whether we will be asking attitude, knowledge, or behavior questions and determine what types of demographic information we need because these decisions can affect our choice of a data collection method. A personal interview or face-to-face survey is probably best if it is essential to (1) hand respondents lists of choices from which they are to select an answer, (2) give them other types of visual aids to help formulate answers (e.g., pictures that we want them to evaluate, response cards to be categorized, etc.), or (3) have them consult personal records or perform other memory assisting tasks, Similarly, if we need to ask a number of open-ended questions, we would not conduct a mail survey because many respondents will not complete a questionnaire that requires a lot of writing. We always want to make the respondent's task as easy as possible, thus minimizing the reasons for not responding.

Determining Available Money and Time

Two other important factors to consider in the preliminary design stage are the amounts of money and time we have for conducting the survey. Money and time determine how many interviews we can afford; whether we can hire interviewers to collect the data and coders to code it, and how many of each; and, in some cases, how large a geographic area we can include in the survey. Generally, mail is the cheapest survey method, followed by telephone surveys; face-to-face surveys are the most expensive. When it is possible to conduct a group-administered survey—for example, with students in classrooms—this may be the cheapest and quickest survey method. In terms of time, telephoning is faster than face-to-face interviewing;

however, the time to complete both is somewhat dependent on the size or geographic distribution of the sample. Mail surveys are less affected by these variables, since the procedures for conducting mail surveys are the same regardless of sample size and geographic distribution. A first mailing is followed by a reminder postcard in approximately two weeks; a few weeks later, a second cover letter and questionnaire are sent, and a few weeks later, a third mailing or a telephone call is made. Thus, the data collection phase of a mail survey usually lasts 8 to 10 weeks, regardless of the sample size and its geographic distribution.

Analyzing Data and Reporting Survey Results

In the preliminary design stage, we must give some thought to the kinds of analyses we need to answer the research questions and the time it will take to prepare a study report, papers, or other products proposed from the research effort. If we ourselves are not doing all of the end-stage work (i.e., data analysis and interpretation, writing, and typing), we must have some idea of how the tasks will be shared and how much time to allocate to them. This step is important not only for estimating the total cost of the survey but also for planning the number of persons and person-hours necessary for completing the work. Time schedules and costs can vary widely, depending on the type and the scope of the survey work.

Stage 2: Pretesting

In stage 2 of the survey process, we begin testing our initial design decisions. This step entails preparing the sampling frame, record-keeping forms, and survey questions and then testing these items to see how well the process is working. To begin, we assemble a sampling frame or, better yet, determine if an acceptable one already exists.

Drafting the Questionnaire

In putting together initial drafts of our questionnaire, borrowing questions from other research studies is acceptable, even encouraged. While we are reviewing past studies with the same or similar research problems, we take notes on how the researchers defined their concepts and the questions they used to measure these concepts.

When we agree with what they did, we are free to use the same wording, unless they copyrighted the questions or scales.[3] If we agree with parts of what they did, we use the parts we agree with and then add our own ideas and wording. Using someone else's questions has another advantage: By asking the same questions, we can compare the results in our survey area with the results from the previous research.

There are two caveats regarding questionnaire development to keep in mind. First, we should never assume that because we are using someone else's questions and they reported no problems with them that these questions will work as well with our study respondents. No matter how many questions we borrow from others, we must always pretest the questionnaire before we start the data collection. Pretesting, like a dress rehearsal before opening night, is one of the most important components of a survey. In fact, if we are developing or asking many new questions, we may want to plan two or three pretests to make sure that the respondents understand the questions and that what we are trying to achieve is working at least on a miniature scale. It is better to keep doing pretest interviews until we feel comfortable with the questionnaire—which may require thirty, forty, or fifty interviews—than to start the main data collection, find problems, and either stop the data collection to fix them (which is nearly impossible) or end up collecting interviews that have obvious measurement problems.

The second caveat concerns the number of questionnaire drafts. Expect to do many drafts of the questionnaire to get to the stage where all the problems seem to be worked out and the respondents' interpretations are incorporated into the questions. Often the difference between a good study and a poor one is that in the former, researchers look for or anticipate problems and, in the latter, researchers assume that if the questions are answered, the data are valid. We should guard against this faulty assumption.

Using Interviewers

For telephone and personal interview surveys, we need to start thinking about how many interviewers we will need and begin assembling and writing training materials that explain how we want

[3]Most survey researchers do not encourage or support the copyrighting of survey questions. The standard procedure is to freely encourage the use of the same questions in order to test the reliability and validity of the items with different populations and at different times.

things done. Both written training materials and the training of interviewers are necessary whether professional interviewers, volunteers, or students are doing the interviewing.

Selecting and hiring interviewers must be closely coordinated with sample selection. For personal interview surveys, we want the interviewers to live reasonably close to the selected households to minimize the amount of travel time and expense required to contact respondents. In a class project, for example, to interview respondents on the north side of town, we would assign students who live close by. Since telephone interviewers usually conduct interviews at a central, supervised location, where they live is unimportant.

The amount of time allocated for pretesting determines the number of pretest interviewers that we will need. If we have a week for pretesting and we need thirty personal interviews, we would probably want to hire and train six interviewers, each of whom would conduct five interviews. For telephone interviewing we might want to use three interviewers, each of whom would average ten completed interviews. We use our best interviewers, if possible, because we want critical feedback on any potential problems with our questionnaire or survey procedures.

Debriefing Interviewers

At the end of each pretest, all interviewers meet with researchers in a debriefing session to go over each question in the questionnaire and all the survey procedures to determine where the problems are and to propose possible solutions. The group meeting encourages an interactive exchange of ideas in which one person's comments triggers a comment or idea someone else may have forgotten. Feedback from the meeting, along with the reading of the actual interviews, provides the basis for revising the questionnaire.

Deciding on Pretest Methods

Pretesting can be done in a number of different ways and steps. In the early phases, the purpose of pretesting is to get feedback on individual questionnaire items. In the later phases the purpose is to test the entire questionnaire and the survey procedures. Questionnaire items are usually tested both informally and formally. As we begin writing questions, we should think about how respondents will react to or interpret specific questions. Colleagues and students may also be asked to try out questions and provide feedback. The first draft of the questionnaire may be tested informally on family, friends, other students, and so forth. When the questions seem to be working well with these people, it is time for a more formal test of the questionnaire with real respondents in the survey area.

Two procedures are now used more and more in the development of questionnaires. One is think-aloud interviews and the other is focus groups.[4] **Think alouds** are one-on-one sessions, with an interviewer and a respondent. Interviewers ask respondents what thoughts occurred to them as the questions were read to them. For example, the questionnaire might contain the following questions:

- What does *food safety* mean to you?
- How important are food safety issues to you personally?
- What does *biotechnology* mean to you?
- What are your impressions of using genetic engineering or biotechnology to change the foods we eat?

As part of the pretest, we want to find out what the terms *biotechnology* and *food safety* mean to respondents and how they arrive at the answers to the survey questions. Understanding the cognitive processes that respondents use in answering questions will help us to write better questions and collect better data.

Another procedure is the use of **focus groups**, small groups of people assembled to discuss topics, issues, or other matters that will help us in writing questions or conducting the survey more efficiently. Groups typically comprise six to eight people with similar characteristics: all men, all women, young black males, working-class people, and so forth. The groups should be constructed so that the members feel comfortable when talking.

In a recent study on families and health, one of the authors conducted two focus groups prior to developing the questionnaire. One group consisted of single parents only, and the other group included married people with children. The purpose of conducting the focus groups was to determine how different family structures, relationships, and experiences affect health care and decision making and how family interactions and relationships influence health. Groups were asked, for example: How do you respond to your child's symptoms? Who takes the child to the doctor? Do you ask other family members or friends for advice? Does your job affect your ability to

---

[4] In chapter 6 we discuss other procedures for testing questions and assessing the results, such as post-interview interviews, taped interviews with behavior coding, and respondent debriefing.

meet family needs? Is health an important issue in your family? What things do you do to promote good health? Of particular interest were the differences among participants and the words and phrases they used to describe their health and health behaviors.

When we either feel comfortable with the draft of the questionnaire or have tried to anticipate how respondents will answer some questions but are still unsure, it is time to try the questionnaire on real respondents. A pretest usually involves twenty to forty interviews, the exact number determined by such things as the number of subgroups of interest, uncertainties we have about how well we are measuring our concepts, the time schedule, and budget. After we complete a formal pretest and debrief the interviewers, we will undoubtedly need to revise the questionnaire and survey procedures. If the changes are extensive, we should conduct informal testing and then another formal pretest. The size of the second pretest is determined by the number of uncertainties we need to resolve. We keep repeating this process until we are completely satisfied with the questionnaire and the survey procedures.

The pretesting phase can last from one month to a considerably longer period. It is not uncommon for the pretesting phase, including the development of the final questionnaire and training materials, to last 2 to 3 months.

Stage 3: Final Survey Design and Planning

The pretest results should be used to improve the survey design and implementation plans. For example, in the pretest of a telephone survey of four physician specialty groups, one of the authors obtained response rates in the range of 40 to 50%. Clearly, these rates were unacceptably low (we discuss why in chapter 5). In subsequent focus groups with physicians, the discussion concentrated on what could be done to increase the response rates. One suggestion that was followed was to give the physicians a choice of how to respond: They could either complete a mail questionnaire or be interviewed by telephone. The rationale was to let each physician choose the method that was best for his or her schedule. The suggestion was a good one because the overall response rate for the main study increased to 67%.

Pretesting may also help to decide how much time to allot between follow-up contacts in a mail survey or whether the final contact in a mail survey should be by mail or by telephone. There are very few hard and fast rules in survey research. Researchers need to be attuned to the factors that can affect response rates and data quality and be prepared to make adjustments.

During this stage, final changes should be made in the sampling plan, the questionnaire, interviewer-training procedures and materials, data-coding plans, and plans for analyzing the data. For example, in sampling we may learn that we need to select more phone numbers to get the desired number of completed interviews because we found more nonworking phone numbers than expected in the pretests. For the questionnaire, we may find that changing the order of some questions improves the flow of the interview, or we may be able to develop closed-ended response choices for some questions that were initially asked as open-ended questions. Another common occurrence is that we find the answers of a particular subgroup in the population, such as those over age 55 or black respondents, to be different from the responses of other subgroups or different from the responses expected. Therefore, we need to decide whether the sample sizes for these subgroups are adequate or whether we need to oversample certain groups.

Stage 4: Data Collection

During this stage, we need to monitor the results of the sampling and data collection activities and begin coding and data file preparation. In sampling, we want to ensure that all the cases are accounted for and that those that have not yielded an interview are being worked thoroughly. Nonrespondents in telephone and face-to-face surveys should be recontacted on different days of the week and at different times of day. It is also important to monitor the results or the dispositions of the completed cases. What are the rates for refusals, noncontacts, ineligibles, and completed interviews? We use biweekly or weekly sample-disposition reports to help spot or anticipate minor problems before they develop into major ones.

Monitoring the interviewers is equally important. Each interviewer's first few completed interviews should be thoroughly checked. We want to ensure that no questions are being missed, that complete information is being obtained, and that all instructions are being followed. It is important to provide feedback to the interviewers so that problems and mistakes can be corrected before they become established patterns. We should also monitor each interviewer's success at converting assignments to interviews. New interviewers are likely to accept respondents' comments of "I am too busy" or "I'm not interested in the topic" as refusals and to give up on the case. It is useful to discuss these situations in training sessions and to instruct interviewers on how to deal with them. If an interviewer has a disproportionate number of refusals, it is a good idea to examine each case with the interviewer and suggest possible ways of recontacting the respondents or ways to handle similar situations in the future. Good researchers attempt to minimize noncooperation by using specially trained interviewers to recontact refusals and convert them to interviews. These interviewers try to convince respondents who are not adamant refusers to reconsider and to grant them an interview. Many times these interviewers convert 20 to 40% of the initial refusals.

As data are being collected, we must code and enter the information from completed interviews into a computer data file. These activities are referred to as **data reduction** and are usually performed by a separate group of people. Prior to entering data into a data file, data reduction staff edit the questionnaires. They look for the same information that the interviewer's supervisor was looking for: skipped questions; incomplete information; and incorrect, inconsistent, or illogical entries. This edit should occur as soon as possible after the interview, ideally within 1 to 2 weeks. Time is important because the interviewer, respondent, or both may need to be contacted to resolve the problem. The sooner this contact occurs, the easier it is to recall the situation and correct the problem.

Stage 5: Data Coding, Data-File Construction, Analysis, and Final Report

The final stage of a survey includes coding and analyzing the data and writing a final report or papers describing the survey results. **Coding** is the assignment of numbers to the responses given to survey questions.[5] Coding respondents' answers to each question allows us to estimate characteristics or to look for patterns among variables. The following example will help to illustrate coding.

In a telephone survey questionnaire used in a study of Maryland adults' attitudes about violent street crime, 824 interviews were

---

[5]Sometimes letters or symbols are used to code responses. This is the exception rather than the rule, and it does not allow statistical analysis of the data. We ignore this type of coding.

completed (see appendix B). Each respondent's answers were individually coded and entered into a data record, usually in the same order that the questions were asked in the survey. A data record includes all the coded responses for one respondent. In addition, each respondent was given a unique identification number between 001 and 824, which was entered at the beginning of his or her data record.

If the respondent with ID number 001 answered question 1 "not very serious," the answer was coded as 3. If the answers to questions 2 and 3 were "very serious" and "stayed about the same," the code values would be 1 and 3, respectively. If the data record begins with the respondent's ID number, the first six numbers of the first respondent's data record would be 001313. In the same manner, code numbers would be assigned to the rest of the first respondent's answers and to the answers given by the other 823 respondents.

Before data analysis begins, the data are checked or "cleaned" to identify and correct coding and data-entry errors. In the cleaning process, the coded response to each question or variable is checked for illegal code values and, when possible, for consistency with responses to other, related questions. If codes for respondents' sex, are 1 for males and 2 for females, then the cleaning process should disclose no code values of 3 or higher for that variable. Interitem consistency is checked in a similar manner. If a series of questions were asked only of male respondents, then we should verify that legitimate codes for these questions are entered for all the male respondents and that a code denoting "not applicable" is assigned to those questions for each female respondent. To complete all the data reduction work, including coding, cleaning, and preparing a data file, typically takes a few days to 4 weeks after the last interviews are conducted, depending on the method of data collection and survey complexity.

The amount of time needed for data analysis and report writing depends on the survey's goals and commitments. After a clean data file is ready, it may take 4 to 6 weeks to write a report documenting the survey procedures and answering one or two research questions. If the plans are more ambitious, then more time must be allocated.

Example of a Time Schedule for a Study

The preceding overview of the stages of a survey gives you an idea of the number of decisions that must be made, the multiple factors that must be considered when making these decisions, the different activities that need to be done simultaneously, and, briefly, the amount of time some survey tasks require. In the example to follow, a more specific time schedule is illustrated. The study is a national RDD survey of 1,000 households with respondents who are 18 years of age or older. The topic of interest is biotechnology and food safety. (Exhibit 2.2 lists the major tasks in the survey and time allocated for each.)

After we decide that a survey is appropriate, that it should be national in scope, and that a telephone survey using RDD is appropriate, we need to make an outline of the research questions and the kinds of survey questions we might ask respondents. While we are doing this, we need to search the literature for articles and books that report on related research. In reviewing these studies, we pay close attention to how the researchers defined and measured their concepts and to the specific questions used in their questionnaires. This information will be used in developing our questionnaire. Although we allocated 3 weeks for the initial literature search and review of past research, the perusal of literature for new studies or for ideas to solve problems is ongoing. Drafting questions and organizing them into a questionnaire follows from this effort. We might spend 4–5 weeks writing questions and developing successive drafts of a questionnaire. We try each draft on a few colleagues or friends,

Exhibit 2.2

**Time Schedule for a Study Involving
1,000 Random-Digit–Dialed Interviews**

Activity	Number of Weeks	Week Number
Review literature and draft questionnaire	8	1–8
Assemble think alouds with ten respondents	1–2	8–9
Revise questionnaire	2	10–11
Conduct pretest 1 ($n = 25$–40)	1	12
Debrief interviewers and revise questionnaire	3	13–15
Pretest 2 ($n = 20$–30)	1	16
Debrief interviewers, revise questionnaire, and develop training materials	4	17–20
Select samples (for pretests and main study)	12	8–19
Conduct main data collection	8	21–28
Code data and prepare data files	12	21–32
Analyze data and write report	open	open

make revisions, retry it on a few different people, revise it, and then try it again. While this is going on, those who will be doing the sample selection need to develop a sampling frame or purchase one from an academic or commercial organization.

Since not much social science research has been done on biotechnology, which has only recently received coverage in the media, we do not know a lot about the public's knowledge of and attitudes about the topic. Thus, it is a good idea to assemble a few focus groups or think-aloud interviews to help in developing the questionnaire. The time schedule allocates 1-2 weeks for this task. Approximately 2 weeks prior to the focus groups or think-aloud interviews, respondents must be recruited.

In weeks 10 and 11 we will revise the questionnaire once again and finish preparations for a formal pretest scheduled for week 12. The pretest will be done with a national, general population sample. Thus, before week 12 we must select the sample, recruit and hire interviewers, and write and reproduce interviewer-training materials. Immediately after completing the pretest interviews, we will have a debriefing with the interviewers. This session may last half a day.

Since we anticipate making major revisions to the questionnaire, we plan a second formal pretest of about twenty to thirty respondents. The revisions and preparations for the second pretest will occur in weeks 13–15, with the second pretest conducted in week 16. Another interviewer debriefing will be held at the end of this pretest.

This pretest and debriefing may uncover no major problems or surprises, or it may reveal that revisions should be made to the questionnaire, requiring additional pretesting. Since a complex research problem or design may require further pretesting, this should not be a source of surprise or alarm. For our example, however, let's assume things went well. Over the next 3 or 4 weeks, weeks 17–20, final revisions will be made in the questionnaire and in the interviewer-training materials. At the same time, we will prepare for the selection and training of coders, develop coding materials, and write specifications for data cleaning and an analysis file. In weeks 8–19 we will conduct sample selection activities for the pretests and the main study. Before week 21, the questionnaires and related materials must be typed and reproduced. Since we plan on completing 1,000 interviews, we will need 1,400 or 1,500 copies of the questionnaire. If the questionnaire is twenty pages, 1,450 copies will amount to 29,000 sheets (fifty-eight reams) of paper for the questionnaire alone. We need to budget an adequate amount of time to type the final copy of the questionnaire; reproduce, collate, and staple the copies; and then integrate the training materials with the questionnaire and sample assignments along with other administrative materials.

In week 21 we will train the interviewers and begin data collection. We have allocated 8 weeks for data collection. A number of factors affect the time allocated to data collection. The time period must be long enough so that we will have a reasonable chance to interview each sample case. We want to allow enough time to reach people who are away on vacation, have very busy schedules, are away from home a lot, are ill or in a short hospital stay, and so forth. Each case must be thoroughly worked so that the sample will represent the diverse nature of the population. We must also consider the interviewers. How many hours a week can we ask them to work? How many interviews can we expect them to complete in an average week? If they work in a central telephone center, are there enough cases to keep them busy for a full shift? If we hire and train 15 interviewers, ask them to work an average of 15 hours per week, and if none leave during the data collection period, then each interviewer must complete about 8.3 interviews per week. This goal is very easy to achieve and, if no major difficulties occur, data collections will be completed in less than 8 weeks.

The same week interviewers are trained, we begin training the coders and writing the specifications for the analysis file. Coding should be concurrent with interviewing; thus, it is important for coders to edit questionnaires as soon as possible. Our schedule allocates four weeks after data collection has ended to complete coding, data cleaning, and preparing the data analysis file. If there are only one or two open-ended questions and the interviewers do a thorough job, it may take less than 4 weeks to produce a complete data analysis file.

The time required to complete a survey depends on a number of factors—project complexity, sample size, method of data collection, and other considerations. Conducting a high-quality survey from start to finish requires hundreds of decisions and a number of stages, and it takes time. In our example, the conceptualization of a research idea, the project implementation, and the creation of a data analysis file take approximately 8 months and reflect the amount of time and level of effort required to properly conduct a moderate-size survey without cutting corners. (This 8-month schedule does not include any data analysis or report writing.) However, we don't always have the luxury of an adequate amount of time to do a survey. Some circumstances require that a survey be conducted more quickly: the need to determine public reaction to a news event (e.g., a military invasion or presidential assassination attempt), or the requirement to complete a survey as part of a class project.

When time is short, the researcher must (1) recognize that by cutting corners the data may have shortcomings that affect the reliability and validity of the results, and (2) determine which compromises may have the least effect on the results. To minimize compromised results, a researcher may, for example, want to buy a sample from a commercial organization rather than to develop a new one. Or, the researcher may want to rely on questionnaire items used in previous surveys and forego a number of pretesting procedures for assessing the validity of the items in the survey population. In both situations, the researcher assumes that things will work well and must be willing to accept the risks involved.

3 Selecting the Method of Data Collection

Once we have decided that a survey is the appropriate methodology for investigating the research problem, the next question to consider is what data collection method is most advantageous. Typically, there are three survey approaches: mail, telephone, and face-to-face. Combinations of any of these are also possible, and we discuss them later in the chapter. A fourth approach is a group administered questionnaire, such as one completed by all students present in selected classrooms or classes on a particular day. This type of survey is usually conducted in conjunction with one of the other survey methods and is also discussed later, under combinations of methods. We begin with a brief description of the three main survey approaches.

Evaluating the Advantages and Disadvantages of the Three Survey Methods

There is no one "best" survey method; each has strengths and weaknesses. It is important to know what these are and to evaluate research objectives with reference to the advantages and disadvantages of each method. The decisions in selecting a method of data collection must be made study by study.

In choosing a method of data collection, three broad categories of factors, with many subcategories, must be considered:

1. Administrative or resource factors
2. Questionnaire issues
3. Data-quality issues

Exhibit 3.1 summarizes the comparative strengths and weaknesses of mail, telephone, and face-to-face surveys. In deciding on a method, we must consider questions relevant to each category of factors.

Exhibit 3.1 **Comparison of Major Survey Methods**

Aspect of Survey	Mailed Questionnaires	Telephone Interviews	Face-to-Face (in home) Interviews
Administrative, Resource Factors			
Cost	**Low***	Low/medium	High
Length of data collection period	Long (10 weeks)	**Short (2–4 weeks)**	Medium/Long (4–12 weeks)
Geographic distribution of sample	**May be wide**	**May be wide**	Must be clustered
Questionnaire Issues			
Length of questionnaire	Short/medium (4–12 pages)	Medium/long (1/4–3/4 hour)	**Long (1/2–1 hour)**
Complexity of questionnaire	Must be simple	**May be complex**	**May be complex**
Complexity of questions	Simple to moderate	Must be short and simple	**May be complex**
Control of question order	Poor	**Very good**	**Very good**
Use of open-ended questions	Poor	Fair	**Good**
Use of visual aids	Good	Usually not possible	**Very good**
Use of household/personal records	**Very good**	Fair	Good
Rapport	Fair	Good	**Very good**
Sensitive topics	**Good**	Fair/good	Fair
Nonthreatening questions	Good	Good	Good
Data-Quality Issues			
Sampling frame bias	**Usually low**	**Low** (with RDD)	**Low**
Response rate	45%–75%	60%–90%	65%–95%
Response bias	Medium/high (favors more educated persons)	**Low**	**Low**
Knowledge about refusals and noncontacts	Fair	Poor	Fair
Control of response situation	Poor	Fair	**Good**
Quality of recorded response	Fair/good	**Very good**	**Very good**

*Boldface indicates that the method has an advantage over one or both of the other methods in the specific survey component noted.

Regarding administrative and resource factors, we need to consider how much time there is to do the research and how much money we have for hiring interviewers and/or coders, purchasing supplies, and buying or constructing a list of the population that we want to sample and interview. Questionnaire issues include how many and what kinds of questions need to be asked to adequately achieve the research objectives. We must decide if one method of collecting the data is more cost-effective or yields fewer reporting errors than other methods. In considering data-quality issues, we must ask whether more respondents are likely to cooperate with one method of data collection rather than another, whether we get more accurate or more complete answers if we use interviewers, and whether one method is more likely to include the population we want to study.

Most researchers start by evaluating the feasibility of a mail or a telephone survey. There may, however, be major, compelling reasons for doing a face-to-face survey; for example, respondents need to be shown lists of answer categories for key questions, the target population has low telephone coverage, or the respondents are likely to have difficulty reading or writing answers to questions. The first two questions we need to ask are "Who are the survey respondents?" and "Is my research question more amenable to one method than to another?" If the answer to the second question is no, then time and money are the next considerations. In addition to thinking about time and money, researchers need to assess several other important factors, as Exhibit 3.1 indicates. The following sections discuss the advantages and disadvantages of each method with specific reference to the factors listed in Exhibit 3.1.

Mail Surveys

Mail surveys involve sending a cover letter and questionnaire to a specific person or address. The cover letter should state the purpose of the survey, who is the sponsor or is collecting the data, who is to complete the questionnaire, an assurance of confidentiality, and when to return the questionnaire (usually within 10 days). Mail surveys require a questionnaire that is totally self-explanatory; the importance of clear and simple statements cannot be overstated, since instructions and questions must be uniformly understood by a wide variety of respondents. If respondents do not understand the task or view it as difficult or too time-consuming, they will probably not complete the questionnaire or will make errors. Cover letters provide a telephone number for respondents to call if they have questions about the legitimacy of the survey or have difficulty interpreting any of the questions. Our experience, however, indicates that very few respondents call, probably fewer than 1%, even if the survey contains controversial or personal items. When respondents have doubts or concerns, they are more likely to not complete the questionnaire or to skip unclear items than to call with questions. Well-designed surveys strive for high cooperation rates by sending reminder letters or a new cover letter and another copy of the questionnaire to nonrespondents.

Advantages

The mail survey is the least expensive of the survey methods. It requires money for postage and envelopes; a list of the names and addresses of the study population (a sampling frame); money to type and print a professional-looking questionnaire; and people to assemble the materials to mail out, keep track of who responds and who does not, do remailings, edit and code the returned questionnaires, enter the data into a computer file, and construct an analysis file.

A major difference between mail and other survey methods is that, in a mail survey, the data are not collected by interviewers. This characteristic has both advantages and disadvantages. A clear advantage is cost. The cost of first-class postage to mail out and return an eight-page questionnaire (printed on four sheets) with a return envelope is under $1.00; an interviewer's pay rate is $5.50 to $8.50 per hour. Another advantage is that since the cost of mailing a questionnaire is the same whether we send it to someone in Alaska or across town, we can cost-effectively survey a national sample of respondents, which is more diverse than a citywide or statewide sample.

The questionnaires used in mail surveys also have several advantages. One advantage is that respondents may consult household or personal records. For example, if we need to know the dollar amount of interest that respondents pay on a home mortgage or how much they paid in doctors' fees within the last 6 months, we can encourage them to consult records rather than to answer from memory. The result is greater response accuracy. A second advantage is that we may use visual aids. If we want respondents to see a list of possible answers before responding, we list the answers with the question. If we want respondents to define the geographic boundaries of their neighborhood or to indicate their travel route to work, we can reproduce a map on the questionnaire or on a separate enclosed sheet.

Mail surveys have also been successful in the collection of data about sensitive topics. Respondents seem to be more comfortable answering questions about intimate medical problems (Hochstim, 1967), personal bankruptcy, convictions for drunk driving (Locander, Sudman, and Bradburn, 1976), and other potentially embarrassing topics in self-administered questionnaires (Aday, 1989). For these types of topics, the more anonymous the method of data collection, the higher the rate of reported behavior. Keep in mind, however, that while a mail survey is better than other methods, it is far from perfect. Many sensitive behaviors remain unreported, even in anonymous mail surveys (Sudman and Bradburn, 1982).

The length of time to conduct a mail survey is fairly constant—usually 8 to 10 weeks—regardless of the sample size and its geographic distribution. As mentioned earlier, we must allow enough time for the questionnaires to get to the respondents, for respondents to complete them, for the return of the questionnaires, and for follow-up mailings and returns. The time required may be either an advantage or a disadvantage, depending on our particular survey. If we have a sample of 2,000 or more, a mail survey will probably take the same or less time than a telephone survey. On the other hand, a telephone survey of 300 to 500 respondents could be completed in 2 to 4 weeks, as opposed to the 8 to 10 weeks that a mail survey would require.

Before we discuss why response rates to mail surveys can vary widely, it is necessary to define the term. We define **response rate** as the number of eligible sample members who complete a questionnaire divided by the total number of eligible sample members. The word *eligible* is crucial to the definition because occasionally people we do not want to include in our survey may receive a questionnaire and may respond. For example, assume we want to measure the attitudes of college males toward abortion. If one of our questionnaires was sent to a female and she responded, we would treat that response as ineligible. In computing our response rate, we would not count the interview and we would reduce the sample size by one. Response rates are an important measure of survey quality; typically the higher the rate, the better the quality. Of course, a 30% response rate is no better than a 20% response rate; both are unacceptably low.

We can achieve reasonably high response rates to a mail survey when the topic is highly salient to the respondent. For example, a survey sent to physicians asking about the burdens of malpractice insurance and actions the government can take regarding the situation would likely elicit a good response. The same survey would not do as well with the general population. Why? Because, while many people in the general population may think the issue is important, they are not nearly as concerned about it as physicians are.

Disadvantages

Response bias occurs when one subgroup is more or less likely to cooperate than another. For example, mail surveys are subject to response bias because they do not achieve good response rates from people with low education, people who do not like to write, those who have difficulty reading, and those who do not have an interest in the topic. Response bias is potentially greater in mail surveys than with other methods because respondents can more easily ignore mail questionnaires than a polite but persistent interviewer. For this reason, the cover letter and the appearance of the questionnaire are critically important in encouraging cooperation and minimizing response bias. Usually, our only contacts with the respondents is through these materials, and, therefore, they must be especially convincing and appealing.

We need to know as much as possible about the nonrespondents (refusals and noncontacts) in order to assess potential response bias. It is important to determine whether those who refuse or who cannot be reached for an interview (noncontacts) are different, in terms of our dependent variable(s), from those who cooperate.[1] When we have a list of our population, we have information that can be used to determine potential response bias. For example, from names and addresses, we can determine if males or females were more likely to cooperate and if those living in large cities were more or less cooperative than people in other areas. Our list may also contain other information to help identify response bias.

A number of characteristics of mail surveys make them less effective than surveys administered by interviewers. Since respondents can look over the questionnaire before deciding whether or not to complete it, the questionnaire cannot be very long, nor can it look

---

[1] It is important to obtain information from the post office on respondents who move. Requesting an address-correction card may assist the researcher in determining if the respondent is no longer eligible because of geographic residence or if follow-up attempts should be made. The post office charges a fee for supplying a forwarding address.

complex or difficult to complete. A mail questionnaire must be completely self-explanatory because no one is present to assist if something is confusing or complex. Even experienced researchers often think that a statement or question is self-explanatory when, in fact, a significant segment of the study population misinterprets it. A lack of understanding by respondents can and does affect the quality of survey responses. It is easy for respondents to skip questions they do not understand or do not want to answer. In addition, the researcher has little control over the order in which respondents answer the questions or over who actually completes the questionnaire. Finally, the answers to open-ended questions are less thorough and detailed in mail surveys than they are in surveys administered by interviewers. Unless prompted by interviewers, many respondents provide only the minimum amount of information to answer the question. This tendency is especially true of respondents with low levels of education and of those who do not like to write.

Telephone Surveys

In a telephone survey, telephone numbers are selected in a variety of ways. Numbers can be selected randomly from a phone book or created by using an existing telephone number and dropping one or more of the last four digits and substituting random numbers. Respondents themselves can be selected from a list—for example, a membership directory that includes telephone numbers. The interviewers are trained in procedures for contacting respondents and administering the questionnaire (Guensel, Berckmans, and Cannell, 1983). They are given an assignment of respondents or telephone numbers to call for interviews. In effect, interviewers are proxies for the principal investigator and are trained to collect information in a uniform and consistent manner. They are to ask questions exactly as written and in the same sequence for all respondents. The reliability of the data depends partly on following such standardized procedures.

Advantages

The telephone survey is the most widely used survey method today. This method has increased in use over the past 2 decades as a number of limiting factors or concerns have been overcome or shown to be overstated.

One factor contributing to the popularity of telephone surveys is the increase in the number of households with telephones. In 1960, 80% of households had a telephone; in 1970, 83%; in 1980, 92%; and in 1990, 94.8% (Frey, 1989; U.S. Bureau of the Census, 1992).

Also of concern to researchers has been the number of households with unlisted telephone numbers, which varies by community. When the proportion of these households is high, excluding them can be a serious omission. Survey Sampling, Inc. (1994) estimates that some metropolitan areas have few households with unlisted telephone numbers—for example, 17.6% in Baton Rouge, Louisiana, and 13.2% in West Palm Beach/Boca Raton/Delray Beach, Florida. In other places a high proportion of households have unlisted telephone numbers—for instance, 47.9% in Jersey City, New Jersey, and 64.6% in Los Angeles/Long Beach, California. Random-digit dialing (RDD) has allowed researchers to overcome this problem, but it costs appreciably more to do an RDD survey than a survey of respondents selected from a telephone directory.

Researchers have also been concerned about the quality of data collected from a telephone survey. A number of studies now show that phone surveys compare favorably with other methods and that the limitations stem from the type and amount of information that must be collected. For example, if respondents must consult records, or if the interview will take much longer than 45 minutes, a telephone survey may not be the best method. However, if the interviewer asks mostly attitudinal and behavioral questions that can be answered accurately from memory, and the interview takes 30 minutes or less, then a telephone survey is a viable approach.

Telephone surveys are intermediate in cost between mail and face-to-face surveys. For a telephone survey, we need:

- Interviewers
- A centralized work center with telephones and space for the interviewers to work
- Monitoring equipment
- A sample of the population, developed or purchased
- Staff to keep track of interview results, to edit and code completed interviews, and to build a computer data file for analysis

Interviewers are essentially proxies for the researcher: We hire people to do interviews for us rather than doing the interviewing ourselves. This has both advantages and disadvantages. On the one hand, the research can be completed much more quickly than it could if the researchers were working alone. On the other hand, interviewers must be selected, hired, trained, and supervised. We must ensure that each interviewer is reading the questions verbatim, coding the responses accurately, and not biasing the survey in any way. Interviewers must also be paid. Both telephone and face-to-face methods are labor intensive, which is the major reason they are more expensive than a mail survey.

There are a number of clear advantages to telephone surveys. Since 94.8% of households in the United States have telephones, **sampling frame bias** is low for RDD surveys. (However, rural areas, some areas in the South, and economically depressed areas are most likely to have lower percentages of telephone households.) Also, most people are willing to be interviewed by telephone, another reason for low response bias. However, some foreign-language groups are not comfortable being interviewed on the telephone, and survey success may necessitate that respondents and interviewers match by nationality and that interviewers speak the respondents' language.

Response rates for telephone surveys are usually in the range of 60–90% when repeated callbacks are used to reach persons who are difficult to contact. We usually recommend 5 to 9 callbacks on different days of the week and at different times of the day. Response rates are usually better for telephone surveys than for mail surveys, primarily because an interviewer personally attempts to convince the respondent of the importance of the research and can schedule an interview at a convenient time for the respondent. Thus, the use of interviewers reduces the burden on the respondent considerably. Location also affects response rates: In an inverse proportion to the size of the cities being surveyed, better response rates are achieved in small towns and cities than in the larger metropolitan areas.

Another advantage is that the length of the data collection period is usually shorter for telephone surveys than for the other methods. Telephoning is the fastest way to initiate contact with a person or household and to make callbacks, an important factor in contacting difficult-to-reach persons.

The geographic distribution of the sample can be wide because it is easy and relatively cheap to purchase a sampling frame of all the area codes and telephone prefixes in the United States from Bell Communications Research ($350) or to purchase a sample of random-digit telephone numbers from a commercial organization ($525 for 2,000 numbers). Nevertheless, the cost of a statewide or national survey is significantly higher than that of a local city survey because the cost of purchasing and/or selecting the sample is higher and we must pay long-distance charges (special rates can be obtained from the phone companies if we make a large number of calls). Costs for interviewing time are about the same for both types of surveys.

The use of interviewers provides a number of advantages to the efficacy of the questionnaire and quality of the data. With thoroughly trained interviewers, the quality of recorded answers should be very high. In addition, because the interviewer is doing all the work—reading the questions and recording answers—interviews can last more than one-half hour if the subject matter is interesting to the respondent. Also, since interviewers are trained in how to ask each question and in what order, the design or layout of the questionnaire can be complex. For example, the questionnaire can employ multiple skip patterns, in which a specific response to certain questions determines whether respondents are asked to answer subsequent questions or not. Well-trained interviewers can handle a variety of situations and formats; they can, for example, clarify for respondents questions that ask about all members of a household together and those that ask about each individual household member separately.

Another advantage to using interviewers is that they are able to control the order of response to the questions. Respondents surveyed by telephone have no idea of what question will be asked next or of the number of questions in the survey. If they saw how many questions were in the survey or that a "yes" response would result in being asked a series of follow-up questions, they might be less inclined to be interviewed or they might answer "no" to the first question of the series.

Finally, it is possible for interviewers to establish rapport with respondents over the telephone and thus convince them to complete the interview, to believe in the authenticity and relevance of the research, and to provide complete and accurate answers to even sensitive questions. Telephone surveys are comparable to the other methods in eliciting responses to nonthreatening questions; they are also quite good for sensitive topics such as sexual behaviors that may lead to certain diseases (Czaja, 1987–88), AIDS and risk behaviors (Binson, Murphy, and Keer, 1987), and similar topics.

Disadvantages

Telephone surveys do have limitations. Questions must be short and fairly simple, and the answer choices that are read to the respondents must also be few, short, and simple. Otherwise, respondents may not keep all the information in mind. Sentences should be limited to twenty words or less, language kept simple, and no more than four or five short answer categories read per question (Payne, 1951). When sentences are long or answer categories are numerous, respondents are more likely to remember only the first parts or the last parts. These are called primacy or recency effects (Schuman and Presser, 1981).

The inability to use visual aids, such as having respondents place response cards into piles, can also be a disadvantage. If we have the respondents' names and addresses, we can mail materials to their homes beforehand. Similar to a combination mail and telephone survey, this method necessitates sending a cover letter explaining the materials before the telephone interview is carried out. This combined method is not possible with RDD surveys unless households are contacted to obtain names and addresses.

A telephone-mail-telephone sequence was reported by Kanninen, Chapman, and Hanemann (1992), but it resulted in a very low final response rate. The survey asked respondents about their willingness to pay for five possible environmental protection programs in the San Joaquin Valley in California. An RDD sample of phone numbers were called, and 1,960 eligible households were identified. During the initial telephone call, the purpose of the survey was explained to respondents and they were asked to provide their names and addresses so that a short questionnaire could be mailed to them. The interview was to be conducted by telephone; the purpose of the questionnaire was to assist respondents in following the question sequence and comprehending the questions. During the initial phone call, respondents were also asked to specify a convenient time for the interview. A total of 1,239 respondents gave their names and addresses, and of those, 1,004 completed the interview. This yielded a final response rate of 51%, with most refusals occurring at the name and address solicitation stage.

The interviewer's inability to control the response situation and the respondents' difficulty in consulting household records during the interview are also disadvantages. When interviewing a respondent, we never know where the telephone is located, whether anyone else is in the room, and how comfortable the respondent is in answering the questions if someone else is nearby. It is also very difficult without advance notice for respondents to consult records when being interviewed by telephone.

Another disadvantage, which may not be obvious, concerns limited responses to open-ended questions. It might seem that a telephone interviewer could probe respondents' answers and record verbatim responses as well as a face-to-face interviewer. In fact, telephone respondents can and do respond to open-ended questions; however, they usually answer in a sentence or in a few short sentences. If the interviewer's probe for "other reasons," explanations, or clarification creates silence or "dead time" and the respondent cannot think of more to say, he or she may begin to feel anxious or edgy. Research shows that long and detailed answers are not elicited as often in telephone surveys as in face-to-face surveys (Groves and Kahn, 1979).

Finally, analysis of refusals and noncontacts is limited with telephone surveys unless the sampling frame includes names and addresses or other identifying information. If we have names and addresses, we can, for example, compare response rates by gender, area of the city, or other available characteristics. With RDD, this is not possible; we cannot be certain that a telephone number is that of a household, much less find out who lives there, unless an interview is completed.

Face-to-Face Surveys

In face-to-face surveys, also referred to as personal interview surveys, information is usually collected by interviewers in the home or in another location that is convenient for the respondent. The key element is that respondent and interviewer are together in the same location.

This is the most expensive of the three methods because of the travel costs involved and the amount of time needed to collect the data. The interview itself takes only about 25–40% of that total; travel, the editing of responses, and other tasks consume the remaining 60–75% (Sudman, 1967). To understand travel time required, assume we need to conduct 800 interviews with persons 18 years of age and older who reside in households in a large city such as Chicago. According to sampling theory, lets assume an average of five interviews should be conducted per selected block. If we want each interviewer to do an average of twenty-five interviews, we need thirty-two interviewers (800 ÷ 25 = 32). Each interviewer will be assigned five blocks to work (25 interviewers ÷ 5 interviews per block = 5 blocks). The city of Chicago is approximately 234 square miles and contains more than 10,000 blocks. Since blocks will be selected randomly, each interviewer may need to travel 1 mile, 5 miles, or even more to each of his or her assigned blocks. Clearly, travel consumes a major portion of the interviewers' total time.

Since the expense of face-to-face designs is greater than that incurred for the postage stamps used in mail surveys or for "letting your fingers do the walking," the main method of "travel" in telephone surveys, why would a researcher ever want to do a face-to-face survey? As we discuss shortly, it is the preferred method of data collection for some surveys because it lends itself well to certain questionnaire items and issues of data quality.

Advantages

Although the face-to-face interview is the single most expensive survey method, the cost disadvantage can be offset by many advantages. The cost is greater than that for the other methods because interviewers must travel to the respondents' homes and are typically paid for both their travel time and the interview time. The following brief description of how the sampling and interviewing are done for a national survey, based on the General Social Survey (GSS) model, illustrates why this method is expensive.

Assume that we want to do a national survey of adults 18 years of age and older who live in households in the fifty states. Considering existing lists, we conclude that no list or sampling frame contains the names or addresses of U.S. residents who are 18 years of age or older. For example, state motor vehicle departments have only information on people who have drivers' licenses; voter registration lists are incomplete because not everyone registers; income tax forms are strictly confidential, and not everyone completes a form each year; and even the U.S. Post Office does not have a complete list of addresses.

Although there is no list of people or households in the United States that is complete enough to serve as a sampling frame, we can use the 1990 U.S. Census of Population and Housing to determine the number of people and the number of households within various political and geographic delineations. For example, we know fairly accurately how many people lived in the city of Chicago; or in Wake County, North Carolina; or in College Park, Maryland, in April 1990.

The GSS design is like a funnel. First, the larger areas are selected randomly, in stages, using the census information. In the GSS, there are eighty-four selections made at this first stage of selection. The second stage of selection is categories or divisions of the first stage. In cities, we might use groups of blocks or census tracts (areas of approximately 2,500–8,000 people); in counties, it might be cities or townships; and in rural areas sections of land might be selected. The number of second-stage selections is 562 and is based on the population or housing units of the first stage of selection. The third stage of selection is usually parts of city blocks or sections of land. In the GSS, units for this stage of selection must have a minimum of fifty housing units.[2] These first three stages of selection are based only on the number of people or housing units within the delineated areas. After the third stage of selection, "listers" are sent to each of the selected areas; their job is to list every housing unit in the selected areas. After all households are listed, a random sample of households is selected.[3] At each, an interviewer randomly selects one person 18 years of age or older to interview. An average of 2.7 interviews are conducted per block or area (Davis and Smith, 1993). Do you know how you obtain an average of 2.7 interviews per block or area?[4]

There are a number of sampling and data-quality advantages to the face-to-face method. Response rates are usually slightly higher than those of telephone interviews. One reason for this is that an advance letter can be sent to the respondent's household prior to the interviewer's visit. The letter is usually printed on the sponsor's letterhead and explains the reasons for the survey, the importance of interviewing each sample household, the use that will be made of the data, and confidentiality of the respondent's answers. This letter legitimizes the interview and makes the task of gaining the re-

---

[2]More units than will be used in one survey are included in the final stage of selection because these areas are used for more than one survey. Conducting multiple surveys in the same areas allows the sampling and listing costs to be spread across studies. For each study, different housing units are selected.

[3]One additional point should be noted. Interviewers should not live on the same blocks that are sampled because it is best if the interviewer does not know the respondent. When personal questions like those about household income are asked, most respondents are more comfortable telling a stranger than someone they know. Therefore, interviewers may have to travel 1 or more miles each time they attempt to obtain an interview with a sampled household, making this type of face-to-face method very expensive.

[4]The same number of interviews are not completed on every block because of different rates of ineligible housing units (e.g., vacant units) and survey cooperation (e.g., refusals, unavailable residents). In an average of ten blocks, one block may have four completed interviews, four blocks may each have two completed interviews, and five blocks may each have three completed interviews—a total of twenty-seven interviews in ten blocks, or 2.7 interviews per block.

spondent's cooperation somewhat easier. Another response rate advantage is that it is more difficult to refuse someone face-to-face than it is to hang up the telephone. There are, however, some drawbacks. Conducting interviews in high-crime areas presents safety problems. Attempting interviews in apartment buildings can also be a problem because of difficulty in gaining access. As is true of telephone interviews, cooperation rates are higher in small towns and cities and lower in large metropolitan areas.

Sampling frame bias is usually low in the face-to-face method. When census data are used as the sampling frame, all individuals in the population, theoretically, have a chance of being included in the sample. Census data become a problem as time passes and the information becomes dated. This is especially true in areas of high growth or decline. Where high growth or decline occurs, the researcher must rely on local government statistics, recent surveys done in the area, or local informants such as real estate agents or banks to help update the population or housing unit counts.

Response bias is also usually low in the face-to-face method. The rate of cooperation is roughly equal for all types of respondents. Since the data are collected by interviewers, the face-to-face method has many of the same advantages as a telephone survey. However, face-to-face surveys allow more control of the response situation than do telephone surveys. For example, if the interviewer believes that the respondent's answers may be affected by others in the room, the interviewer can suggest moving to another part of the home to ensure privacy. Rapport is also better in face-to-face interviews because the respondents get to see the person they are talking to. Interviewers are trained to be courteous and attentive and to build rapport with their respondents. The quality of recorded responses in face-to-face surveys is rated as very good because interviewers receive extensive training in asking the questions and recording the answers. In addition, their work is thoroughly checked by both supervisors and the coding staff.

Many advantages of the face-to-face method relate to the questionnaire itself. The questionnaire can be more complex because it is administered by a trained interviewer. For the same reason, and because both interviewer and respondent are in the same location, complex tasks or questions can be asked. For example, assume we have a list of twenty-five behaviors that vary by degree of risk, such as bungee jumping, sky diving, riding a mountain bike, and so forth. These twenty-five behaviors are listed individually on twenty-five cards, and we want each respondent to put them into one of four piles. The piles are "would never do," "would consider doing," "have done at least once," and "have done more than once." This task is much easier for the respondent if an interviewer is in the same room explaining and illustrating the task. Face-to-face interviews also allow for the use of visual aids. For long questions or long answer categories, the interviewer can hand the respondent a copy of the question or the answer categories and have the respondent follow along as the items are read, making it easier for the respondent to understand what is being asked. Interviewers also have control of the question order in face-to-face interviews.

The face-to-face survey method is also best for open-ended questions, since these surveys allow a more relaxed atmosphere and tempo than do telephone interviews. As a result, it is easier for the interviewer to probe for additional information, and respondents are not as uncomfortable with long pauses between answers because they can see what the interviewer is doing (Groves and Kahn, 1979).

A face-to-face interview can be longer than a telephone interview for several reasons: It takes place in the respondent's home; respondents do not have to hold a telephone receiver while they listen to the interviewer; "dead time" or long pauses are not a problem; and the interview questions and tasks can be more varied and interesting.

Another positive aspect of the face-to-face method is that, since the interview takes place in the respondent's home, he or she has the opportunity to consult records. Still, the respondent may not be able to locate the appropriate information while the interviewer is present unless the respondent has been given advance notice that records need to be consulted. In this regard, mail surveys may be more advantageous because respondents can locate and consult records at their convenience. Finally, the face-to-face method is as well suited as the other methods to the asking of nonthreatening questions.

Disadvantages

There are four major disadvantages to the face-to-face method. The first is cost. As we showed earlier, it is expensive to complete the listing of housing units and to compensate the interviewers for travel time and other expenses. A national face-to-face survey with interviews lasting 45–60 minutes probably costs at least $250 per completed interview. Although cost data comparing the three methods are not readily available, a national face-to-face study probably costs more than twice as much as a similar telephone survey.

Another obvious disadvantage is the amount of time it takes to complete a face-to-face survey. Groves and Kahn (1979) reported that the entire interviewing process for a face-to-face interview is 2.6 times longer than that for a similar telephone interview. Considering the widespread distribution of interviewers across the survey area, training time, the transfer of completed questionnaires and materials to and from the interviewers, and other logistical considerations, the data collection phase of a face-to-face survey could easily take three times longer than that of a similar telephone survey.

To achieve some cost advantages, researchers attempt more than one face-to-face interview per selected block. If one respondent is not home, the interviewer can try another sampled household. There is a penalty, however, for *clustering*, or doing more than one interview per block. People of similar characteristics (such as income, demographics, attitudes) tend to live on the same blocks or in the same neighborhoods. Thus, when we sample more than one respondent per block, we collect similar information for some variables. Think about it. People with similar incomes and lifestyles have similar values and behaviors. A respondent may not be exactly the same as his neighbors, but he is probably more similar to them than he is to people who live on different blocks or miles away. Thus, when we do more than one interview per block, we are not capturing all the diversity in the sample population. However, all residents on a block are not going to be exactly alike on all the variables for which we are collecting information. Sampling statisticians have shown that the optimum design has some clustering rather than none. As a compromise between cost and a lack of diversity on a block, most social science surveys try to average between three to eight completed interviews per block. The more similar people may be on an important variable, the fewer the number of interviews we would want to complete per block.

Another possible disadvantage with face-to-face interviews is the hesitancy of respondents to report very personal types of behavior. The expectation is that the more personal the method of data collection, the less likely respondents are to report sensitive behaviors. The findings, however, are mixed. A few studies have found lower rates of reporting in face-to-face interviews for depression (Aneshensel, Frerichs, Clark, and Yokopenic 1982), sexual behaviors (Czaja, 1987–88), and alcohol consumption by women (Hochstim, 1967). On the other hand, Bradburn, Sudman, and Associates (1979) found no significant differences by method for the reporting of declared bankruptcy or arrests for drunk driving, and Wiseman (1972) reported no differences about questions on abortion and birth control.

Another related drawback is that respondents are more likely to provide socially desirable responses in a face-to-face interview. This is especially true in studies of racial attitudes, and the outcome appears to be affected by the racial characteristics of respondents and interviewers. Campbell (1981) and Hatchett and Schuman (1975–1976) found that answer patterns were different when the interviewer and respondent were of the same race. When the racial characteristics are different, the respondent is much more likely to give a socially desirable response. Sudman and Bradburn (1982) indicate a small effect by method of data collection, claiming that respondents are most likely to **overreport** socially desirable behavior in face-to-face interviews and less likely to do so in mail surveys.

Combinations of Methods

There is no requirement that a survey must use only one method. Sometimes, depending on the research question and an evaluation of the factors listed in Exhibit 3.1, the best approach is a combination of methods.

A few examples will illustrate the possibilities. Assume we want to do a survey of the students at a university about their desire for more student recreation facilities and the fee increases they are willing to pay. Let us also assume we have limited funds to conduct this project. One possible cost-effective means of surveying the students is by classes. We would be taking advantage of groups of students and, in the time it takes to complete one interview, we can obtain responses for an entire class. Assuming that most professors will allow us to use part of their lecture time to administer the questionnaire, this is a very efficient survey design. However, what do we do about students who are absent on the day of the class visit? If the number is large, the results of the survey may have a serious response bias. Thus, we need to include those missing from class, or at least a subsample of them, and **weight** their responses.

Since it is very unlikely the professors will let us come back a second time to interview the missing students, we need to contact them using one of the three previously described methods. All of these methods will be more expensive than the classroom method. Therefore, we want to subsample these nonrespondents. How many students we interview and how we do it will depend on our time schedule and resources. The quickest way would be by telephone. What would you decide?

One of the authors used a combination of methods in a national survey of physicians that was mentioned briefly in chapter 2. The original plan was to do a national telephone survey. Resources, time schedule, and survey questions indicated this was the optimum approach. In the pretest phase, the response rates were poor—less than 50%—even when there were more than fifteen attempts to contact some physicians. This response rate was unacceptable. To find an approach to improve it, the researchers conducted two focus groups with physicians from the survey population. One important finding of the focus groups was that physicians (and other very busy professionals) need a method of responding that is compatible with their schedules. The suggestion was to let them pick the way in which they wished to be interviewed: by telephone or a self-administered mail questionnaire. This strategy worked. The response rate in the main study was about 40% higher than in any of the three pretests.

Finally, there are a number of different ways methods can be combined. Sometimes we start with the least expensive method, such as a mail survey, and then make the final contacts by telephone. Another combination frequently used when multiple interviews are required in a household (of married couples, for example) is to hold an initial face-to-face interview with one member of the household and leave a self-administered questionnaire for the other household member. The possibilities are limited only by the imaginations of the researchers.

4 Questionnaire Design: Writing the Questions

The survey questionnaire is the conduit through which information flows from the world of everyday behavior and opinion into the world of research and analysis; it is our link to the phenomena we wish to study. The focus of chapters 4–6 is on how to transform research questions into serviceable questionnaires. Chapter 4 is divided into two main sections: factors in questionnaire design and writing questions. Chapters 5 and 6 cover organizing the questionnaire and testing the questions.

Most, though not all, of our examples will be drawn from two projects: a telephone survey of Maryland adults to determine their attitudes toward violent street crime, and a self-administered survey of University of Maryland students about several current issues on the College Park campus. These two studies provide questionnaire examples for surveys of the general population and of a special population and allow us to note important differences between instruments that are interviewer-administered and those that are not. Yet, while there are a number of differences in both design and execution between telephone surveys and mail surveys, the fundamental issues of questionnaire design are the same. We begin with these. Some will seem simple, even mundane; but as we shall see, they are neither.

We must approach the task of developing a questionnaire not as an isolated effort but in the context of achieving our research goals within our resources. At the end of our task, we will have answered several questions and learned how to make a number of key decisions about the development of our instruments, including:

[1]The telephone survey was actually conducted by the University of Maryland Survey Research Center; the student survey is a composite of several separate studies that were conducted with University of Maryland students.

- Are respondents able to provide the information we want?
- How can we help them provide accurate information?
- What must respondents do to provide the information that is needed?
- How is each research question rewritten as one or more survey items?
- What questionnaire items should we include?
- Do the selected items measure the dimensions of interest?

Factors in Questionnaire Development

In our examination of developing a questionnaire and writing questions, we focus on the response process, on the utility of individual questions, and on the structures of both entire interviews and individual survey questions. To this end, we begin with a brief overview of where the questionnaire fits into the survey research process and how the roles of researcher, interviewer, and respondent are related in the collection of the data.

Over about the last 10 years, there has been extensive interdisciplinary research by cognitive psychologists and survey methodologists collaborating on issues of survey research design, particularly on the question-response process (Jabine, Straf, Tanur, and Tourangeau, 1984). While most aspects of this collaboration are well beyond the scope of this book, a model suggested for the overall survey process (Tourangeau and Rasinski, 1988; Presser and Blair, 1994), including respondent tasks, is a useful guide for our decision making in instrument development. By *model* we simply mean a formal description of how a process or phenomenon works. Models may be mathematical or, as in this case, diagrammatic. The purpose of a model is to describe the components of the process and to show how they operate together.

In this model of the survey process (see Exhibit 4.1), the researcher develops the survey question and specifies its analytic use. The question is administered by the interviewer or is self-administered. Then the respondent has to do four things: interpret the question, recall relevant information, decide on an answer, and report the answer to the interviewer. These answers are entered into a data set, and the researcher analyzes the results, coming full circle back to the originally specified analytic use of the item. In designing the

Exhibit 4.1
Model of the Survey Data Collection Process

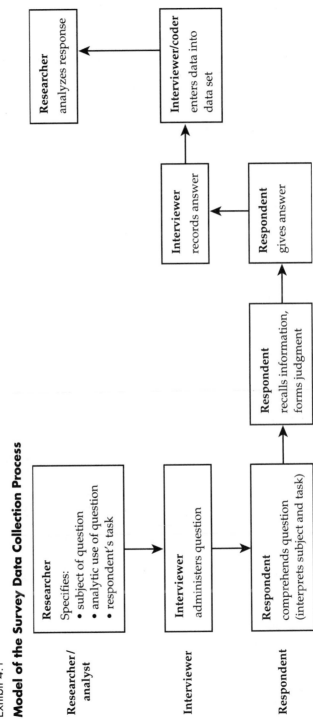

questionnaire, we will need to keep in mind the roles of these players and their tasks, as well as the analysis plan, which is the analytic use to which the question will be put.

Before starting down the road of the procedures, techniques, research, folklore, and craft that go into questionnaire design, we need a sense of our destination. What are the characteristics of a good questionnaire? How do we know when we have reached our goal? The survey model will be our guide.

In this chapter we will note many characteristics of a good questionnaire, but three are so fundamental they share equal billing at the top of our list: It is a valid measure of the factors of interest; it convinces respondents to cooperate; and it elicits acceptably accurate information.

When the researcher specifies the subject and analytic use of each question, clearly the underlying expectation is that a valid measurement will be obtained in the survey. Above all else, the instrument must measure the attitudes, behaviors, or attributes required by our research questions. Each research question may require one survey item or several. But if, in the end, we have not measured the factors of interest, along appropriate dimensions, our other efforts are useless. So the specification of the analytic use of each item has to be clear before we can write (or borrow) survey questions.

Assuming our questions are valid measures, respondents must then be convinced to cooperate and to provide acceptably accurate information. If we develop a questionnaire, however valid, that few respondents are willing to answer or, if willing, cannot answer reliably, we fail. Respondents must understand the question as the researcher intends, have the necessary information, and be able and willing to provide an answer in the form the question requires.

To accomplish these goals, we must not cling so tightly to the language of our hypotheses, constructs, or research concepts that few people other than experts can understand us. Neither can we be satisfied with a questionnaire that obtains cooperation and is easy to answer but at the price of distorting the measures we are after. Other factors contribute to a good questionnaire, but these three are paramount.

Suppose one of our research questions is, Do most people think that the criminal justice system is performing well? We might imagine a very crude first pass that simply tries to use this question as a survey item:

```
Would you say that most people think the criminal
justice system is performing well?
     1. YES
     2. NO
     3. DON'T KNOW/NOT SURE
```

Assume that through pretesting, or just further reflection, the following criticisms of the question come up:

- Respondents cannot report very well about how people in general assess the criminal justice system.

- Respondents have different ideas about what is meant by *criminal justice system*.

- Respondents resist choosing between just "yes" and "no" options; they express feelings that fall in between these alternatives.

- Respondents want to address specific aspects of the system, rather than judging it in general.

More might be said about this question, but these criticisms give an idea of the types of problems that come up. Although the question is exactly the research question of interest, it does not work as a survey item. Now consider the following revision, which addresses the three criticisms.

```
Do you think that people charged with crimes are
fairly sentenced almost always, most of the time,
some of the time, or hardly ever?
```

This item also has problems—as an exercise after reading this chapter, you should try to list what they are. But this modification does address the three criticisms of the original version: It asks what respondents themselves think, rather than asking for a judgment about the opinions of others. It eliminates the ambiguous and complex term *criminal justice system*. It provides a range of response categories to measure shades of opinion. But, in making the question more palatable to respondents, we have all but abandoned the research question—Do most people think that the *criminal justice system* is performing well? Why is that?

The new question fails in at least three ways, and possibly in others. First, it is too limiting. The criminal justice system involves more than sentencing—it also has arrest and rehabilitation functions, among others. Second, factors having nothing to do with the system, such as the financial resources of the accused, may determine how "fair" a sentence, if any, is received in particular cases. Third, the item does not get at the notion of a system, parts of which may work better than others. This research question is complex, and a large part of the survey could be devoted to it alone. If that is not an option, we might consider the following version, which has an introduction, multiple items, and open-ended follow-ups:

```
Three important parts of the criminal justice sys-
tem are the police, the courts, and the prisons.
I'd like to ask you about the job each is doing.

    A. Do you think that the police are doing an ex-
       cellent, good, fair, or poor job? {if fair or
       poor} What would you like to see them do?

    B. How about the courts? Are they doing an ex-
       cellent, good, fair, or poor job? {if fair or
       poor} What would you like to see them do?

    C. How about the prisons? Are they doing an ex-
       cellent, good, fair, or poor job? {if fair or
       poor} What would you like to see them do?
```

In this version, we avoid the problems in the first question draft yet do not lose sight of the central research question. We define the term *criminal justice system* to help ensure that all respondents answer about the same thing. We ask about the components separately; if people feel differently about some of them, we capture that. For those who do not think a particular part of the system works well, we find out why. While these multiple questions add complexity to our analysis, they also add richness to it—and realism.

When **operationalizing** the research questions as survey items, we are forced to be concrete, to specify exactly what information we expect from respondents. This task may force us to reexamine some of our research questions. There is nothing wrong with this, providing we do it deliberately and consider the effects of such a reexamination on our analysis plan. At this key decision point, we need to ask the following questions: Exactly what data do we need? What will we be able to obtain? How do we plan to use it?

We turn now to the respondent's role in the model: comprehending the question, recalling relevant information, and forming and reporting an answer. First, note that respondents' comprehension requires interpreting both the question's subject and the task. For example assume that, in the study of college students, we want to know how many courses in mathematics a college senior has taken since entering the university. We write a draft question: "How many college mathematics courses have you taken?" The respondent must understand not only the subject of the question, college mathematics courses, but must know exactly what to count (the task) in arriving at an answer. This may seem a simple task, but it isn't. Consider whether the following should be included in the courses counted:

1. courses being taken now, but not yet completed
2. college-level mathematics courses, such as calculus, taken in high school
3. remedial courses taken in college
4. courses taken by transfer students at their previous college
5. a course taken but failed last semester
6. a course that primarily involves mathematics but is given by another department or is not listed as a math course, such as econometrics
7. an audited course, not taken for credit
8. a course taken on a pass-fail option

It is often useful to construct such a list when a term might be commonly understood to include different things. As an exercise, try to write a new question that includes courses in categories 3, 4, and 8, but not the others.

Even this simple question on college mathematics courses requires a number of decisions by the researcher, decisions that affect how the question is finally written and what the results will mean. Thus, in writing questions, we must carefully consider exactly what we want respondents to do when we pose tasks such as counting or estimating. If the choice of what to count is left to the respondents, different people will include different things, introducing measurement error into the resulting data.

As the model indicates, the respondent must first comprehend the question, then recall relevant information. So many survey questions rely on the respondents' ability to recall information that it is useful to consider this area in some detail. In considering the role of memory in a survey interview, we tend to think of respondents remembering and reporting particular facts, events, or behaviors. However, we should also recognize that even opinion questions involve memory. If the respondent is asked for an opinion about something the respondent has thought about prior to the interview, then the response is simply a matter of recalling that previous judgment. If the respondent has not considered the subject before, or if something in the interview prompts additional consideration, then the respondent must recall information relevant to reaching an opinion. That new information is used to form the judgment, which is then reported (Tourangeau and Rasinski, 1988).

In developing a questionnaire, we are concerned not that some respondents have poorer memories than others but that certain recall tasks are intrinsically more difficult. Respondents' particular past experiences, their general memory aptitude, and the cognitive effort and recall strategies they use all interact to affect their ability to remember information. In deciding what we can ask in an interview, we rely first on our judgment of how plausible we think it is that respondents can remember the requested information. Second, we try to confirm this judgment by pretesting the questionnaire.

Returning to our example of the college student survey, assume we want to know whether students think that there are adequate treatment programs on campus for alcohol and drug abuse. Some students will have thought about the issue or will have more knowledge about it, perhaps because of contact with such a program. They will respond easily with a previously formed judgment. Respondents who have not formed an opinion will need to think about such things as what they have read about such programs or, perhaps, about the experiences of people they know.

If, in another instance, we ask seniors in college to list the courses they took the previous semester, we expect all of them will be able to do so quite easily. What if we ask those same students to list the courses they took in the ninth grade? Although some will be able to do it and others will not, it is inherently more difficult for all of them. Many factors conspire to make the task harder: the passage of time; intervening events, such as other courses; and the low salience to college seniors of their ninth-grade courses. What if we now ask them to list the grades they received last semester? Again we would expect that all of them could do it, though it might take slightly longer than remembering what courses they took. What about their grades in junior high school? Again this is a harder task for all, and we would anticipate differential performance. In the task of remembering grades, another factor—uniformity—comes in. For the student who got all As (or all Cs for that matter), the task is much easier—the student does not have to try to remember each individual course.

We see that while the memory abilities of respondents is a factor, so too are the task characteristics. We often know a good deal more about the latter. Survey researchers, in the course of designing a study, frequently discuss (with or without evidence from research studies) how difficult particular recall tasks are for respondents. What questions are included and how they are asked depend partly on that assessment.

We must also admit that it may not be possible to address every research question of interest through a survey. Sometimes a task will simply be too difficult for most respondents, resulting either in poor cooperation, inaccurate data, or both. For example, while it might be very interesting to an epidemiologist to interview people age 65 and over about the details of their adolescent health history, the low salience of many of the relevant events and the many years elapsed since their occurrence are likely to make these data too difficult to elicit in an interview.

In developing our questionnaire, we will frequently use reasoning of the sort just described. This approach will facilitate our decisions not only about what questions to include but also how to structure them to aid respondents' memory. For example, consider the question about mathematics courses. Rather than try to construct a single item, which presents respondents with a possibly difficult recall task, we might break up the task, asking either about courses semester by semester or about different types of math courses (e.g., regular, audit, pass-fail) in separate items.

The decisions we make will affect how well respondents can answer the questions we pose and whether they are willing to try. One sure way to obtain poor response rates is to ask questions that are difficult for many respondents.

Writing Questions

Now that we have at least a general sense of our goal of operationalizing our research questions into survey items, how do we begin to construct a questionnaire?

We can borrow questions other surveys have used or we can develop our own. Neither method is inherently better than the other. An advantage of borrowing questions from previous studies is that we can (or may need to) compare our results to previous findings. Such a comparison is much more problematic if our questions are different from those used previously. If our findings differ from the earlier study, we cannot say how much of the difference is due to the changed question. In addition, questions from other surveys may—depending on the former use—have already undergone a great deal of testing, saving us some effort.

One category of questions that it may indeed be important to borrow is that of **screening questions,** the items at the beginning of a questionnaire used to determine eligibility for the study. For example, assume we are looking for a particular characteristic, say adults who were crime victims, and our estimate of the proportion of households with an eligible person is based on a previous survey. One of the first questions asked should determine if the potential respondent is a crime victim. If we ask the question about victimization differently than the previous study did, we may well find a different incidence of crime victims, affecting our screening rate and related costs. That is, if we expect a certain percentage of respondents to screen into the interview and, in fact, find a lower percentage, then either our costs increase to obtain the desired sample size of crime victims or we must settle for fewer such cases.

In general, we need to take care that borrowed questions truly measure the variables we intend. Using a question that is "close" in order to save time or effort can result in false savings when it comes time to analyze the results.

Even borrowed questions need to be pretested. Language usage and connotations change over time, and the context in our questionnaire is likely to differ from that of the question's previous use (Converse and Presser, 1986). The pretesting of borrowed items is also necessary if our administration mode differs from the original one. A question that worked well in a self-administered questionnaire may not be clear, or may have other problems, when heard over the telephone. Finally, we should note the population for which the original question was used. A question that was suitable for a survey of physicians may not work at all for a survey of patients, or for the general population. Despite these caveats, there are many very good survey questions available, and it would be foolish to ignore them. However, since borrowed questions must pass the same standards for inclusion in the study as do the questions we write ourselves, we will discuss some of those standards next.

Criteria for Survey Questions

Within the limited resources we have to design and conduct our study, not every question can be included in the study. Each question has a cost and must be justified. In Exhibit 4.2, we specify some criteria that a question should satisfy before it is used in the study. This key decision guide summarizes many of the issues discussed to this point and links them in a step-by-step procedure that can be applied to each question considered for inclusion in the study. Determining whether questions meet these criteria depends on judgment. Some survey questions may require pretesting before this determination can be made; for others, the answer will be obvious. This set of simple criteria may be consulted throughout the course of questionnaire development.

Exhibit 4.2

Key Decision Guide: Question Utility

A. Does the survey question measure some aspect of one of the research questions?

B. Does the question provide information needed in conjunction with some other variable?
{IF NO TO BOTH A AND B, DROP THE QUESTION. IF YES TO ONE OR BOTH, PROCEED.}

C. Will most respondents understand the question and in the same way?
{IF NO, REVISE OR DROP. IF YES, PROCEED.}

D. Will most respondents have the information to answer it?
{IF NO, DROP. IF YES, PROCEED.}

E. Will most respondents be willing to answer it?
{IF NO, DROP. IF YES, PROCEED.}

F. Is other information needed to analyze this question?
{IF NO, PROCEED. IF YES, PROCEED IF THE OTHER INFORMATION IS AVAILABLE OR CAN BE GOTTEN FROM THE SURVEY.}

G. Should this question be asked of all respondents or of a subset?
{IF ALL, PROCEED. IF A SUBSET, PROCEED ONLY IF THE SUBSET IS IDENTIFIABLE BEFOREHAND OR THROUGH QUESTIONS IN THE INTERVIEW.}

The first two points in the guide have to do with the need for the survey question; the remainder have to do with the feasibility of obtaining the information. Clearly, if the item measures some facet of one of the research questions, we should consider including it. If the item itself does not address a research question but is needed to complement another item, we should also consider including it. For example, assume we asked question A: "Since living in this neighborhood, have you ever had to call the police?" And, those respondents who answered "yes" would get the follow-up question B: "How many times?" In order to compare respondents, an additional item would have to be asked, question C: "How long have you lived in this neighborhood?" While item C may not be of interest in itself, it is needed to analyze item B.

The Structure of Survey Questions

A very wide variety of question types are available to the researcher, but relatively few types are needed in most surveys, and, on their surface, most of these are uncomplicated. But as we will see, many items that at first glance appear boringly simple pose serious problems for respondents, require difficult decisions for the researcher, and consume many resources for testing and revision, often more time and other resources than the novice researcher allocates to questionnaire development.

In writing questions, we must consider two components of our model of the data collection process—respondent and interviewer. We want to pose tasks that both players can perform reasonably well. Although we focus primarily on the respondents' tasks, we should keep in mind that interviewers have to be able to read the questions smoothly, pronounce the words clearly and unambiguously (especially in a telephone survey, when interviewers cannot rely on visual cues that convey that respondents are puzzled), and have clear instructions for recording the responses. To these considerations, we add a very important factor: We do not want to influence the respondent's answer in one direction or another. Therefore, while we develop our questions, we must constantly ask ourselves whether we have introduced bias into the data-gathering process.

We want to write questions that are unadorned and uncomplicated, as explicit and single-minded as a lawyer's interrogation. While we want survey questions to sound natural if administered by an interviewer or to read smoothly if self-administered, it is important to recognize that a survey question is a very special construct with a clearly focused purpose. As much as we labor to make them sound natural, survey questions are not simply forms of conversation. Ideally, survey questions are shorn of the vagueness, ambivalence, asides, and digressions of everyday speech. Conversely, although we take pains to ensure that our questions reflect our research goals, these questions do not typically contain the language of social science either. That is, words used in questions are simpler than the scientific intentions that drive them. Unlike either everyday conversation or scientific discourse, survey questions must function without supplementary explanation. Once the survey question is arrived at, we require that interviewers ask the question in exactly the same way each time, neither adding, deleting, nor changing words. While we often do not know why different wording of questions produces different results, that such effects occur is not disputed (Schuman and Presser, 1981). The reliability of the data obtained through survey research rests, in large part, on the uniform administration of questions and their uniform interpretation by respondents.

For those questions we choose to write from scratch, there are several options for how we articulate them, in what order we present them, the response dimensions, and the form of respondents' answers. We begin by defining some options, noting the generally preferred approach, then discuss why deviations from that approach are sometimes necessary or desirable.

Whether for telephone, face-to-face, or self-administered surveys, the questions can be broadly defined, open or closed. In the former, respondents are not given explicit answer choices; in the latter they are. For reasons that will become clear, we recommend using closed questions as much as possible. Data from open questions are essentially narratives that must be interpreted and coded; after the survey is over, the researcher is still a step away from having results that can be analyzed quantitatively. We will make some limited use of open questions, but our focus is on closed items.

A closed question has two parts: the statement of the question and the response categories. We need to devote equal attention to each part. We state the question as directly as possible, and we require that the answer be given in terms of one, and typically only one, of the answer choices provided. Often, specific qualifiers or conditions are part of the question. These added components restrict the meaning of the question to match our research objective. The simplest example is the yes-no response option. For example:

In the past year, has anything happened to you or
your property that you thought was a crime or an
attempt at a crime?
 1. YES
 2. NO

While the choice of response options is relatively straightforward,
even in this case we have made certain decisions, for example not to
include "don't know" or "not sure" options. Whether we include
such options depends on our judgment about whether many respondents may not be able to answer simply "yes" or "no."

For example, imagine that a respondent returned home one day
and found a broken first-floor window. Does it mean that someone
attempted to break into her home, or was it an accident caused by
children playing? However much thought she gives to the question,
she may remain uncertain. Now consider a situation in which several months ago, a respondent's calculator was stolen at work when
she left it unattended for a moment. It was of little value, and she
saw no hope of getting it back, so she did not report the theft to the
police or to her insurance company. When she hears our survey
question, she cannot recall exactly when this rather minor theft occurred. Was it in the past year or not? Again, she may be uncertain.

For this question then it may be reasonable to add a "don't
know" option. But these examples illustrate more. They show that
we need to think through each question from the perspective of
plausible situations to judge whether all or most respondents will be
able to answer it in the expected manner. Often, thinking through a
few hypothetical examples yourself or posing the question to a col-
league will quickly reveal such problems. Such informal judgments
and conversations are not substitutes for formal pretesting but a
complement to it.

As an exercise, consider what kinds of difficulties some respondents might have with the following survey questions. Pay particular attention to the response categories.

BECAUSE OF CONCERNS ABOUT CRIME, how often do you
avoid certain areas that you'd like to go to?
Would you say:
 1. Always
 2. Frequently
 3. Seldom

4. Never
8. Don't know [volunteered][2]

In the past year, would you say that the VIOLENT crime situation in YOUR NEIGHBORHOOD has gotten better, gotten worse, or stayed about the same?
   1. Gotten better
   2. Gotten worse
   3. Stayed about the same
   4. Don't know [volunteered]

The Use of Qualifiers in Survey Questions

As noted, many times we need to qualify or restrict a question in one or more ways. This is often done to make a respondent's task (such as recalling past events) easier, to simplify a complex phenomenon or judgment (such as rating different components of satisfaction), or to tailor the survey item to fit the research question (such as focusing on things that occurred in a particular time period). Here is a list (by no means exhaustive) of common components of survey questions and examples of them.

1. Specific reference period

Quite often research questions may concern events occurring only in a particular time frame, for example:

How often have you shopped at the Book Center *this semester—that is, since January?*

or

In the past year, did anything happen to you or your property that you thought was a crime or an attempt at a crime?

---

[2]Typically, "don't know" or "dk" responses are coded 8 (or 88), and refusals to respond are coded 9 (or 99). This allows the same code to be used for these outcomes throughout the questionnaire, regardless of the number of response categories, which simplifies data analysis. In the example shown here, the interviewer does not offer the "don't know" response as an option, but the respondent may volunteer it.

In some instances, the time period needs to be limited to make it possible for respondents to provide reasonably accurate counts of a behavior or an event. Deciding what time frame will work for most respondents is a combination of what we think has worked in other surveys and of judgment.

In other instances, we may be interested only in a particular time period for substantive reasons. If we want to compare attitudes about crime in the past year to data from previous years, clearly we must limit interview reports to the past year.

2. Summary judgment

Sometimes, to avoid the use of an excessive number of qualifiers or to recognize the complexity of an issue, we ask respondents for a summary judgment.

In general, would you say that crime in your neighborhood is very serious, somewhat serious, not too serious, or not at all serious?

Overall, how satisfied are you with your academic advisor?

Without these qualifiers, some respondents may balk at responding, saying that some kinds of crime have gotten better and other types worse. Similarly, some students will say that they are sometimes very satisfied with their advisor and dissatisfied at other times. These qualifiers are intended to elicit an "all things considered" type of judgment.

3. Adjectives and other restrictions

Just as we can limit reporting to a particular time, so too can we limit it to a particular place (precisely or generally defined) or to one category of events.

In the past year, would you say that the *VIO-LENT* crime situation in *YOUR NEIGHBORHOOD* has gotten better, gotten worse, or stayed about the same?

This approach is often used when the research question calls for comparisons of different aspects of the same issues—for example, different types of crime in different places.

4. **Reasons for behaviors**

If the research question or hypothesis posits reasons for behaviors (or, much more difficult, opinions), then the question must attempt to elicit those reasons.

BECAUSE OF CONCERNS ABOUT CRIME, how often do you carry a weapon for protection?

As an exercise, for the question, "How many times have you gone to a physician?" write four versions: one that adds a reference period, one that includes only visits for a particular reason, one that includes only certain types of doctors, and one that does all three. To keep things interesting, *don't* borrow from the examples given above.

More on Response Categories

Usually response categories are explicit. Their choice determines, to a great extent, what our data will look like. Before considering some characteristics of effective response categories, let us examine some of the kinds of things response categories measure.

Survey questions can measure an enormous range of issues: attitudes, such as favoring or opposing abortion, the effectiveness of local police, or rating job satisfaction; behaviors, such as frequency of moviegoing; personal attributes or facts, like age, income, or race; and knowledge, such as how AIDS is transmitted. How well such measures are obtained in a survey interview depends not only on how precisely the question is asked but also on how suitable the response categories are. Sometimes the appropriate categories follow naturally from the question. For example, in asking "What type of school did you attend just before coming to the University of Maryland?", we need simply to think of the possible places a student might have come from, such as:

High school
Transferred from a 2-year college
Transferred from a 4-year college
Returning after an absence

If we are uncertain that we have covered all the possibilities, a "Somewhere else (please specify)" category might be added. When the question concerns a fact or attribute, it is often clear what the response alternatives must be. In questions about opinions, the categories, and even the correct dimension, may not be obvious. For example:

```
Depending on the circumstances of the case, some
students found responsible for the possession
and/or use of illegal drugs are given the option
of random drug testing for a period of 2 years
in lieu of actual suspension from the university.
How satisfied are you with this policy? Very
satisfied, somewhat satisfied, somewhat dissatis-
fied, or very dissatisfied?
```

We could focus on which "satisfaction" categories to use, but something more fundamental is amiss. Is *satisfaction* the word that we want? Perhaps students who have had experience with this policy could say how satisfied they were with the result, but that's a somewhat different issue. And for other students, satisfaction with a policy they have never encountered is imprecise at best. Maybe what we really want to know is do students think the policy is *fair*.

In other instances, response categories are integral to the question and just have to be listed for coding. A simple example would be "Do you sell your books after completing the course or do you keep them?" The categories are obviously "sell them" and "keep them." But even in this relatively straightforward case, we need to be sure all the possibilities are covered. Examining this question more closely, we see that a student could also choose to "sell some and keep some"; so we need to add this option. Are there any other possibilities?

A more complex question with integral response categories comes from the crime study. Suppose we want to find out what respondents think about alternative sentences for criminals—that is, a sentence other than being sent to prison. We might develop a question such as:

```
Do you think people convicted of robbery should be
sent to prison, required to report to a parole of-
ficer once a month, required to report daily, or
monitored electronically so their whereabouts are
known at ALL times?
```

Once again, the response categories are the heart of the question and are developed with it. But many times, in asking about attitudes, ratings or evaluations, or behaviors we have quite a choice of ways to structure the response options. In Exhibit 4.3, we list a number of common response categories for measuring attitudes, behaviors, and knowledge. While this exhibit is far from exhaustive, it serves as an introduction to response categories. (For more examples of scale and question construction, see Sudman and Bradburn, 1982.) Note that some of these categories are easily adapted to other dimensions. For example, the "very/somewhat/not too/not at all" quantifiers work well with measures such as "helpful," "serious," "concerned," "likely," and "interested," among others.

It is important to be aware that many of these terms do not have an absolute meaning. They are ordered relative to each other, but their meaning is left to the respondents' judgment; one person's "good" will be another's "fair." (Also see Bradburn and Miles, 1979, on vague quantifiers.)

Most of the response categories listed in Exhibit 4.3 use three or four choices and do not present a neutral category. We recommend keeping the number of categories small, especially for telephone interviews. Respondents have to keep the categories in mind while deciding their answer. Similarly, many respondents may take the easy out with a neutral or "no opinion" category if they do not feel strongly about an issue. Many of these respondents will, however, lean one way or another, which can produce useful data. Still, if, after pretesting, we find respondents pushing for a middle alternative, providing one might be advisable. There are widely divergent views on the number of categories and the use of a neutral category, which are beyond the scope of this book (see Sudman and Bradburn, 1982; and Schuman and Presser, 1981 for a full discussion of the issues).

In another type of response format , only the end points of a scale are labeled, as in:

```
On a scale of 1 to 10, where 1 means not at all
serious and 10 means extremely serious, how seri-
ous a problem is crime on campus?
```

This approach elicits a finer partitioning of responses (variance). However, it does introduce complexities into the analysis. Does one compute average ratings; combine parts of the scale into high, medium, or low categories; or use some threshold level (such as any rating greater than 7) to indicate that crime is perceived as a problem? All these and others are possible. If there are many points on the scale, it will probably be somewhat easier for respondents if the instrument is self-administered and they can see the range.

Exhibit 4.3

Some Common Response Category Quantifiers

Opinions

Very satisfied/ Somewhat satisfied/ Somewhat dissatisfied/ Very dissatisfied

Very important/ Somewhat important/Not too important/Not at all important

Oppose/Support

Strongly oppose/Oppose/Support/Strongly support

Knowledge

Very familiar/ Somewhat familiar/ Not too familiar/ Not at all familiar

True/False

A lot/Some/A little/Nothing

Frequency of Events or Behaviors

Never/ Less than once a semester/ Once a semester/ Twice a semester/ Three times a semester/ More than three times a semester

Per day/Per week/Per month/Per year/Never

Always/ Frequently/ Seldom/ Never

Always/Sometimes/Never

All/Most/Some/A few/None

Often/ Sometimes/ Rarely/ Never

Ratings

Gotten better/ Gotten worse/ Stayed about the same

Excellent/ Good/ Fair/ Poor

A great deal above average/Somewhat above average/Average/ Somewhat below average/A great deal below average

Very fair/Fair/Unfair/Very unfair

High/Medium/Low

Small/Medium/Large

We should recognize the subjective nature and the inherent complexity of opinion questions (see Turner and Martin, 1984, for a full treatment of these issues). When two student respondents independently answer the question "How satisfied were you with the book center's special-order service?" the word *satisfied* may well have somewhat different connotations for each of them. That is, the dimension of satisfaction has multiple aspects, which may be given greater or lesser emphasis by different people (or in different situations). For one student, the satisfaction rating may be dominated by a particular, unpleasant encounter with a cashier; for the other, the perception of average costs of goods may determine the rating. Each respondent understands the term *satisfaction*, but each puts his own spin on it.

Some additional lessons for questionnaire design and interviewing come from this observation. First, if obtaining a good understanding of, in this case, respondent's satisfaction is central to the study, multiple questions are probably necessary. After obtaining the general measure, some follow-up items would be asked. In this example, we might follow with a question such as "What was the MAIN reason you were {satisfied/dissatisfied}?"

Second, respondents may want to know what aspect of satisfaction is intended. When they ask an interviewer, the standard response should be "Whatever it means to you," letting the respondent make the choice of what kinds of things to consider (Fowler and Mangione, 1990).[3] There is a great potential for interviewers to influence responses in such situations, especially if the respondent does not have a strong opinion about the particular issue. This is one more reason why we emphasize that interviewers read questions verbatim and refrain from interpretive "helpful" comments.

Finally, in seeing, once again, the complexity lurking within another seemingly simple situation, we may choose to add to our pretest agenda methods to explore how respondents understand such terms as *satisfaction, serious,* and others in specific question situations. This need may also affect our choice of pretest methods. We will return to this in some detail in chapter 6.

In constructing categories for frequencies of occurrence of events or behaviors, our choices of both the number of categories and the number of times denoted by each one is guided by our perception of the range of times the event or behavior is likely to occur. If we overestimate or underestimate this frequency, most respondents will be

---

[3]Notice that this is the opposite strategy than we take for factual questions about attributes or the occurrence of certain events or behaviors, where the "objects" of inquiry are well defined, such as car ownership, and we want to ensure uniform reporting across respondents.

grouped into one category and we learn nothing. In such a situation, we say the measure has little or no variance. The semester-based response scale in Exhibit 4.3 (under "Frequency of events or behaviors") may work quite well for a question about visits to an academic advisor or trips to the bookstore; it would probably not work for visits to the library. Presumably, most students will go to the library many more than three times a semester, so our responses would be bunched into that one category. The choice of response scales is still another instance in which the questionnaire is guided by our perception of how the world (in this case, the world of academia) works; and in pretesting, we will evaluate those perceptions.

Sometimes we don't have even an initial impression of the correct choices to provide. In such a case, we may choose to ask an open-ended question (without explicit response alternatives) in the pretest to learn what frequencies of behavior (or other categories) are likely. We then use this information to construct closed categories for the main study questionnaire. So, for example, if we are not sure how often, on average, students see an academic advisor each semester, the pretest question might be simply: "All together, how many times did you visit your academic advisor last semester?" After checking what respondents reported in the pretest, it may be possible to create categories such as "never," "once a semester," "twice a semester," "three times a semester," or "more than three times a semester." On the other hand, if the pretest data show that many students meet with an advisor many more than three times a semester, then a set of categories that take this information into account might be constructed.

If we are not confident, even after pretesting, what frequency range makes sense, it may be best to ask the question open-ended, even in the main study, and code the responses later.[4] This situation could arise, for example, in a question that only a subset of respondents are asked, in which case pretesting does not obtain enough information to develop categories.

Some Final Advice on Potential Pitfalls

One type of question we suggest avoiding is the agree-disagree format. In this type of question, respondents are given a statement and asked whether they agree or disagree with it. There are usually two,

---

[4]Note that this type of open-end elicits a single number, or a number of times per some time period, and so does not present the difficult coding issues of open-end narratives.

four, or five categories provided. The following is an example of the agree-disagree format:

```
I am going to read you some statements about the
criminal justice system. For each one, please tell
me if you strongly agree, agree, disagree, or
strongly disagree.

The police are doing an excellent job. Would you
strongly agree, agree, disagree, or strongly dis-
agree?
```

Although this form is quite popular, it is also problematic and has been strongly criticized by survey methodologists (Converse and Presser, 1986). Research has shown that there is a tendency (called "acquiescence response set") toward agreement, regardless of the question's content. Further, there is evidence (Schuman and Presser, 1981) that this tendency is related to education, with less-educated respondents showing the tendency toward agreement more frequently than better-educated respondents.

Another type of question to avoid is the **double-barreled question** which, often unintentionally, has two parts, each of which the respondents may feel differently about. For example, "Do you think the police and courts are doing an excellent, good, fair, or poor job?" A respondent who thinks the police are doing a poor job but the courts are doing a good one has no way to answer. Unlike the agree-disagree items, double-barreled questions do not reflect bias or the researcher's preference; rather, they are structurally flawed. The solution is almost always to break up the item into two questions. Double-barreled items often result from a misguided attempt to save space by piling multiple topics into one question. The result is questions that are unintelligible and unanswerable and cannot be usefully analyzed.

Ambiguity is the ghost most difficult to exorcise from survey questions. In testing a question on respondents, we find that they arrive at different interpretations of it so often that it almost seems willful. If first we banish ambiguity, all our remaining work is easier. Payne (1951), in his classic work *The Art of Asking Questions*, ends with an excellent checklist of things to consider in writing questions, many of which have to do with ambiguity.

5 Questionnaire Design: Organizing the Questions

Questionnaires are typically organized into sections that follow the logic of the sampling plan, the data collection procedure, and question administration. Most questionnaires consist of an introduction, a respondent-selection procedure, substantive questions, background or demographic questions, and, possibly, a few post-interview items. While the form and methods for each of these components will vary by particular survey and by mode of administration, their purpose, as described below, generally remains the same.

Introduction. When respondents (or household informants) are contacted for the interview, they must be given enough information about the survey to induce their cooperation. This step is necessary even when there has been prior notification about the study.

Respondent selection. This step usually occurs in general population surveys when the unit of analysis is the individual. Typically, housing units are selected—in one or several stages—from the sampling frame; then, within each sampled household, an individual is randomly chosen for the interview. Omission of a careful respondent-selection procedure can introduce serious bias into the sample.

Substantive questions. In this section we ask questions to address each aspect of our research goals. This is the heart of the questionnaire, accounting for the majority of the data and, hence, the majority of our effort and costs.

Background questions. It is common practice in general population surveys to obtain some background information, usually demographic, about the respondents. There is no standard set of such questions, but sex, age, race, education, marital status, and income are frequently used. (See the crime survey questionnaire in appendix B for a formatted set of several common demographic items.) There are three general reasons for obtaining these data. First, our analysis may require them. If we want to compare the attitudes of whites and nonwhites on, for example, the effectiveness of the criminal justice system, we need to know each respondent's race. Second, we may want to compare the demographic distributions in our study to census data in order to assess the representativeness of our sample. Third, if we decide to use poststratification weights (see chapters 7–10 on sampling and report writing), these data will also be needed.

For surveys of special populations such as students, background questions may also be included, depending on the analysis needs. Our student omnibus survey in appendix A, for example, might ask class rank, grade point average, and other such items. But we should have a clear idea how each item will be used before adding it, since background questions also have a cost.

Post-interview questions. After the interview proper, there may be a few additional questions for the respondent, the interviewer, or both. Such questions generally fall into two categories. First, we may want some information about the interview just completed. For example, we might ask the interviewer to rate how well respondents seemed to understand particular questions or whether respondents were reluctant to answer some items. Respondents might similarly be asked whether there were any times when they were not sure what a question meant, or why they refused or could not answer some items. These sorts of scripted post-interview questions can be particularly useful on pretests of potentially difficult or sensitive instruments (see the discussion of pretesting below) but may also be included in some main data collection as well. We must, however, keep in mind that post-interview items add to the cost of the survey, so such questions cannot be idly included. They must pass the same tests of usefulness as any other questions.

Second, after the interview, in some cases, we may ask respondents for the names of secondary sources (relatives or others who will know the respondents' whereabouts should they move) if we plan to recontact the respondents or to send them a copy of the survey results.

Transitions and auxiliary information. In addition to these main parts of the questionnaire, we sometimes need to give respondents information before they answer a question—for example, descriptions of the two social service programs we want to ask their preference about. In other instances, we need to write transition statements that precede questions about a new topic.

One possible by-product of trying to provide helpful information, or transitions, is the introduction of bias. One must take care that the information given to respondents to assist them in answering a question does not bias their responses. To the general public, bias often suggests intentional efforts to affect answers. Certainly that can happen; but unintended effects are much more common. Bias is also a concern in writing transitions, which should be short, neutral statements to bridge the gap between sections of a questionnaire, alerting the respondent that the next questions are about a new topic.

Some things to watch out for in providing information or transitions in a questionnaire are listed below. Each type of problem is followed by an example of a transition statement or section introduction.

- *Social desirability.* "The student health service is developing a new program to educate students about the dangers of alcohol. These next questions are about your drinking habits."

Questions about drinking are generally somewhat sensitive. It is not socially desirable to report drinking to excess. This transition would very likely add to that sensitivity. Respondent **underreporting** of the frequency and amounts of their drinking might well result.

- *Adjectives conveying positive or negative qualities.* "Over the past year, the student government advisors have worked hard to improve the referral service provided by academic advisors. The referral service is an integral part of the advising process. Part of the purpose of this survey is to find out how good a job students like yourself think advisors are doing in providing referrals."

Again, the transition and information may have the effect of encouraging positive evaluations in the questions that follow. Not all respondents will be so affected, but some, particularly those without strong prior opinions about the advising service, might be.

- *Links to authority.* "The president of the university and the board of trustees have proposed a plan to reorganize the academic advising system. Some groups oppose this plan. The next questions are about your opinions about the plan."

In this instance, the prestige and authority of important administrators are on one side, while on the other side are vague opposition groups. In what direction might some respondents be swayed in their assessment of the plan?

What are some ways to avoid the potential bias of transitions and background information? The simplest is to minimize their use. Often they may not really be needed. Second, avoid language that is likely to arouse strong feelings; interviews do not need to be colorful. Never indicate a position on an issue. If transitions and information are necessary, keep them brief, balanced, and bland. Finally, in the questionnaire-testing phase, don't forget that transitions and information are also part of the questionnaire and should be evaluated with the same scrutiny. Every part of the questionnaire has the potential to affect answers and needs the same attention given to the questions themselves.

Introducing the Study

One objective in designing the questionnaire is to convince potential respondents that the study is important enough for them to devote their personal resources of time and effort to it. We want the respondent to take the study seriously and try to provide complete and accurate responses. Convincing respondents to do this is one of our first tasks, and it begins with how we introduce the survey.

It is important to realize that there is a distinction between the survey topic, per se, and our particular study. It is not enough that the *topic* appeal to respondents; the *study* must seem worthwhile as well. A respondent may, for example, be very interested in the problem of crime and think that it is an important societal issue. It does not follow, however, that the respondent thinks that our study about crime is important.

Although, for the sake of brevity, we will not repeatedly refer to "potential respondents," it is important to keep in mind that this is the case. Each person selected into the sample is a potential respondent; but he or she is also a potential refuser or other type of non-interview.

Introducing the study to the respondent can begin with the cover letter sent with a mail questionnaire, with an advance letter preceding a telephone or personal visit study, or with the interviewer's introduction in a "cold" contact at the respondent's household. We will discuss key aspects of each of these forms of initial contact in turn. First, let's set down some guiding concerns.

As we consider how to develop introductions appropriate to each method of interview administration, we want to keep in mind the kinds of questions that respondents often have about a survey. These include:

What is the study about?

Who is conducting it?

Who is the sponsor?

Why is the study important?

What will be done with the study results?

These are typical things that respondents want to know before agreeing to participate in a study. The respondent's interest in these questions should seem self-evident, but many researchers overlook the common-sense basis of the respondent's decision to participate in the study. Other questions respondents may want answered include:

Why is the study pertinent to me?

Why was I selected?

Some respondents may want to know even more about the survey, but there is a limit to how much information can be conveyed quickly in the introduction. The questions listed are those that come up in most surveys of the general population, and of many special populations as well. We may find that for a particular study additional information is essential. For example, if the study requires asking about sensitive or illegal behaviors, it will probably be necessary to give special assurances of confidentiality. If the sample was selected from a special list, such as patients in an HMO (health maintenance organization), it may be advisable to inform respondents where their names were obtained.

Telephone Introductions

How do we decide what information to include in the introduction to a telephone interview and how do we best convey it? The following is a draft of an introduction for an RDD survey about crime in the state of Maryland:

```
Hello, my name is _____. I'm calling from the Uni-
versity of Maryland Survey Research Center. The
Survey Research Center is conducting a survey for
the governor's 1991 commission on violent street
```

crime. The survey results will be used to help
plan programs to reduce crime through prevention,
education programs for young people, and better
law enforcement. Your household was chosen through
a random-selection process. Your participation is
completely voluntary but is very important to the
representatives of the survey. All your answers
will be kept in strict confidence.

Take a moment to check whether all the questions that potential
respondents typically want the answers to, listed earlier, have been
addressed in this draft introduction. Then, before reading further,
take a moment and try to imagine how *you* might react if you heard
this introduction on the telephone. Remember, the respondent did
not expect the call, and no advance letter was sent. All that is known
about the survey comes from what is in this introduction.

All the key questions have been answered, but the introduction
is far too long. The respondent picks up the phone and is asked to
listen to a paragraph. Remember, we want to convey these key
points, but quickly.

Here is a first pass at revision. Let's compare it to the original and
analyze the reasons for the changes we have made.

Hello, I'm calling from the University of Maryland. My name is _____. We are doing a study about
crime for the State of Maryland's Summit on Violent Street Crime. The results will be used to
help plan ways to reduce crime. Your household was
chosen through a random-selection process. Your
participation is completely voluntary. All your
answers will be kept in strict confidence. For
this study, I need to speak with the adult in your
household who is 18 or older and will have the
NEXT birthday. Who would that be?

First, we mention *where* the call is from before giving the interviewer's name. Remember, many refusals come at the very outset of
contact. If the first thing the respondent hears is an unfamiliar name,
it could be a negative signal. Hearing the name of an organization,
and one that sounds legitimate, alerts the respondent that this may
be some type of business call, rather than a wrong number or a sales
call. This is a small matter, but many of the decisions in designing

the questionnaire are in themselves small, yet they have a cumulative effect.

Next, we substitute the word *study* for *survey*. There is some evidence (Dillman, 1978) that the word *survey* carries some negative connotations. Also, sales calls are often disguised as surveys, which many respondents are now alerted to.

The details about the use of the study results have been cut back. There was too much of this in the first version. The mention of the governor was also removed. While mentioning the governor may have helped get many respondents to cooperate, others may have negative feelings toward the governor, which would lessen their likelihood of cooperation. Limiting the sponsorship to the state of Maryland should provide the broadest appeal.

Additionally, the information about how the respondent's household was selected and the assurance of confidentiality were deemed nonessential for this particular study. Note that although we do not say how long the interview will take, if the respondent asks about interview length, the interviewer must give a truthful response. Interviewers should say how long the average interview is but that it may be somewhat shorter or longer for any particular person. Similarly, the other information we decided not to keep in the introduction should all be available to the interviewers to use as individual respondent situations warrant.

The within-household, random respondent selection was incorporated into the revised introduction. This allows a smooth flow from providing information about the study into making the first request of the respondent. So we end the introduction with a subtle transition into the question-asking phase of the interview.

The final version of the introduction was shortened still further to the following:

```
Hello, I'm calling from the University of Mary-
land. My name is _____. We are doing a study for
the state of Maryland's Summit on Violent Street
Crime. I need to speak with the adult in your
household, who is 18 or older, and will have the
next birthday. Who would that be?
```

Advance and Cover Letters

Advance or cover letters can be an important part of the survey. An advance letter is sometimes sent to respondents before they are contacted by the interviewer. A cover letter accompanies a mailed questionnaire. Although their focus is somewhat different, the purposes of advance and cover letters are quite similar, so we will treat them together. (See Dillman, 1978, for a complete treatment.)

In both cases, the purpose is to use the letter to help obtain cooperation. To this end, both provide information very much like that in interview introductions, but with crucial differences. First, unlike the interviewer-administered introduction, advance or cover letters must stand on their own. Second, letters are much more easily ignored than an interviewer. For both these reasons, such letters must be eye-catching (yet professional), clear (but brief), and compelling (but neutral). The letter must stand out from the welter of junk mail most people receive and must speak for the researcher to the respondent, addressing the key obstacles to cooperation.

As suggested by Dillman (1978), these letters generally include the following content in the order specified:

- What the study is about; why it is important; how the study results will be used
- Why the respondent is important to the study
- How the respondent was selected
- Promise of confidentiality
- A phone number to call if the respondent has questions and who will be reached at that number

In mail surveys, the cover letter serves the function of introducing the survey, so it is advisable not to repeat this information in the instrument itself. In the questionnaire itself, respondents should be given a simple set of clear instructions for answering, and each section of the instrument should be labeled in a different typeface to clearly signal transitions.

What Questions Should the Questionnaire Begin With?

Having guided the respondent through the introduction, we are ready to ask the first questions. What guidelines do we want to follow to select those questions? There are two things to keep in mind: first, the respondent's decision to participate occurs in stages; and second, there may be a logical relationship between the questionnaire items or sections.

There is not a large body of research literature on what motivates respondents to participate in a survey (see Groves, 1989, and Groves, Cialdini, and Couper, 1992, for a summary). But we do have a lot of evidence that most refusals occur at the introduction or during the very first questions in interviewer-administered surveys. It may be helpful to think of the respondent as making an initial *tentative* decision to participate (or at least to keep listening) based on the information in the cover or advance letter and in the introduction.[1] Next, the respondent hears (or reads) the first question. Besides beginning to obtain data, what should that first question accomplish? It should have all the following characteristics:

- *Relevant to the central topic.* We do not want to tell the respondent the study is about crime and then ask a first question about how many years of education, for example, the person has completed. While this may be very relevant to the analysis (and will be asked later), many respondents will ask themselves (or the interviewer), "What does my education have to do with the issue of crime?" This is one reason we do not usually ask demographic questions first.

- *Easy to answer.* Most surveys include questions that vary in the degree of difficulty respondents have in answering them. It is best to begin with a question most respondents will find relatively easy to answer. While some respondents may find a difficult question intriguing, many others will wonder what they've gotten themselves into, and they will feel frustrated and, perhaps, terminate the interview. Remember, we want to get the cooperation of a wide range of respondents. As an exercise, after reading this chapter, go through the questionnaires in appendixes A and B and note which questions *you* would find easy to answer, and which you would find difficult.

- *Interesting.* Little in the survey research literature speaks directly to the issue of interesting questions. Some investigations of interviewer-respondent rapport touch on the issue of interest indirectly, but they seldom address it as an independent factor. Yet, common sense should dictate that, other things being equal, anyone would prefer to answer an interesting question than a

---

[1]When asked, at the end of a telephone interview, the main reason they chose to participate, a nontrivial number of respondents reported being caught unaware and beginning the interview without really thinking about it. In those cases, it was really the absence of a decision not to participate (Blair and Chun, 1992).

mundane one. In general, it is more interesting to give an opinion ("Do you think the amount of violent crime in your town is increasing, decreasing, or staying about the same?") than a fact ("Do you read a newspaper everyday?").

- *Applicable to and answerable by most respondents.* One way to begin an interview that would definitely not seem to hold respondents' interest would be a series of questions to which many people will answer "don't know" because the questions do not apply to them. Such a question would be, "In general, how reasonable do you think the price of software is at the University Book Center?" Many respondents will have to respond that they don't know because they've never purchased software.

- *Closed format.* While some respondents will enjoy the chance to answer an open-ended question that does not limit their response choices, many others will find this a difficult way to start an interview. This may be especially true if, prior to the interview, the respondent has not thought much about the issue at hand.

Although these guidelines help us in deciding what questions to begin with, sometimes we have to deviate from this ideal. It is important to know when this is the case and what to do when it happens. Perhaps the most common situation of necessary deviation occurs when screening is involved. When the survey target population is not identical to the frame population, questions have to be asked at the outset of the interview to determine whether the household or individual fits the population definition. For example,

```
How many children under the age of 18 live in this
household?
_____   ENTER NUMBER AND PROCEED
(None) END INTERVIEW
```

One note of caution in asking "screener" questions like this is to not make it obvious what type of target households are eligible for the survey. Some respondents will answer one way with the intention of opting out of the study (e.g., a man with children answering "no" to the above question). A way to avoid this is to balance the question so it is not obvious what answer will terminate the interview (e.g., "Of the people who live in this household, how many are adults 18 or older and how many are children under 18?").

Many times the screening questions will be rather innocuous. For example, when the target population comprises households in a particular geographic area, such as a county or school district, the screener will simply ask place of residence. In other cases, the questions may be relatively sensitive—if, for example, only households in particular income categories are of interest. In a few cases, such questions could be so sensitive as to make their feasibility (without severe underreporting) doubtful—for example, in a survey of homosexuals.

Sudman and Bradburn (1982) note that sensitivity is often determined as much by the response as by the question. For example, a question about illegal drug use is not sensitive to a respondent who does not use drugs. Other items, however, such as questions about sexual behaviors, are sensitive to most people. In general, we recommend that the novice researcher steer clear of sensitive items, especially as screeners. When mildly sensitive questions must be asked early, the following guidelines should be followed.

- Ask as few sensitive questions as absolutely necessary to establish the respondent's membership in the target population.
- Make clear to respondents why it is necessary to ask such questions.
- If costs permit, consider inserting an opening nonsensitive "buffer" question or two before the screening item(s) to establish some rapport with the respondent.

Finally, it may be necessary to deviate from the guidelines for the opening questions if sections of the questionnaire apply only to respondents with certain characteristics. For example, if the first section of the questionnaire is about people who smoke, then we must first ask respondents whether they smoke to know whether to ask the section about smoking.

Grouping Questions into Sections

Now that we have some notion about how to begin the questionnaire, we have to decide the order of the remaining substantive questions. There is little research on this issue, so we will again employ a set of guidelines. We begin with the same qualities of relevance, ease, interest, and available knowledge that we considered in choosing our first interview question. Since most terminations occur early in the interview, these same concerns should guide the choice of the first set of questions and may also direct the order of subsequent questions as well.

To these considerations we add internal logic and a smooth progression, or flow, through the questionnaire. Certainly, if some questions depend on prior responses, the order of these items is dictated by that logic. It is also useful for the respondent to sense the flow, or natural progression, of the instrument. This is worthwhile in both interviewer-administered and self-administered instruments. As Dillman (1978) points out for mail surveys, the respondent should have a sense of progressing smoothly and, one hopes, rapidly through the questionnaire. We want to avoid having questions on a particular topic scattered through the questionnaire. Also, if a set of questions uses the same scale, it is easier for respondents to answer them together.

Now we'll apply these guidelines to the crime survey cited survey. Exhibit 5.1 lists the survey topics. How might we arrange them in the questionnaire?

We want the first set of items to be easy. Certainly it is easier for respondents to answer questions about subjects they have thought about before than about those they haven't. Some respondents will have thought about the criminal justice system, but many others will not. Also, as we have already seen, that set of items may be moderately difficult to answer. Personal experiences with crime meet the

Exhibit 5.1

Topics for the Maryland Crime Survey

A. Background (demographic) questions

B. Personal experiences with crime

C. Opinions about the criminal justice system

D. Fear that they or their family will be victims of crime

E. Perceptions of the violent crime problem in their neighborhood and in the state

F. Perceptions of the nonviolent crime problem in their neighborhood and in the state

G. Things done to protect themselves from crime

H. Opinions about alternative sentencing

I. Perceptions of the crime problem, generally, in their neighborhood and in the state criterion of ease, as do things respondents have done to protect themselves against crime. Both these topics, however, have the drawback of being somewhat sensitive. Alternatively, given the media attention to the crime problem, many people will have perceptions about how serious crime is, and the topic is also clearly relevant to the survey's purpose. Thus, we might begin with the questions on perceptions of crime.

It is more likely that people have thought about the crime problem where they live than somewhere else. So it is probably easier to ask first about neighborhood crime, then crime in the state. Should we ask about violent crime first, then other types of crime, and crime in general last, or should we follow some other order? What guides our choice? Sometimes the answer to one question can influence the answer to a subsequent item. That is, responses can be affected by the context in which they are asked. These context effects are often difficult to anticipate.

For example, a general assessment can be affected by the context of having already given more detailed ratings. When providing the general assessment, respondents will sometimes not consider the relevant detailed answer they have already given. Sudman and Bradburn (1982) speak of this as a "redundancy effect" and recommend that "overall, then, if you are asking a series of questions, one of which is general and the others more specific, it would be better to ask the general question first" (p. 144).

Following this advice, we might first ask about crime in general (I), then about violent crime and nonviolent crimes (E, F). Since perceptions are strongly influenced by personal experience, it will probably be easy for respondents to recall any experiences with crime at this point in the interview. Keeping in mind the concerns about the role of respondents' memory in answering questions, this might be a good place in the interview to ask about any personal experiences with crime (B). A minority of respondents or their families (though more than you might guess) will have been victims of a crime, but this question should certainly trigger their concerns about being victims (perhaps by bringing to mind an incident they read about or something that happened to a friend. So the question about fear of crime seems natural to ask at this point (D). Then, since actions taken to protect themselves and their families would, in part at least, be based on perceptions, experiences, and expectations about crime, logic would seem to point to this section next (G).

Finally, we are left with the items about the criminal justice system and alternative sentencing. Which order do we choose here? We again have a situation of a general and a specific aspect of an issue. So, following the advice of Sudman and Bradburn (1982), we ask first about the criminal justice system in general (C) and then about sentencing, the specific part of that system (H). As we shall see, the alternative sentencing questions are also somewhat more difficult, reinforcing the argument for placing them last. We end, as is typical in telephone interviews, with the demographic items (A). The final order (at least until we pretest) is shown in Exhibit 5.2.

Having walked through one question-ordering problem, we turn to the survey of undergraduate students about a wide range of topics for different sponsors. Rather than being driven by a set of research questions, the focus of this study is to obtain information for planning purposes by different campus administrators. Such a multipurpose study is called an **omnibus survey.**

The questionnaire is designed to be self-administered in a sample of classrooms. Responses are anonymous, rather than confidential. Unlike a confidential survey, in which the researcher can link respondents by name, phone, or address to their interviews, the procedures of an anonymous survey prevent anyone, even the researcher, from linking respondents individually to their answers. This approach is sometimes used when there are questions about very sensitive issues or illegal behavior. Given the topics shown in

Exhibit 5.2

Order Determined for Topics in Maryland Crime Survey

Perceptions of the crime problem, generally, in their neighborhood and in the state

Perceptions of the violent crime problem in their neighborhood and in the state

Perceptions of the nonviolent crime problem in their neighborhood and in the state

Personal experiences with crime

Fear that they or their family will be victims of crime

Things done to protect themselves from crime

Opinions about the criminal justice system

Opinions about alternative sentencing

Demographic questions

Exhibit 5.3

Topics for the Omnibus Survey of Students

Use of the university book center, shopping habits, and satisfaction

Use of academic advising and opinions about the advising system

Demographics

Alcohol and drugs: use, opinions on campus policy, perceptions of needs
for education and treatment services

Race relations on campus

Exhibit 5.3, decide what order they might be arranged in. Then see
the questionnaire in appendix A for an example of one way they
might be ordered.

Questionnaire Length and Respondent Burden

Telephone interviews typically take from 10 to 20 minutes or so to
administer, although some may take only 5 minutes and others as
long as an hour. In-person interviews commonly run 30 minutes to
an hour, although interviews of 2 or more hours are possible. Mail
questionnaires tend to be four to eight pages, but, again, many are a
bit shorter and some a great deal longer. Why all the variation? How
long should a questionnaire be?

Like many of the decisions in survey design, interview length requires balancing several factors, often without a clear rule for how to
do it. The money and other resources available and the amount and
type of information needed are primary concerns. But the expected
interest or motivation of respondents and the limitations of the
mode of administration are also very important.

Regardless of the available resources or the amount of information we feel we need, respondents must be willing to spend the time
required to complete the questionnaire. Putting aside the possibility
of monetary compensation, what motivation do respondents have to
devote time to our study? If the study is interesting, people are more
likely to want to do it. If it seems an important societal topic, they
may have additional motivation; and, if some action will be taken on
the basis of the survey, that motivation may be increased (Dillman,
1978; Groves, 1989).

For mail and other self-administered surveys, it is paramount that appearance be carefully considered. The appearance of length can be as important an influence on respondents as the actual number of pages or questions. Dillman (1978) gives the most complete treatment of self-administered questionnaire formatting. We will note only a few key aspects of such formatting, taking the perspective of the survey-response model.

In making the decision to participate in the survey or not, the respondent has only a general idea of what is in store. At this point, the *perception* of burden guides the respondent's decision to participate or not. Respondents can quickly see the layout of a self-administered questionnaire, including spacing, type size, and question length. An instrument that is closely spaced, with tiny print or long questions, will be forbidding to many respondents.

Respondents can also be quickly put off by long or complex instructions for answering questions. We want to require as little work as possible of respondents in providing the necessary information. Unclear instructions can also have the effect of increasing respondent errors or item nonresponse among those who do participate.

We suggest (based on the work of Dillman) the following guidelines for the formatting of self-administered questionnaires:

- Limit instruments to six to eight pages.
- Precode response categories by assigning a number to each possible answer for the respondent to circle.
- Space the categories so that it is easy to circle one response without touching an adjoining one; arrange the categories vertically, one under another, rather than horizontally spread across the page.
- Provide simple instructions of no more than two sentences describing how to answer questions—for example, "Please circle the number of your answer unless otherwise instructed."
- Use a different typeface for questions, response categories, and transitions or section headings.
- Whenever possible, use arrows to indicate skip instructions.

Avoiding Other Flaws in Mail Questionnaire Design

Two inadvisable design tendencies in self-administered questionnaires are so common that they deserve special mention. First, as in questionnaire design in general, we recommend minimizing the use of open-ended questions. While these questions are easy to write and seem natural in an instrument that the respondent is going to write on, they present many problems. In addition to those discussed earlier, there are the added problems of illegible handwriting, unclear abbreviations, and ambiguous answers (which an interviewer is not available to probe). These can combine to cause serious problems in coding and analysis.

Second, inappropriately complex terms, whether jargon or "ten-dollar words," often find their way into self-administered questionnaires, perhaps because self-administered instruments are often (especially for mail surveys) pretested without the questions being discussed with respondents. Additionally, such surveys are often used with a special, rather than the general, population. We suggest putting the language used in self-administered questionnaires to a reality check by asking:

- Is the word found in everyday use, such as in the general section of a newspaper?
- Is there a simpler word that conveys essentially the same thing?
- If the term is purported to be the specialized language of a professional group, has it been checked with some members of that group? (Often, especially outside the physical sciences, even technical terms are not uniformly understood or used by all.)

Finally, the pretesting method(s) selected for a self-administered questionnaire should allow for feedback from respondents. Obtaining completed questionnaires, even those that look reasonable, is no guarantee that the instrument worked as intended. Respondents will often guess or take a stab at answering questions they don't fully understand. In our question about university drug policy, the term *in lieu of* may be known to most student respondents, but a nontrivial number may be unsure of its meaning and answer the question anyway. Without using a pretest method that obtains respondent feedback, this situation may pass unnoticed.

6 Questionnaire Design: Testing the Questions

The pretest is a set of procedures used to determine whether the questionnaire works in the manner intended by the researcher, providing valid and reliable measures of the attitudes, behaviors, and attributes of interest. Typically, but not invariably, pretesting involves trying out the questionnaire, in some manner, on respondents like those who will be interviewed in the main study. Everyone agrees that pretesting is essential, but it is useful to examine, in some detail, why this is so. Not only will this examination provide a better understanding of survey questionnaires, but it will also help us choose wisely from the array of available pretesting methods.

In designing a questionnaire, we make many decisions and assumptions, some conscious, others not. Underlying the first questionnaire draft is our judgment about what respondents will know, what words they will understand, what sorts of information they can and will provide, and what response tasks they can perform. When we pose alternative choices to the respondent, we have in mind some notion of the appropriate dimensions for an answer; we start to envision what our data might look like. Much of our effort is subtly informed by our feelings about how people will respond to our queries, by a notion that what we ask is sensible, by some vision of how the respondents' world works.

In a first draft of a survey question, one or more of these assumptions are likely to be wrong for many respondents. For example, do most people know how many total miles they drive each week? Will the typical respondent understand the word *export*? Can most people remember how many times they went to a restaurant in the past 6 months? All of these represent possible items we might use in a survey. Clearly, respondents differ in their knowledge, memory, and willingness to try to answer difficult questions.

In writing the first draft of the questionnaire, we have assumed that the vast majority of respondents will be able and willing to do the things the survey requires of them—our results depend on this being true. It is difficult, especially for novice researchers, not to use themselves as a model, albeit often unintentionally, in writing questionnaires. In so doing, we assume that respondents can do the things we can do, understand the words we know, are willing to work to answer difficult questions we feel are important or interesting.

After the first pretest, we have data to assess some, though usually not all, of these presumptions. Many a questionnaire composed in cool solitude melts under the heat of real respondents' answers in the pretest.

Importance of Respondents' Comprehension of and Ability to Answer Questions

One thing we want to assess in the pretest is the respondents' ability to provide good answers to our questions. By "good" answers, we mean those that are valid and reliable. Validity requires, first, that the questions measure the dimension or construct of interest; and second, that respondents interpret the question as intended. Reliability mainly refers to the degree of variation among responses in repeated trials. For example, if another researcher uses our questionnaire on a sample survey of the same population (at the same time our study is conducted), following all our procedures, that researcher should obtain (within sampling error) the same results.

There are a number of pretesting methodologies available to determine how respondents understand survey questions. Although there has been some research comparing these methods (Bischoping, 1989; Presser and Blair, 1994; Cannell, Fowler and Marquis, 1989; Campanelli, Rothgeb, Esposito, and Polivka, 1991), there are no definitive answers about which method is best in particular circumstance. Once again, we must develop our own judgment and make use of general guidelines on how to proceed in best allocating our resources.

Since the methods for determining respondents' comprehension vary so greatly by mode of administration, we will divide our discussion by data collection method, beginning with telephone. The key resources in telephone survey pretesting are mainly, but not exclusively, labor (primarily interviewer hours) and available time.

Other resources, such as materials, telephone charges, and the investigator's time to analyze the results, are needed, but the total costs are mainly driven by the project schedule and field staff labor.

Conventional Pretests and Interviewer Debriefings

In a conventional pretest, a small number of respondents, usually twenty to forty, are interviewed. The exact procedures planned for the main study are followed. After this interviewing takes place, a debriefing meeting is held with the interviewers. This practice is so common that it is what most people generically think of as pretesting. But it is only one of several available methods.

Bischoping (1989) notes differences of opinion about the ideal group of interviewers for the pretests. Some researchers favor using only the most experienced interviewers (Fowler, 1984; Converse and Presser, 1986); others suggest a mix of interviewer experience (Demaio, 1983) on the belief that less-experienced interviewers may uncover problems that the more experienced staff handle almost automatically. We suggest the former course. In a controlled experiment, Bischoping (1989) did not find significant differences between interviewers of varying levels of experience in the number or kinds of problems they mentioned.

The interviewer debriefing is generally organized as follows:

- *Overview of the pretest,* including any serious problems of respondent resistance to participation or to particular interview topics.
- *Question-by-question problem identification,* in which each interviewer is asked in turn about any problems the respondents had with the item.
- *Question-by-question suggestions for revision,* in which each interviewer may suggest alternatives for handling identified problems.
- *Summary comments* on how well or badly the pretest went and on the main issues to be addressed before actual data collection or additional pretesting commences.

Notice that, although we are interested in respondents' comprehension (as well as other respondent issues), the debriefing consists of a series of reports and opinions of interviewers. It is important to keep in mind that, in effect, the interviewer serves as a proxy for the pretest respondents. During the debriefing, it is often useful to separate interviewers' perceptions of *potential* problems that respondents might have from *actual* problems encountered.

Additionally, in a debriefing, it is important to get all the interviewers' comments and reports about their respondents' experiences in the interviews. Debriefings can often be dominated by one or two talkative interviewers, while others with useful information never speak up. One way to deal with this is to ask each interviewer to comment on each questionnaire item.

Another problem to be alert for is what we might call the aberrant anecdote. Extreme interview situations are vividly remembered and almost always reported in the debriefing. Two common examples involve the extremely knowledgeable respondent and the outlier respondent. In the first case, say for our crime survey, an interviewer might have interviewed a lawyer who takes technical issue with many of the survey questions, points out alternative response categories, and raises many issues not included in the questionnaire. In the second, for the same study, an interviewer might encounter a respondent who recounts a large number of various crimes committed against household members, resulting in an unusually long interview and, perhaps, a suspicious reluctance to answer questions about household behaviors and precautions concerning crime. Such cases are likely to be raised at length in the debriefing, especially if they happened to one of the talkative interviewers. While we learn some things from these two respondents, we must keep in mind that they are atypical and must not let them dominate our thoughts on questionnaire revisions.

On the other hand, pretests often reveal instances of respondents' resistance to questions they believe are unrealistic. Consider our question about alternative sentencing:

```
Do you think people convicted of robbery should be
sent to prison, required to report to a parole of-
ficer once a month, required to report daily, or
monitored electronically so their whereabouts are
known at ALL times?
```

While many, even most, respondents may have been willing to answer the question in this form, others might have insisted that their answer depends on the circumstances. They want to know if a gun was used, if anyone was hurt, if the robber had prior convictions, and so forth. We might decide to go ahead with the general form of the question. But if this topic is central to the study and we know, perhaps from other research or from pilot work, the key factors that affect respondents' choices, we may choose to develop a more complex form of the item. In this case, we might provide a vignette[1] before asking the opinion alternatives. For example,

```
Suppose a [20]-year-old is convicted of robbing
someone of $100 on the street. He threatened the
victim with [a gun]. He has [4] prior convictions.
```

We then ask the respondent's opinion about what should happen to the person. The items in brackets are varied across interviews following a pattern to produce a data set in which we can analyze how opinions vary under different circumstances. Clearly, this question is much more complex to administer and to analyze than the version with which we began; it is also more realistic and informative. We learn more about the issue at hand, but, as always, at a cost.

Post-Interview Interviews

Another common method of obtaining information about comprehension is through post-interview discussions with respondents about the interview they just did. This method is based on the work of Belson (1981), in which respondents to a survey were recontacted by a different interviewer and asked questions *about* the meaning of items in the first interview. Belson found that many respondents did not understand the original interview questions as intended. The current practice is to ask the post-interview questions immediately after the interview proper is finished. The interviewer says something like "Now I'd like to ask you about the interview we just completed."

Typically, we will want to use prepared post-interview questions but not limit the discussion to them. If it is clear from the interview

---

[1]See Converse and Presser (1986) for a discussion of the role of vignettes in surveys, sometimes called factorial surveys. When this approach is used, the factors (in brackets in the example) are varied. With multiple factors, the number of versions can increase very rapidly. Careful pretesting is needed to decide which factors will serve to separate groups of respondents with different positions on the issue.

that certain items caused problems or confusion, the interviewer should be given the latitude to include those issues as well.

The following is an example of a post-interview script:

```
Those are all the questions I have about the issue
of crime in the state. Now, I'd like to ask you
just a few questions about the interview.
  1. First, were there any questions you were not
     sure how to answer?
     If YES, which ones were those?
        Why were you not sure how to answer the
        question about [subject of question]?
  2. When I used the term criminal justice system,
     what did you think I meant by that?
  3. When I asked the question about the quality
     of your neighborhood, what sorts of things
     did you consider?
  4. Are there any questions you think that many
     people would find difficult to answer?
     If YES, which ones were those?
        Why do you think people would have diffi-
        culty with the question about [subject of
        question]?
  5. Were there any important things related to
     these issues that we failed to cover?
```

Notice that, unlike the questions in the questionnaire, the items in the post-interview script are largely open-ended. Because we do not know exactly what types of problems respondents might identify, we do not want to overly constrain their answers. If this were part of a series of pretests, it may be that issues identified in the first pretest might be explicitly asked about in the subsequent ones. Also note that we try to keep the post-interview brief.

For example, early post-interviews on the student omnibus survey might reveal such things as the importance to students of the availability of walk-in advising and their belief that peer advisors should be of at least the same class rank as the students they advise. These are the sorts of things that the researcher, not being a member of the population, might not be aware of, but such opinions can be uncovered quickly by allowing pretest respondents to comment on the study issues. (This is also a strength of focus groups.)

There are two ways to involve respondents in this sort of discussion. One way is to tell them at the outset of the interview that afterward we will be discussing the interview with them. Converse and Presser (1986) call this a **participating pretest.** The other is to conduct the interview as planned, then ask the post-interview items. This is called an **undeclared pretest.** Converse and Presser recommend beginning multiple pretests with a participating pretest, then moving on to an undeclared one. But there is little in the literature that addresses how well these two pretest methods work in combination.

Cognitive Interviews

Still another approach to pretesting to determine respondents' comprehension is to do one-on-one or **cognitive interviews.** In this participating arrangement, respondents are recruited and asked to come to a central location. The questionnaire is administered to each respondent separately. Borrowing a procedure called the think aloud from cognitive psychology, respondents are instructed to think out loud as they answer each question. The idea is to determine what things respondents consider in answering the question. This method can provide insights into comprehension problems or other problems, such as difficulties recalling required information. The instruction given to respondents is of the form (closely following Ericsson and Simon, 1993):

```
We are interested in what you think about as you
answer some questions I am going to ask you. In
order to do this, I am going to ask you to THINK
ALOUD. What I mean by think aloud is that I want
you to tell me everything you are thinking from
the time you first hear the question until you
give an answer. I don't want you to plan out what
you are saying or try to explain your answers to
me. Just act as if you are alone in the room
speaking to yourself. It is most important that
you keep talking. If you are silent for any long
period of time, I will ask you to speak.
```

The interviewer will then prompt the respondent with probes such as, "What were you thinking about?" or "How did you come up with that?" Typically, in the course of the interview, the interviewer also asks a set of prepared, that is scripted, probes to determine the respondent's understanding of particular items immediately after an answer is given. Although this latter procedure is at variance with the recommendations of many cognitive psychologists, it is widely used by survey researchers. The resulting method is a hybrid of the think-aloud procedures and the Belson-type "intensive interview" (Belson, 1981).

This method can show how respondents are formulating their responses based on their understanding of the question. In the question, "How often in the last year did you drink alcohol? Would you say, more than once a week, about once a week, once or twice a month or less than once a month," a respondent, thinking aloud, might mention something like: "Last year I didn't drink very much. There was a party on New Year's Eve, then probably the last time before that was Thanksgiving break, when a bunch of us got together to watch the Notre Dame game . . . " In examining this think-aloud transcript (called a **protocol**), the researcher realizes that the respondent is apparently thinking about the last calendar year, rather than the 12 months previous to the interview. If the latter is intended, the question might be revised to "How often in the *last twelve months*, since [GIVE DATE ONE YEAR PRIOR TO DATE OF INTERVIEW], did you drink alcohol?" One advantage of cognitive interviews is that this sort of problem can be uncovered very quickly. However, because of the very small samples typically used, it is hard to know how frequently respondents are likely to have a particular difficulty.

In cognitive interviews what the respondent was thinking at the point of answering the question is fresher in mind than it would be in the post-interview method. The disadvantage is that the resources required for this type of interview are greater. More people have to be contacted to find respondents willing to come in for the interview. Typically, in one-on-one interviews, unlike cold-call interviews, respondents are paid to participate. The remuneration generally varies from $10 to $50, depending on the amount of time required. So our trade-off, given a fixed budget, is to do fewer of these interviews and more of the cold-call interviews.

Cognitive interviews can be useful when the respondents' tasks or the question concepts are potentially difficult. The most complete discussion of these methods and their theoretical basis is given by Ericsson and Simon (1993). Another source of survey application examples is Royston (1989).

Interaction Coding

Interaction coding is a method developed by Cannell, Fowler, and Marquis (1968) at the University of Michigan to quantitatively assess how well a face-to-face or telephone survey interview is conducted. In this procedure, it is assumed that in the ideal interaction between an interviewer and respondent, the interviewer reads the question verbatim, and the respondent replies with an answer. They then proceed to the next question. In interaction coding, a third party uses a simple set of codes to indicate deviations from this model: nonverbatim reading of the question, respondents' requests for clarification, requests to reread the question, or inadequate answers. Each time each question is administered, each problem type is coded 0 if it does not occur and 1 if it does. Then the percentage of times a problem occurs for each question is calculated.

While this method was originally developed to investigate interviewers' performance, it has also been used to identify problem questions. Fowler (1989) recommends that questions that are coded 15% or more of the time into one of the deviation categories be considered problematic. While the 15% cutoff is somewhat arbitrary, it has proved useful in practice. An advantage of this procedure is that it can be done in conjunction with conventional telephone pretesting, at little additional cost, using monitoring facilities in a centralized telephone facility. If such a facility is not available, then added cost does become a factor. For personal interviews, tape recording and later coding is typically used.

Respondent Debriefing

Respondent debriefing is a slight variation on the post-interview interview. In this instance, respondents, after completing an interview, are taken back through the entire interview, question by question, and asked their reaction (and other scripted probes) to each item. These debriefings are usually done face to face, which usually means bringing respondents to a central office. The initial interview is often tape-recorded (or videotaped). The tape can be played back as a way to help respondents remember what they were thinking at the time they originally answered the questions. The costs are very similar to those for the intensive interview procedure, with the addition of the cost of the recording equipment.

We should note that all these special methods require additional training of interviewers beyond that needed to conduct the actual survey interview. Further, while the methods are increasingly used in combination, though at additional costs, there is little research on optimal combinations. For studies with many new or potentially difficult items, we suggest beginning with a method that probes problems related to respondent comprehension and recall fairly directly, such as the post-interview methods or cognitive interviews, then moving on to conventional pretesting with behavior coding. For very simple instruments, conventional pretesting alone may be sufficient.

Expert Panel

Finally, Presser and Blair (1994) found that the use of an expert panel was very effective compared to other methods in identifying respondents' problems with a questionnaire. An expert panel is a small group of specialists brought together to critique a questionnaire. The participants are primarily survey professionals, but subject-matter experts may also be included. The group, consisting of three to eight members, is given a copy of the draft instrument several days prior to the meeting. Then, in a group session, the panel reviews the questionnaire item by item, a process similar to conventional pretest debriefing. The difference is that the panel's recommendations stem from their research experience and knowledge of questionnaires (or subject-matter issues) rather than from the reactions of pretest respondents. In an experimental comparison to other methods, Presser and Blair (1994) found that such panels were efficient in identifying many of the types of problems identified by other pretest methods and uncovered other questionnaire flaws (such as potential analysis difficulties) as well. The strengths of expert panels come from their diversity of expertise as well as their interaction in the meeting. The Presser and Blair panels consisted of a cognitive psychologist, a questionnaire-design specialist, and a general survey methodologist. Clearly, other combinations should be tried as well. It is important to note that consensus on either potential problems or solutions is sometimes not reached by the panel, but this is also true of conventional methods. However, we strongly suggest resisting the temptation to use experts as a substitute for pretesting with respondents.

Even the novice survey researcher, without substantial financial resources to pay panel participants, still has options that permit the use of the expert panel. Because the amount of time required is small—usually only 3–4 hours in total—it is often possible to find people who will participate without payment. Faculty members at a university may be called on (particularly for a class project on campus), as may colleagues at other universities. Another resource may be survey professionals at nearby survey organizations. Finally, researchers who have done surveys in the subject area may be asked to help. (These last may be identified during the project's literature-review phase. If travel time and costs are a limitation, it is possible to conduct the panel meeting relatively cheaply via a conference call.

Examining Interviewer Tasks

An interviewer's performance is also a crucial part of the survey's quality. As we have noted, the interviewer can be a major contributor to total survey error. Fortunately, given limited resources, many of the procedures that uncover sources of respondent error are also effective identifiers of interviewer error and problems as well.

Interviewer debriefings are obviously an opportunity for interviewers to report difficulties such as awkward questions, logic errors with skip patterns, words that are difficult to pronounce, or questions that come across differently when read aloud than when seen on the page. In fact, one has to take care during the conduct of the debriefing session that interviewer problems are not dwelled on at the expense of reports of respondent issues.

Monitoring telephone pretest (as well as main) interviews is a standard procedure at most survey organizations. Telephone-monitoring equipment allows a supervisor or investigator to listen to interviews in progress without either the interviewer or the respondent being aware that they are being monitored. This is done for quality control during main data collection, to see that procedures for administering questions are being followed. It is also a good way to detect rough spots in an interview during the pretest. Therefore, we urge researchers to monitor interviews. Questions sometimes come across quite differently when heard than when read; phrases that may seem moderately awkward or complex on the page often are unbearable in the interview. For the novice researcher, monitoring is also an invaluable aid to learning how to write questions that sound natural.

Revising and Retesting: Deciding Which Pretest Problems to Address

It is not always possible, or advisable, to address every problem identified in pretesting. First, we may decide that an identified "problem" is not really a problem or is too trivial to warrant the cost of a change and the additional testing then required. It is common—often to the chagrin of the interviewing staff—that issues raised in pretest debriefings are not incorporated into the next draft of the questionnaire. In other instances, we may feel that the problem will seldom occur and that addressing it may introduce other problems. For example, assume that in pretesting the question "Most of the time you drank alcohol, on average, how many drinks did you have at one time?" a single respondent reports that when she is out with her boyfriend she sips from his drinks rather than having her own. So she finds it difficult to provide an answer in terms of "how many drinks" she had. It would require an extensive revision to accommodate such a respondent and in the process would make the question needlessly complicated for the majority of respondents. In this case, it makes sense to leave the item unchanged.

Those situations aside, we suggest returning to the question-utility guide in Exhibit 4.2 to help decide on changes. If, based on these criteria, the problem discovered in the pretest affects the question's usefulness, the question needs to be either revised or dropped. Sometimes, we find that a question is simply too difficult to ask, perhaps because the level of complexity of the research goal requires multiple items. If the question is central to our research, then the multiple items are sensible. But if the item is less central, we may decide that the questions that need to be added are not worth the resources. In other instances, the question may not be suited to the administration mode: It may be too long or have too many response categories for a telephone interview. In such situations, if a question cannot be effectively revised, it is wise to drop it.

Deciding How Much Testing Is Enough

The different kinds of testing we have described can obviously become quite elaborate, time-consuming, and costly. We should anticipate the amount of pretesting we will need and devise a plan based on the complexity of the instrument, the proportion of new items, and, to some extent, the skip-pattern structure. If there are numerous branches to sections asked of only some respondents, larger pretests may be necessary to ensure complete testing of all sections of the questionnaire. After we have completed the amount of pretesting we decided we can afford and have evaluated the results using the question-utility guide, we must make the hard choice either to drop items that do not work or to shift resources (both time and money) from other parts of the project to do further testing. This last course should be taken only if two conditions hold: The problematic instrument items are central to our research questions, and we will not reduce other parts of the design (such as main sample size) below the point of usefulness.

Pilot Tests

One last method of design and instrument development is the pilot test. In a pilot test, a relatively large number of interviews are conducted using the exact procedures planned for the study. Pretests are a necessary preliminary to pilot tests. As we have seen, in the pretest, we use a small number of cases to detect flaws in the questionnaire. We try to develop the instrument and interview procedures to maximize cooperation and to aid the respondent in the required response tasks. But there are aspects of the data collection process that pretesting alone may not address.

For example, pretest samples are usually too small to use to estimate cooperation or screening eligibility rates. Additionally, some field procedures may not be testable with small samples. There may be unknown characteristics of the sampling frame, or of the target population's response to aspects of the instrument, that can be examined only in a large field test. When the cost of the main study is high, or when some of the procedures are innovative or unusual, it may be risky to proceed to main data collection without a pilot study.

Since most small-scale studies cannot afford pilot studies, it is best to stick to well-tested field and sampling procedures. To this end, it is useful to spend some time at the outset of the study searching the literature for both survey questions, as noted earlier, and for studies that have surveyed our target population. Consider how well the mode of data collection worked; whether there were cooperation or data-quality problems; and whether special interviewer-training procedures were used (e.g., in handling sensitive questions) that we might adopt.

Some Last Advice

The questionnaire is the indispensable means by which the opinions, behaviors, and attributes of respondents are converted into data. The focus in chapters 4–6 on the development and testing of the questionnaire reflects the instrument's central role in the survey process. Still, there is much more that could be said, and the first questionnaire the reader attempts to construct is likely to present issues that were not addressed here. Thus, it is very important to consult the references provided in this and other chapters. Often a point that was omitted or only touched on here is treated in detail elsewhere.

We end with four final points. First, to the extent resources permit, use multiple pretesting methods and multiple rounds of testing. Every flaw that is found during testing is one less problem to confront during analysis and interpretation. Second, learn to assess survey questions by reading them aloud and developing your ear. A question that sounds awkward or unnatural or is hard for you, the researcher, to read will surely cause problems for respondents. Third, consider no question's wording sacrosanct. If a question does not pass muster in pretesting, its flaws must be confronted, however difficult that may prove or however enamored you may be of its original form. Finally, seek out examples of questionnaires written by experienced researchers. You cannot consult too many examples while learning the art of questionnaire design. In addition to texts and journal articles, copies of questionnaires from surveys conducted by major survey organizations or federal government statistical agencies are often available for free (even through on-line databases).

It has been remarked that all computer programs have one thing in common: They can be improved. The same is equally true of survey questionnaires.

7 Designing the Sample

Most of what we do in surveys relies on common sense. In sampling, for example, we need to think about which population we want to study, what list or resource we can use that includes this population, how good this resource is, what problems we might encounter, and how we can overcome them. Knowing a few basic principles and using common sense can greatly help the researcher in addressing these concerns.

In the first part of this chapter, we define sampling, explain why it is more efficient than interviewing everyone and illustrate the differences between nonprobability and probability samples. Since probability designs are the preferred method, the remainder of the chapter focuses on them. Particular attention is given to the key tasks of defining the population, constructing and evaluating sampling frames, and handling unexpected situations and common problems. We also address the commonly asked question, "What sample size do I need?" Finally, a number of examples are presented showing how to use census data to plan a survey and to determine whether the number of interviews with important subgroups will be adequate for analysis.

The Basics

Sampling is the selection of elements, following prescribed rules, from a defined population. These elements are usually the subjects of the study: They can be individuals, households, farm animals, sections of land, business transactions, hospitals, and so on. There are two main reasons for sampling. One is to generalize to or make inferences about the population of interest for research questions (e.g., How many people were unemployed but looking for work in March?

What proportion of adults in Maryland believe that violent crime in their neighborhood has gotten worse?). A well-executed probability sample allows us to estimate these numbers and percentages.

A second reason for sampling is that it is more efficient and less expensive than a **census,** which attempts to include or ask questions about every element or member in the population. It took about 10 years to plan, carry out, and report the results of the *1990 Census of Population and Housing* at a cost of about $2.6 billion. From 1988 through 1990, the Census Bureau created about 635,000 temporary jobs and hired about 565,000 people (U.S. Bureau of the Census, 1989). Think about the difficulties involved in hiring this many people, especially well-qualified people. Then, think about training them and building in quality-control checks. While the Census Bureau does an outstanding job in accomplishing this feat, the logistics of this task contribute to proportionately more errors, higher costs, and a less capable staff than would a large sample survey. In fact, this alternative has been discussed on a number of occasions, but since it would require a change in the U.S. Constitution, it is very difficult to convince members of Congress and state legislators of the advantages of a sample survey. So, the debate goes on.

There are two types of samples: probability and nonprobability samples. **Probability samples,** or *random* samples, are those in which every element has a known, nonzero chance of selection and the elements are selected through a random procedure. While elements do not need to have an *equal* chance of being selected, every element must have *some* chance and that chance must be *known*. By fulfilling these two conditions and using the correct statistical formula, we can estimate values for the entire population and the margin of error of that estimate. For example, assume we want to estimate the number of students on a university campus who had at least one cold during the past winter. (The potential measurement problems inherent in this seemingly simple research question are ignored here but covered in chapter 4.) Let's assume that winter is defined for our purposes as November 15 through March 15; that the school has a total of 28,000 enrolled students; that we can obtain a list of every student and this list has no missing or incomplete information; that we want to select a sample of 1,000 students; and, finally, that all students who are sent a questionnaire will respond (perfect cooperation). A random sample of 1,000 students out of 28,000 gives each student a 1 in 28 chance of being in the study or a **probability of selection** of .0357. This is just saying the same thing in two different ways.

Probability of selection = 1,000 ÷ 28,000 = 1 ÷ 28 = .0357

If 62% or 620 of the students in the sample say they had a cold last winter, we can estimate the percentage or the number of students in the total population who had a cold last winter by using the probability of selection to compute an estimate of the range of possible values wherein the true population value may lie, otherwise known as the **sampling error.**[1] To make this computation, we multiply the reciprocal of the probability of selection (1 ÷ .0357) by the number of students who said they had a cold, and we compute a **confidence interval** for this number. A confidence interval for a numeric variable is a range of values above and below the sample estimate that should contain the population value. In order to compute the confidence interval, the researcher sets a probability—for example, 90%, 95%—that the confidence interval includes the true population value. The reciprocal of .0357 is 28. Does this look familiar? We multiply this number by the number of students who had a cold (620). This gives us an estimated total of 17,360 (620 * 28 = 17,360). Next, we must compute a confidence interval because this is only one sample out of many, many possible samples of 1,000 students that could be selected from a population of 28,000. Using a 95% probability level, the confidence interval for our sample estimate is 18,202 to 16,518. This means that if we were to survey repeated samples of 1,000 students as in our example, the confidence intervals for 95% of the samples would contain the true population value for the number of students that had a cold last winter. We will say more about estimating population values later. The major point to understand from this exercise is that to have a statistical basis to estimate a population value from a sample, the sample must be a probability sample.

A second type of sample is a nonprobability design, which includes convenience, purposive, quota, and snowball samples. The names for these samples suggest the method by which respondents are selected for the study, as the following examples illustrate.

In a study to see who studies more outside of class—juniors majoring in engineering or juniors majoring in a social science—a convenience or purposive sample could be used to select two junior

[1]Sampling error is not error in the sense that we have made a mistake. It is an estimated range of values, computed from our sample, that indicates where the population value may be. The estimated range of values is computed because only a sample of the population, not everyone, is interviewed.

level classes in engineering and two junior level classes in the social sciences without a random procedure or known probability of selection. We would ask all the students in each class how many hours of homework they do in an average week. The classes would be purposefully selected—junior level classes in engineering and social sciences—and we might select classes that would be convenient for our schedule or because we know the instructors and it would be easy to gain their cooperation. In these situations, all juniors in both disciplines would not have a known chance of selection, and there is no way of estimating how representative the results are of all junior engineering or social science majors.

In a quota sample, before interviewing begins we determine what characteristics of the population being studied, such as gender, race, age, and employment, might be related to our dependent variable. Before we conduct the study, we want to know what proportions of the population have these characteristics so that our final interviews reflect these population distributions. If the population is 50% male and 50% female, we want half the final interviews to be with males and half to be with females. If the study is being conducted in a specific city or county, we may find information about the population from U.S. census data or a recently conducted study. For studies of students, information is usually available from the registrar or the office of records and admissions. Let's assume that we are doing the study in a city and that gender and race are important variables. Census data indicate that for adults 18 years of age and over, 52% are females, 48% are males, 27% are African American, 68% are white, and 5% are some other race. Assume that we need 200 face-to-face interviews and that the distribution of the population by race is the same for both genders. Knowing these percentages, we can now estimate interview quotas for the sample:

	Number of Interviews	
	Women	*Men*
White	71 (.68 * 104)	65 (.68 * 96)
African American	28 (.27 * 104)	26 (.27 * 96)
Other	5 (.05 * 104)	5 (.05 * 96)
Total	104 (.52 * 200)	96 (.48 * 200)

Interviewers would be assigned the above quotas, and they would be sent to designated areas, such as street corners, shopping malls, or selected city blocks. At the assigned areas, the interviewers would be instructed to fill their quotas. When the study is completed, the interviewed sample usually matches the population exactly on the important variables.

There are three major problems with this design. One is the lack of control over who is interviewed. The interviewer is told the *type* of person to interview, but not who. For example, at a shopping mall, interviewers can exclude specific individuals whose looks they do not like or who seem to be in a bad mood or in a hurry. Thus, those who are included may be different in important ways from those who are excluded. A second problem is that records are usually not kept of the number of people contacted or the number who refused to be interviewed. The only records are the number of completed interviews, and we know that the sample characteristics of gender and race match the population. Again, the group that agreed to be interviewed may be different from the rest of the population. They may be more cooperative, they may have more money, or, depending upon the day and time that interviews are conducted, these respondents may overrepresent the elderly or unemployed people. We also have no assurance that other important variables, which were not used in defining the target groups, will be distributed in our sample as they are in the population.

The third and most critical issue is that the probability of selection of these 200 respondents is unknown. If the study was done at a shopping mall, those in the eligible population who never visit that mall would have no chance of selection. Conversely, people who visit the mall two to three times a week would have a greater chance of being in the study than those who visit it less often. These same criticisms apply to "street-corner" and other types of haphazard designs. In short, if you wish to generalize to a population, all the elements in the population must have a known, nonzero chance of being in the study.

Another frequently used nonprobability design is snowball sampling, used when the sample units are rare or hard to find. One assumption underlying this method is that people with similar characteristics or attributes are likely to know each other. A more general assumption is that individuals without the characteristic may know others who have it. Suppose we are interested in interviewing people who are HIV-positive to see what aspects of their lifestyle they may have changed to forestall the onset of AIDS. Clearly, this is a rare and hard-to-find population group. No sampling frame exists for this group and, while its numbers are increasing, it still represents a very small percentage of the total population. To conduct such a study, we might combine two nonprobability designs. First, we need to locate or gain access to organizations or groups where HIV-positive people can be found—for example, organizations of gay men or AIDS support groups. Depending on the survey's time schedule and resources, a convenience or purposive sample of organizations might be contacted. Access to some or all of an organization's members is obtained usually by posting announcements on bulletin boards or by giving a presentation to members at an open meeting. A few respondents will volunteer to these requests, and this gives the researcher a starting point. The next step is to conduct the interviews. At the end of the interview, using the "snowball" tactic, the interviewer asks the respondent for names and telephone numbers or addresses of people the respondent knows who satisfy the eligibility conditions for the interview. That is, identified members of a population are asked to identify other eligible people.

While there is truth to the underlying premise of the snowball design—that people with similar characteristics associate with each other—it also has the flaws typical of a nonprobability sample. How well does the final sample represent the population of HIV-positive people? We are unable to answer this question because we don't know the probability of selection and can't estimate the boundaries or limits of sampling error. In addition, we don't know how limiting our initial selection of organizations and volunteers was. Do the cooperating organizations or volunteers know all the other HIV-positive people in the study area or are organizations and friendships closed cliques? The inability to estimate a range of error for our sample results seriously undermines the credibility of the final study.

Nevertheless, nonprobability samples can serve useful purposes. Not every research study is designed to estimate some characteristic of or generalize to a population. In an exploratory study, a researcher may only want to get a sense of what respondents are thinking, believe, or feel about a topic, information that may be useful in designing a larger and more comprehensive study at a later time. Nonprobability samples are also useful in the early stages of testing questionnaire items. We may be uncertain how specific types of individuals will interpret the wording of certain questions, and thus, we may want to focus our efforts only on these individuals. Or, if we have prior knowledge about the population or groups of interest, we can use that information to better focus the study resources. For example, if we are developing an education module for health care workers dealing with the most misunderstood aspects of AIDS, we might survey groups that have some knowledge about AIDS rather than to survey all health care workers. The assumption in this case is that misunderstandings of a group such as nurses who have cared for AIDS victims will also be present in other groups of health care workers. Thus, the results of a study of AIDS nurses would be generalizable to all health care workers.

Defining the Population

Let's return to a discussion of probability samples. Two key tasks in creating probability samples are defining the population and selecting or constructing the sampling frame. The population is the group or aggregation of elements that we wish to study, the group to which we want to generalize the results of our study. We begin the process by referring to the research problem. What is it that we wish to study? We may want to know, for example, "What proportion of adults believe a woman should be allowed to have an abortion for any reason?"

There are two components of the population definition that must be specified: the units or elements of analysis and the defining boundaries of the units. For units of analysis we must decide if the research problem focuses on individuals, households, group quarters, or something else. The term *individuals* is self-explanatory, but the other two terms may not be. According to the U.S. Census Bureau (1993b) definition:

> A household includes all the persons who occupy a housing unit. A housing unit is a house, an apartment, a mobile home, a group of rooms, or a single room that is occupied as separate living quarters. Separate living quarters are those in which the occupants live and eat separately from any other persons in the building and have direct access from the outside of the building through a common hall. The occupants may be a single family, one person living alone, two or more families living together, or any other group of related or unrelated persons who share living arrangements. (p. B-13)

Group quarters are all other types of living arrangements. The Census Bureau has defined two types of group quarters: (1) institutional and (2) noninstitutional. Institutions are places where occupants are under "formally authorized, supervised care or custody" such as prisons, federal detention centers, military stockades, local jails, police lockups, halfway houses, nursing homes, mental hospitals, schools or wards for the mentally retarded, homes for neglected children, and training schools for juvenile delinquents. The Census Bureau defines noninstitutional group quarters as living arrangements of ten or more unrelated people, such as rooming houses; group homes that provide care and supportive services, such as maternity homes for unwed mothers; religious group quarters; college dormitories; agricultural workers' dormitories; emergency shelters for homeless people; crews of maritime vessels; and staff residences of institutions. Investigators must decide in the design phase of the research which types of residential living arrangements contain the eligible respondents for their research.

How do we decide whether we want to study individuals, households, or some other units? It depends on the objectives of the research problem. If we are studying attitudes about abortion, individuals would be the appropriate units of analysis. Because attitudes might differ by gender or age, it would not make sense to designate households as the units of analysis. If attitudes differed within households, for example, between spouses or between adults and children, there would be no convenient way to report the attitude of the household. While attitudes are individual in nature, total income or the number of durable goods owned or purchased in the last year, such as refrigerators and automobiles, may best be studied by household. Although individuals and households are common units of analysis, other possibilities include organizations or institutions such as labor unions, banks, colleges, environmental groups, hospitals, and clubs. The appropriate unit of analysis for studying the types and quality of science facilities in elementary schools is elementary schools. Hospitals would be the unit of analysis for estimating the number and types of organ transplants in the last 5 years. Deciding the unit of analysis is up to the researcher, and it is a decision that must be made in the design phase of the research.

The second task in defining the population is to specify the defining boundaries. For a population of individuals, this usually involves specifying the geographic boundaries of the study area, the demographic characteristics of the study population, the age of respondents, and the residential units included. The geographic boundaries of the study area are determined by the population the study will generalize to and the amount of available time and resources. Depending upon these constraints, the study area may be defined as a city, county, metropolitan statistical area, state, or some other geographic entity. The geographic area must be specified early in the design phase because it has implications for many other activities, such as obtaining a sampling frame, hiring interviewers for a face-to-face survey, and estimating telephone charges for a telephone study.

We must also define the characteristics of eligible respondents and the residential units in which they may live. For example, the General Social Survey (GSS) is a national probability sample of English-speaking adults who reside in households in the fifty U.S. states. There are a number of points to note about this definition. First, this survey includes all fifty states. For many face-to-face studies, Alaska and Hawaii are excluded because of the higher costs to train, supervise, and maintain interviewers in these states. These two states comprise only 0.67% (less than 1%) of the U.S. population (U.S. Bureau of the Census, 1993c), and many investigators are willing to live with the more restricted definition of the population. Second, the survey includes only English-speaking adults. This excluded about the 2.5% of the sample households for the years 1987–1991 (Davis and Smith, 1991). The excluded households represent about thirteen language groups, 60% of which speak Spanish. To include these groups in the survey would require a number of activities that would significantly raise the cost per interview. To include non–English-speaking respondents, we first need to anticipate what language groups or dialects may fall into the sample. Will they be German, Chinese, Turkish, Arabic, Vietnamese, or some other groups? After anticipating the groups, we need to have a double translation of the questionnaire performed for each language. The questionnaire is translated from English into the foreign language and then the foreign language version is translated back into English, ensuring that language subtleties and innuendos have not been overlooked. Additionally, interviewer-training manuals need to be developed and/or modified and bilingual people in each of the languages must be hired, trained, and sent to the non–English-speaking households. Clearly, these activities not only increase the survey costs but may also increase the time required to complete the work.

A third consideration is the age of an eligible respondent. Adults may be defined as any person 18 or older, 19 or older, or 21 or older. It all depends on the objectives of the research and the group to which we wish to generalize. Sometimes, only people within a specified age group are eligible, such as all persons 18–64 or women 21–49. In the former age group, the interest may be in adults who are not retired; in the latter, the goal may be to study women after high school to see whether they joined the labor force, at what age, and in what occupations.

The type of dwelling unit in which the eligible respondents reside is a fourth consideration when defining the population. The GSS surveys households; this means that people residing in dormitories, shelters, nursing homes, and in other types of group quarters are excluded from the survey. In 1985, about 2.7% of the U.S. population resided in group quarters, but the percentage varies considerably by age group (Davis and Smith, 1991). In 1980, people living in group quarters represented about 9.4% of people 18–24 and 11.4% of those 75 and older, but only slightly more than 1% of the population between 25 and 64.

Decisions about how broadly to define the population depend on several considerations. A number of questions must be asked: Which groups do I want to generalize to? How have other researchers defined the population when they have investigated this issue? What are our resources for doing this study, not only in terms of time and budget but also in personnel and facilities? Is there a "best method" of data collection for the research issue or the defined population? Is there a list or resource available that contains the eligible members of the defined population?

Constructing a Sampling Frame

Once we have defined the population in probability sampling, the next task is to find or construct a sampling frame. The frame is the list(s) or resource(s) that contains the elements of the defined population. For a telephone survey, the frame may be a telephone directory or a list of all the telephone prefixes for the geographic area. For mail surveys, the frame is usually a list with the names and addresses of all the elements, such as an organization's membership list. If the research objective is to determine the satisfaction of recent graduates with the academic training they received at a college or university, a list of the names and addresses of graduates in the past 5 years might be obtained from the alumni office or from the registrar's office. Can you think of any problems with using these types of lists? (We will discuss these issues shortly.)

A frequently used sampling frame is a compilation of census data. These data are used when no reasonably complete list(s) exists for the defined population. Census data are usually used as a frame for face-to-face, general population studies—for example, of adults 18 years of age and older. You might believe that lists of all adults in the United States do exist. However, there are only two relatively complete lists, and both are confidential and not available to the public: census forms that are completed every 10 years, and income tax forms that are filed each year. Other lists that might be available all have major exclusion problems. For example, telephone directories do not include households without telephones or those with unlisted telephone numbers; lists from state driver's license bureaus do not include people who do not drive; voter registration lists exclude about one quarter to one third of all adults; and property tax records or utility company files are not inclusive of all adults and may not be public information.

How do you select a sample of adults using census data when the names and addresses are confidential? That is a good question. A brief example that avoids complex sampling theory will be useful. (However, parts of the process described involves sampling theory that is beyond the scope of this book. Therefore, you will need to accept certain decisions on faith.)

We begin with the research problem. Assume that we want to study the attitudes of adults toward abortion. What is the next step? We need to define what we mean by *adult* and specify the defining boundaries. Let's assume we are interested in interviewing people 18 and older who reside in households and we have enough resources to conduct a statewide face-to-face interview survey. Assume further that our required sample size is 1,000 completed interviews and that the average number of completed interviews per city block or final stage of sampling is five.[2]

We select the sample in stages, using census information. At the first stage, we select counties or groups of counties; for this project, we want to sample twenty-four counties. The twenty-four counties will be selected with probabilities proportionate to the number of people 18 years of age and older in each county.[3] Within each county,

---

[2] The reasons for conducting five interviews per block are explained further in chapter 8.

[3] Selecting places with probabilities proportionate to a measure of size in the first stage of sample selection gives larger places a higher chance of being in the sample. For example, we propose to select 24 counties from a total of 100 counties. The population of persons 18 and older in North Carolina in 1990 was 5,024,507. We create a sampling interval by dividing 5,024,506 by 24, which gives 209,354. Onslow County had 113,577 persons 18 and older, and Ashe County had 17,412. The probability of being selected in the first stage of selection is higher for Onslow ($113,577 \div 209,354 = .54$) than for Ashe ($17,412 \div 209,354 = .08$). To equalize the overall probability of selection, the same number of units must be selected at the last stage of selection. This point is illustrated in chapter 8.

we will select two to four places with probabilities proportionate to the number of adults. "Places" can be cities, towns, census tracts, or some other county subdivision. At the third stage, we select city blocks or sections of land in rural areas. This stage will also be selected with probabilities proportionate to the number of adults.

Note that we have conducted three stages of selection based only on census data, and without names and addresses. At the next stage, however, we must count the households in the blocks or sections of land selected in the third stage. A person called a lister is sent to each block or area to compile a list of the addresses or locations of every household. A comparison is then made between the number of households found by the lister and the number that was used to select the block or area (census data). If we expect a 70% response rate, then approximately seven households per block ($5 \div 7 \approx 71\%$) are selected for interviewing. Using counts of people or households within defined geographic areas, and then at the last stage of selection going out and making a count, is one way in which a probability sample can be selected without having a list of the population before you start. One final note of caution: The numbers used in each stage of selection must be reasonably accurate or unknown biases can result.

Matching Defined Populations and Sampling Frames

Many times a perfect match is not possible between the defined population and an available sampling frame, and compromises must be made. A telephone survey of adults illustrates this problem. Since every adult does not have a telephone and many have unlisted numbers, a perfect frame does not exist. Let's go back to our study about the attitudes of adults toward abortion to illustrate the point.

Let's assume that we have decided to do the study in Wake County, North Carolina, the county that includes the city of Raleigh, and we have decided to do the study by telephone. What can we use as a sampling frame that would give every adult in the county a known chance of being in the sample? The first thought, and actually a good one, is the white pages of the telephone directory. However, as a frame, the telephone directory has a number of weaknesses. First, it excludes people without telephones. However, when we decided to do this survey by telephone, we accepted this potential bias. In Wake County, North Carolina, 3.4% of the occupied households do not have a telephone. The key question is, "Are the individuals in these households different from those who do have telephones for the variables being investigated?" In general, the answer is yes, they are different. However, in this case, they are a small percentage of the total and the cost to include them (by face-to-face interviews) far outweighs their value to the final results. For these reasons, we will live with this potential bias.

Second, a telephone directory excludes people who do not list their telephone number in the telephone book. In the Raleigh-Durham Metropolitan Statistical Area, which includes Wake and four other counties, this group represents approximately 23% of all households. Clearly, this number is too large to ignore. Random-digit dialing (RDD) sampling procedures, however, described in chapter 8, overcome this problem. A third problem with the telephone directory as a frame, or with telephone surveys in general, is that some households have more than one telephone number, and hence, higher probabilities of selection. This problem can be offset by adding a question to the survey that asks how many different telephone numbers the household has, excluding business numbers. The survey data from each household with more than one residential number are weighted by the reciprocal of the number of residential numbers so that when we analyze the data, each household has the same probability of being in the survey.[4]

A fourth problem involves the geographic coverage of the Raleigh telephone directory. How much of the county is included: Is all, most, half, or maybe even more than Wake County included? This needs to be determined. Inspection of the telephone book indicates that there are two residential sections. One section includes the city of Raleigh and a number of surrounding towns and unincorporated areas. This section covers about 75% of the county and is serviced by one telephone company. The second section covers an area that is serviced by at least two other companies. This area includes the remainder of the county and a few small cities (population less than 5,000) and rural areas outside the county.

We have three options. One is to use only the first section of the telephone book, which includes Raleigh and approximately 75% of the county's population. We could redefine our population as adults that live in the city of Raleigh and in nearby areas. At the conclusion

---

[4]Weighting is discussed later in this chapter and in chapters 8 and 10.

of our study, we would need to describe the characteristics of this population. We might note the proportion of adults living in cities or urban areas, the proportion in rural areas, the median income of this population, the mean years of education completed, and so on.

A second option would be to use both sections of the telephone book. To make the sampling frame match our population definition, we would need to screen some of the telephone numbers. Although the telephone directory lists all the telephone prefixes in the county and notes the prefixes unique to each city, it does not indicate whether the prefixes extend beyond the city and town boundaries. Thus, for interviews in all towns that are on the county border, it would be necessary to ask each respondent whether his or her household is in Wake County or an adjacent county. From census data, we estimate that approximately 8% of the sample numbers would have to be screened in this manner. If the respondent's household is not in Wake County, it would be ineligible, and we would not attempt an interview.

A third option is to define our population frame as both sections of the telephone directory. Once again, after consulting census data, we estimate that approximately 4% of the telephone numbers in the book come from the adjacent counties of Johnston and Harnett. The simplest and most complete procedure then, would be to define the population as households listed in the Raleigh telephone directory— that is, all of Wake County and a few small towns and rural areas beyond the county border, which add an additional 4% to the population size. Since the county of Wake has no unique relationship to our research problem, there is no need for the sampling frame to exactly match the county boundaries. It is important, however, when we report our survey results, to provide the reader with a precise and accurate definition of the survey population and to describe the demographic characteristics of this population.

Recognizing Problems with Sampling Frames

One thing we have learned in our many years of survey experience is never to trust a sampling frame. Since incomplete and inaccurate information are inherent in sampling frames, the researcher needs to recognize the potential problems and to know how to handle them when they occur. The following problems often arise when the frame is a list:

- The list contains units that are not members of the defined population—these units are called ineligibles.
- Information about individuals or units on the list is not accurate.
- Information about individuals or units on the list is missing.
- Some individuals or units are listed more than once.

Ineligibles

A common problem is ineligibles. What should you do about them? The answer is simple: Ignore them for purposes of interviewing, but include them in the sampling rate. The **sampling rate** is the number of selections that must be made from a frame to achieve the desired sample size divided by the total number of selections in the frame. An example will help to explain this. Assume we want to interview recent graduates from our university to determine their satisfaction with curriculum changes that were instituted 5 years ago. We want to interview only graduates of the past 3 years, but the only frame we can get includes people who have graduated in the past 6 years. What do we do? We use the 6-year frame, but we determine what proportion of the graduates come from the last 3 years and what proportion come from the previous 3 years. To make matters simple, let's assume that the proportions are equal, 50% from each period. If there is no order to the list by year of graduation—people from both periods are randomly distributed throughout—we would expect a random sample of 1,000 names to include approximately 500 people from each period. Since we are not interested in interviewing people who graduated more than 3 years ago, every time such a person is selected, we simply ignore him or her and go on to the next selection. However, we still need to estimate the number of ineligibles in the list so they may be accounted for in the sampling rate. Having ineligibles on the list and ignoring them does not affect the probability of selection. Here is why. If 18,000 students graduated in the last 6 years and 9,000 graduated in each 3-year period, the sampling rate would be 1,000 ÷ 18,000 (1 in 18) or .055. We assume we will end up with 500 eligible graduates from the total of 9,000 eligible graduates for a probability of selection of 500 ÷ 9,000 = .055. Ineligibles are part of the sampling rate, but they do not affect the probability of selection, at least not in this situation.

Frequently, however, the probability of selection *is* affected by ineligibles because of incorrect sampling procedures. Another example will illustrate this. Assume that eligibles and ineligibles are mixed together on a list. Instead of adjusting the sampling rate based on the proportion of ineligibles on the list, researchers make the typical mistake of ignoring the ineligible person and selecting the next eligible person on the list. Can you guess what is wrong with this procedure? It gives eligible people who are preceded on the list by an ineligible person a double chance of selection: their own probability of selection and the ineligible person's chance of selection.

This incorrect procedure is commonly used when sampling from a telephone directory. Although the objective is a sample of telephone numbers, the sample selection process usually takes a sample of lines and telephone numbers. Since many telephone directories mix residential listings with business listings, to select a sample of households, you must treat business listings as ineligibles. Another common occurrence is that people with long names or addresses take up two lines. There are also other reasons why not every line in a telephone book has a telephone number (see Exhibit 8.2 in chapter 8).

No one counts all the eligible telephone numbers in a telephone directory and then selects a simple or systematic random sample of the listings. Think about the telephone directory for a large city such as Chicago. It contains more than 1,400 pages of listings, with five columns per page. Every column comprises more than 110 lines. It might take a week to count all of the people in the book. What researchers do, instead, is to estimate the proportion of lines that do not contain an eligible household number, include this proportion in the sampling rate, and then select a sample of lines from the telephone directory. Although this is the correct procedure, you must be careful to give each listing the same chance of selection. So, if business and residential listings are mixed together, you need to estimate the proportion that are business listings. The same must be done with blank lines or other ineligible lines. In essence, an estimate of the total number of ineligible and blank lines must be obtained before a sampling rate is established. This estimate becomes part of the sampling rate.[5] The key is to ensure that the probabilities of selection for the elements do not change because of the selection procedures.

Inaccuracies

A second common problem with sampling frames is that they contain inaccuracies. Thus, we may select an element that we thought was eligible but it turns out to be ineligible. Since all sampled cases

[5]These points are illustrated in chapter 8.

must be worked completely, and we do not know in advance which cases are eligible, ineligibles become a problem because each one takes time and money to work, reducing the number of eligible cases that can be obtained within the allotted time and budget. Therefore, it is important that this type of problem be found early, before or at pretesting, so that corrective actions can be taken.

Another potential problem with sampling frames is that, instead of finding one eligible element at a household or telephone number, more than one eligible element is found. Assume that we listed all households on a city block and then selected a sample of households at which to conduct interviews. The interviewer arrives at one address and, instead of finding one household, finds two: a front, listed apartment and a back, unlisted apartment. What should the interviewer do? In this case, the correct decision is to interview both households because the second household is eligible, even though it was not part of the initial frame. We want all eligible units to have a chance of being selected into the sample, and this is the only way the second unit has a chance of selection. In addition, we want to generalize to all eligible units, and this second unit is a member of the eligible units. In most situations, we can usually assume that mistakes are random. Since we happen to find one (random) error, there are likely to be others. It is also likely, as illustrated above, that some elements that were thought to be eligible are ineligible. If the frame is current and of good quality, these situations should be infrequent. However, knowing the proper corrective actions is still necessary.

Missing Information

Surprise elements can become a major problem. In a study designed by the authors in 1987–88, the best available sampling frame was census data. We decided to use the census data but to update it in areas of high growth because it was already 7 years old. We used a number of sources—statistics compiled by the city—on new housing starts and demolitions, and we contacted banks and real estate agents to ask them about areas of new growth. From past experience, we knew that no one source would have all the information we needed and that using multiple sources would be the best strategy. Using information from these sources, we updated the 1980 census data and made our block selections based on these data. Almost all the selections worked out well except for one block. We estimated that this block had about 50 households on it. When the lister arrived at the block, he found that a high-rise building had been erected and was now occupied. Instead of 50 households, there were now 450 households. In the previous example, when two households were found where one was expected, both were interviewed. Following a similar procedure in this case would mean using the same sampling rate for the 450 households that was to have been used with the 50 households—1 in 7 households. If we used a 1 in 7 rate, instead of selecting 7 households, we would end up selecting approximately 64 households. With a 70% cooperation rate this would yield about 45 interviews from this one block. Since we planned on doing a total of 500 interviews, this one block would contribute a disproportionate amount to our total number of completed interviews. In a situation like this, we might allow a double or triple number of interviews to be conducted in this block and then weight the results to reflect the number of interviews that should have been done in the block. If, for example, we allow 15 interviews to be conducted from that block, we would weight those interviews by a factor of 3 $(45 \div 15 = 3)$.

Other surprises can occur when sample respondents are selected. In most general population surveys of individuals, only one respondent per household is selected for interviewing. In a study of individuals, what do you think of this? Do all eligible respondents have the same probability of selection? The answer is no. In a one-person household, the one person is selected for interviewing. In households with three eligible people, only one person is selected, and the probability of selection for each person is one-third, at this stage. Thus, the probability of selection differs by the number of eligible people within the household. To make the probabilities equal for all individuals, the data must be weighted to reflect the number of eligible people in the selected households. In a one-person household, the weight is one; in a two-person household, it is two; in a three-person household, it is three, and so on.

Multiple Listings

Another common problem with frames is that some individuals are listed more than once, giving them higher probabilities of selection, unless some corrective action is taken. This situation occurs in telephone samples of households because some households, for a variety of reasons, have more than one telephone number. There can be one telephone number for the teenagers and one for the adults; the household may have a second telephone number that is given only to very close friends or relatives; or one of the numbers may be used for a business. The Federal Communications Commission estimates that approximately 6–8% of households in the United States have more than one residential telephone number.[6] The way to correct this situation is to add a question to the survey that asks about the number of different telephone numbers in the household and to weight the respondent's data by the reciprocal of the number of nonbusiness telephone numbers in the household. If there are two, the data are given a weight of .5; if there are three, it is .33; and so on.

A similar situation results from the use of university directories, which list the names and addresses of faculty, staff, and students. Some students or staff members may be listed in more than one section of the directory; graduate students who have assistantships may be listed as both students and staff. Many times staff members take courses, and thus they may be listed as both staff and students. In these situations, two things can be done. Every time a graduate student or staff member is selected, we would look in the other section of the directory to see if this person is listed a second time. We can assign all those who are listed twice a weight of .5, or we can randomly delete one-half of these cases. These procedures equalize the probabilities of selection.

Finally, one question that is frequently asked and for which there is no definitive answer is, "How accurate and complete should the sampling frame be?" The major problem with inaccuracies is that it takes time and money to work each case to find out that a respondent is ineligible or maybe that he or she is eligible but has moved to a new location within the target geographic area. It usually takes additional time to obtain current information and then to attempt an interview. These efforts take resources that could be used to interview eligible cases. Thus, time and effort spent on inaccurate information usually reduces the number of eligible cases that can be interviewed.

How complete the sampling frame should be is also a difficult question. The researcher must ask a number of questions. How different are the missing elements from the included elements? How might the final results be affected because of the missing elements? Will only the outcomes for single variables be affected or will relationships between variables be affected? Before adopting a frame, we need to investigate its inadequacies and assess how they may affect our results.

---

[6]This information was obtained through a telephone call to the Industrial Analysis Division at the FCC. It does not include households that have both residential and business telephone numbers.

Determining Sample Size

One of the most frequently asked questions in survey research is "What sample size do I need?" As usual, there is not a simple answer to this question. Sample size is a function of a number of things: the research design being used; the variability of the key variable(s), if we are trying to estimate a population value; or, if we are testing hypotheses, the size of the differences between two variables and the standard error of their difference. When testing hypotheses, the researcher tries to set a sample size that minimizes making two types of errors when drawing conclusions from the data: (1) to claim that variables are related when they are not (called Type I error); or (2) to conclude the opposite, that two variables are unrelated when, in fact, they are (called Type II error). Resolving these issues and determining sample size is a complex problem that is discussed in detail by Cohen (1988), Fleiss (1981), and Moser and Kalton (1972). To give an idea of the information required to begin solving for sample size, we will illustrate the classic method of determining sample size when estimating a population percentage.

An approximate formula (Cochran, 1977) for determining the sample size for a variable expressed as a percentage is:

$$n = \left(1 - \frac{n}{N}\right) * \frac{t^2(p * q)}{d^2} = \frac{\text{finite}}{\text{population}} * \frac{\text{probability level } * \text{ variance}}{\text{confidence interval}}$$
$$\text{correction}$$

Where:

n = The sample size or the number of completed interviews with eligible elements

N = The size of the eligible population

t^2 = The squared value of the **standard deviation** score that refers to the area under a normal distribution of values

p = The percentage category for which we are computing the sample size

$q = 1 - p$

d^2 = The squared value of one half the precision interval around the sample estimate

Expressed in words, the formula states that sample size is an expression of a finite population correction factor $(1 - n/N)$ times the probability level for this sample occurrence times the **variance** or the variability of our variable in the population divided by the size of the confidence interval that we want for our estimate. Let's talk more in depth about these components and then look at an example.

Finite Population Correction

The finite population correction (fpc) is an adjustment factor that becomes part of the formula when sample elements are selected without replacement.[7] However, the fpc has very little effect on the end result when the size of the sample is less than 5% of the total population. In most sample surveys, this is the case, and the fpc is excluded. We will have more to say about the relationship between sample size and population size in a later example.

Probability Level

The formula now has three components. To solve the equation, we set the values for two components (probability level and confidence interval) and we approximate the third (variance). The value for t, **probability level,** is the standard deviation score that expresses the percentage of a variable's values that fall within a set interval when the variable is normally distributed. One standard deviation includes about 68% of the sample values and its score is 1.0; two standard deviations include about 95% of the sample values and its score is 1.96; and three standard deviations include approximately 99% of the values and its score is 2.58. By using these values or scores, we assume our variable is normally distributed. When we set t, we are setting a probability level for our sample result. We are saying that out of 100 samples of the size that we are going to conduct, we want to be x percent confident (we set x) that our sample confidence interval (d) includes the population value. Lets move on to the next component.

Variance

The formula is for a variable expressed as a percentage. Typically this means that we are interested in a variable expressed as two

---

[7]Sample elements can be selected with or without replacement. With replacement works as follows. If we want to randomly select a sample of three numbers from the set of numbers 1–10, after each number is selected, it is returned to the group of numbers and it can be selected again at the next selection of a number.

categories: those who do and those who do not or those who have and those who do not have. For example, we may want to estimate the percentage of the population that smokes cigarettes, owns a handgun, rides public transportation, makes more than $30,000 per year, and so forth. Each of these variables is expressed as the percentage that do or have and the percentage that do not. Any variable can be expressed as a percentage. We may be interested in a variable which has response categories of strongly agree, agree, disagree, and strongly disagree. We can dichotomize this variable by deciding what category or categories we are interested in determining the sample size for. If we were interested in the proportion that agree with a statement, we would combine into one category those that strongly agree and those that agree and combine the two disagree categories into a second category. The percentages in the final two categories must sum to 1.0. The variance of a percentage variable is the product of the two percentages.

If we want to do a study to estimate the number of adult smokers in Raleigh, to determine the sample size, we need to come up with a good guess or estimate of the percentage of smokers before we do the study.[8] This estimate is a necessary component of the formula. While this seems incongruous with our task, there are a number of methods that can be used to make this estimate. One is to use the results from a previous study. If the characteristics of the study site are not similar to those of Raleigh, the researcher can adjust the estimate. Another method is to make a conservative guess at the proportion of smokers. As we will see shortly, the variance component does not affect the solution of the formula as much as the confidence interval. Thus, an incorrect guess does not affect the required sample size as much as the setting of the precision of a confidence interval around the estimate. A third method for estimating the variance is to conduct a small pilot study. Depending on one's resources, a short phone call to a random sample of 25 to 50 households should provide a reasonable estimate. In this example, p would be the proportion of adults who smoke and q would be 1 minus that percentage.

---

[8]While we work through the example step-by-step, the reader might want to think through the steps using a different example, such as determining the sample size to estimate the proportion of adults in your home town that eat breakfast at least five times a week or who exercise for 30 minutes at least three times per week. These alternate examples will help to reinforce the step-by-step procedures.

Confidence Interval

The third component of the formula, which is determined by the researcher, is the confidence interval, or d. This interval is the margin of error that we require or will tolerate. The only way, theoretically, to estimate a population value without sampling error is to include or interview every element in the population. When we interview a sample of cases, we can only estimate the population value within a range of values. The component d is expressed as plus and minus and represents one-half of the range. Thus, if we assume that 30% of the adults in Raleigh smoke, d is how large or small we need the estimated range to be around 30%. As we will see shortly, the smaller the range, the larger the required sample size.

Let's go back over the components of the formula and then go through an example. The variance is the value we must guess or estimate. The percentage of the population with the characteristic is p, and the remaining percentage of the population is q. The probability level, t, which we select, represents in how many repeated samples of 100 that total the same size as ours, the population value is likely to fall within the specified confidence interval. The confidence interval, d, is the width of the range in which we want our estimate to fall.

Putting It All Together

Let's finish the example on estimating the number of adult smokers in the city of Raleigh. The question is "What sample size do we need *if we assume the following components*?" Let's assume that Raleigh is similar to the U.S. population in the proportion of adults who smoke. Our assumptions are that Raleigh is the home of a major university—its residents have an above-average level of education—but it is also the capitol city of a tobacco-growing state. We assume these factors are offsetting and believe the percentage of adult smokers in the United States is a good estimate for Raleigh. We assume $p = .30$ and, therefore, q is $1 - .30 = .70$. We want our probability or confidence level to be 95%—that is, to include the population value in 95 out of every group of 100 samples of the same size. And, we want the confidence interval to be ±5%. In summary, the problem is stated as follows, "What sample size do we need if we want to be 95% confident that the population value lies in the interval between 25% and 35%?" Substituting these values into the formula gives:

$$n = \frac{(1.96)^2(.30)(.70)}{(.05)^2} = \frac{.8067}{.0025} = 323$$

The number of interviews we need is 323. Remember that our estimate of the variance was a guess or a rough estimate. If we do 323 interviews and find that our estimate is wrong, what effect does that have on our calculations? The answer is that the confidence interval will be affected. The purpose for doing these calculations is to get some idea of the required sample size within the constraints we have established for the research problem. But these calculations are only a guide. We don't need to do exactly 323 interviews. However, if our estimate of variance is correct and we want to achieve the stated level of precision, we should strive to complete about this number of interviews.

Once the study is conducted, we always compute confidence intervals for the key variables. The confidence intervals are based on the variability of each variable, the number of completed interviews, and the probability level we established. In the above example, if our estimate of the proportion of smokers was too high, meaning less variance in the population, our final confidence interval would be smaller than ±5%. This would give our sample estimate more precision than we required. If our estimate was too low, meaning there are more smokers than we estimated, it would make our confidence interval larger than we planned for. Two examples will illustrate this. We use the same formula as before. This time we solve for d. We use the actual percentages or variances in the data and the number of interviews completed. If we found that 20% of the population smoked, the results for d would be

$$d^2 = \frac{(1.96)^2(.2)(.8)}{323} \qquad d = \sqrt{.00190} = .0436$$

The confidence interval would be ±4.4% around the sample estimate rather than ±5%. If our survey found 40% of the adults to be smokers, d would be

$$d^2 = \frac{(1.96)^2(.4)(.6)}{323} \qquad d = \sqrt{.00285} = .0534$$

Rather than ±5%, the confidence interval would be ±5.3%.

These examples illustrate an additional point. The formula has four components. By setting or knowing three of the components, you can solve the equation for the fourth.

Formula Assumptions

We should also point out other important aspects of the formula. It is based on selection of elements by simple random sampling (srs), which means that all elements and combinations of elements have an equal chance of selection. In reality, few samples are srs; thus, the formula is only a guide to sample size requirements. Second, the formula applies only to a variable in percentage form. Metric variables such as income require the more traditional method of calculating a variance, which is taught in data analysis or statistics classes. Third, the formula gives a sample size solution for only one variable. Most surveys have many important variables. The fact that each variable in a survey has its own variance and, thus, that each can require different sample sizes forces researchers to make tough decisions. Typically, a compromise is fashioned between sample size requirements, the method of data collection, and the resources available.

A fourth assumption of the formula is that the sample comes from a large population or that the sample is a small proportion of the population. When this occurs, you can ignore the fpc, which we did in the above solutions. Many times, researchers believe incorrectly that a sample must be a certain percentage of the population if it is to accurately reflect the population. Sometimes we hear researchers ask if they should take a 1%, 5%, or some other percentage sample of the population. The only time the population size is important is when the sample represents more than 5% of the population, an arbitrary standard used by many sampling statisticians. Let's illustrate this with an example. Our sample size requirement for the smoking study is 323. The population correction factor is represented by (Cochran, 1977)

$$n' = \frac{n}{1 + \left(\dfrac{n-1}{N}\right)}$$

Our sample size requirement is $n = 323$ and the population of adults 18 years and older in Raleigh in 1990 is $N = 167,193$ (U.S. Bureau of the Census, 1992). Substituting these values into the equation, we get

$$n' = \frac{323}{1 + \dfrac{322}{167,193}} = \frac{323}{1.00193} = 322$$

The solution gives us a difference of 1, which is really no difference. What might happen if the population of adults numbered 50,000?

Substituting this number into the equation for N gives us a result of 321. Again, no real difference. Let's do one more example. What if the size of the population is 2,500? Substituting this into the equation gives a sample size requirement of 286. This represents 37 fewer interviews, or an 11.5% reduction. Note that a sample of 323 is 12.9% of a population of 2,500, which exceeds the 5% standard. This returns us to an earlier point: Population size does not affect sample size unless the population is small and the sample is more than 5% of the population. This is the reason that, if the variance and the other components of the formula are assumed to be the same, a study done in Raleigh or in the entire state of North Carolina or in the entire United States, requires the same size sample!

What Most Affects Sample Size

Now that we have an idea of how to determine sample size and we know that population size is usually not a factor, we next want to examine what component or components of the formula have the greatest effect on sample size. Exhibit 7.1 presents the sample sizes for different combinations of variances, probability levels, and confidence intervals. Part A presents the results for 95% confidence (probability level), and Part B for 90% confidence (probability level). The results for a third frequently used probability level, 99%, is left for the student to solve. Within each part of the table, we present the maximum variance for a percentage variable (.50/.50), a middle range variance (.70/.30) and a low estimate of variance (.90/.10). We also present three confidence intervals: ±5%, ±4%, and ±2%.

Let's first look at Part A, which gives the 95% probability level. For a variable with the maximum variance of .50/.50 and a confidence interval of ±5%, the sample size requirement is 384. Going down the first column, the requirements for a variable with a variance of .70/.30 is 323, and for one with a variance of .90/.10, 138. Note that the smaller the variance, the smaller the required sample size.

In each row, the confidence intervals change. For the maximum variance and for a confidence interval of ±5%, the sample size required is 384. As we demand more and more precision around the estimate, the required sample size increases. At ±4% the requirement is 600, but at ±2% the requirement jumps to a sample size of 2,401. Going from ±5% to ±2% causes more than a sixfold increase in sample size. This increase is the same for each level of variance.

Exhibit 7.1

Required Sample Sizes for Different Variances (expressed as percentages), Probability Levels, and Confidence Intervals[a]

A. 95% probability level with different variances and confidence intervals

$$\frac{(1.96)^2(.5)(.5)}{(.05)^2} = 384 \qquad \frac{(1.96)^2(.5)(.5)}{(.04)^2} = 600 \qquad \frac{(1.96)^2(.5)(.5)}{(.02)^2} = 2401$$

$$\frac{(1.96)^2(.7)(.3)}{(.05)^2} = 323 \qquad \frac{(1.96)^2(.7)(.3)}{(.04)^2} = 504 \qquad \frac{(1.96)^2(.7)(.3)}{(.02)^2} = 2017$$

$$\frac{(1.96)^2(.9)(.1)}{(.05)^2} = 138 \qquad \frac{(1.96)^2(.9)(.1)}{(.04)^2} = 216 \qquad \frac{(1.96)^2(.9)(.1)}{(.02)^2} = 864$$

B. 90% probability level with different variances and confidence intervals

$$\frac{(1.64)^2(.5)(.5)}{(.05)^2} = 269 \qquad \frac{(1.64)^2(.5)(.5)}{(.04)^2} = 420 \qquad \frac{(1.64)^2(.5)(.5)}{(.02)^2} = 1681$$

$$\frac{(1.64)^2(.7)(.3)}{(.05)^2} = 226 \qquad \frac{(1.64)^2(.7)(.3)}{(.04)^2} = 353 \qquad \frac{(1.64)^2(.7)(.3)}{(.02)^2} = 1412$$

$$\frac{(1.64)^2(.9)(.1)}{(.05)^2} = 98 \qquad \frac{(1.64)^2(.9)(.1)}{(.04)^2} = 151 \qquad \frac{(1.64)^2(.9)(.1)}{(.02)^2} = 605$$

[a]These calculations do not include the finite population correction factor.

When we go from a low variance to a maximum variance, the required sample size increases by a factor of 2.77; however, when we go from a moderate confidence interval to a small confidence interval, the increase is a factor of 6.25. These changes are comparable across all variances, confidence intervals, and the two probability levels. Thus, for a percentage variable, the size of the confidence interval or the precision of the sample estimate affects sample size requirements the most. The Current Population Survey is a real-life example of this requirement for a metric variable that must be estimated with a high level of precision. This survey is conducted monthly to estimate the unemployment rate in the United States with a confidence interval that is a fraction of 1%. To achieve this percentage rate, approximately 60,000 households are interviewed each month.

Using Census Data

As pointed out frequently, census data can be helpful in planning a survey, especially for estimating how many interviews we will obtain with people from various demographic subgroups and whether these sample sizes will be adequate for purposes of analysis. To ensure that we have adequate sample sizes, we must plan ahead. We need to review our research questions again: What are the objectives of our survey? What are the questions that we want to answer? Do we need answers for the total population? Only for specific subgroups? If so, which ones? Or, do we need answers for both the total population and certain subgroups? Let's continue the discussion of our survey about adult smokers in Raleigh.

Research Objectives

We need to think about our research objectives and the types of analyses we feel are important. As we do this, we want to consult census data to see what the interview outcomes might be. Again, we begin with: What is the research question? We want to estimate the number of adult smokers in Raleigh because we want to develop and test an intervention program to see whether it is successful in helping people to quit smoking. A natural follow-up question is whether we need to consider specific types of people. Are we interested only in an estimate of the total number of smokers, or do we want to get estimates for specific subgroups defined by gender, age, race, or combined gender and race? We ask these questions because research tells us that smoking behavior differs among these subgroups and it will be more effective if we tailor the intervention programs to specific needs of certain subgroups, rather than developing one general program for everyone. Therefore, we are interested not only in total population estimates but also in estimates for specific subgroups.

Analysis Groups

The next step is to ask ourselves in what specific subgroups we are interested. Let's assume we are interested in estimates for both males and females; for three age groups—18–39, 40–64, and 65 and older; by race; and maybe by gender and race. Next, we need to find out how many people there are in Raleigh in these various groups, determine how many interviews we can afford to conduct, and then put these pieces of information together. This last step will allow us to estimate the confidence intervals for all the subgroups and to determine whether the levels of precision are adequate for our purposes.

Assume that our resources will allow us to conduct 600 thirty-minute telephone interviews. To estimate how these interviews will be divided among our subgroups of interest, we need to find data that describe the adults in Raleigh by the characteristics of interest, and we need to make assumptions about whether a telephone survey will adequately represent these groups.

Consulting Census Data

It is at this point that we consult census data. The U.S. Census Bureau conducts censuses on population and housing, agriculture, and government; economic censuses on retail trade, wholesale trade, service industries, transportation, manufactures, mineral industries, and construction industries; and censuses on foreign trade and other subjects. Censuses are taken every 5 or 10 years, depending upon the topic. Data are presented for two types of areas: governmental—United States, Puerto Rico, states, counties, cities, villages, townships, congressional districts, Indian reservations, and so forth; and, statistical areas—regions of the United States, metropolitan areas, urban areas, census tracts, blocks or block groups, ZIP codes, and other types of geographic areas. Data are available in printed reports and on computer tapes, CD-ROM laser discs, and microfiche. In addition to these censuses, the bureau conducts about 250 sample surveys each year. In short, the U.S. Census Bureau gathers and disseminates a treasure trove of information.

For our survey on smokers in Raleigh, we are interested in information that comes from the census of population and housing. Conducted every 10 years, this census collects data from every housing unit. A short-form questionnaire includes questions about the sex, race, age, marital status, and household relationship of all residents of the unit. The long-form questionnaire, which is distributed to a sample of people, includes additional questions, on social and economic characteristics such as education, place of birth, ancestry, language spoken at home, disability, fertility, employment characteristics, and other topics.

The information we need can be found in the printed report entitled "General Population Characteristics—North Carolina," Volume CP-1-35 (U.S. Bureau of the Census, 1992). Table 61 in this volume provides detailed information on the age and sex, by race, of all of the people in the city of Raleigh in 1990. (Exhibit 7.2 is a reproduction of this table.) The table provides detailed information about the total number of people in the city of Raleigh by specific ages and age groups, by race and Hispanic origin, and by one gender group—females. To determine the number of males by age and race we need to subtract the number of females from the total number of people. By doing a little addition, subtraction, and division, we can obtain from this table all the information that we require.

Making Choices

Exhibit 7.3 provides an estimate of the number of completed interviews, by subgroup, for a sample survey of 600. Before constructing this table, we first consulted the Census of Housing (U.S. Bureau of the Census 1993a) and learned that only 3.6% of the occupied housing units in Raleigh do not have a telephone. Therefore, we are assuming that telephone coverage is fairly uniformly distributed among the subgroups in the population and that none of our subgroups of interest are significantly underrepresented. We are also assuming that a telephone survey will reach each of these subgroups in the same proportions in which they are distributed in the population—that is, if our sample is truly random and we do not get differential rates of interview cooperation by subgroups, the final results of our survey by subgroups should closely approximate the percentages in the population. We don't expect our numbers to exactly match those in Exhibit 7.3, but we assume that they will be reasonably close to these estimates.

Exhibit 7.3 shows a common situation for gender in that the population is fairly evenly divided between males and females. A survey should give us approximately equal sample sizes by gender if cooperation rates are the same. For most surveys, however, this is a dubious assumption because females are more likely to cooperate than males. Final interview results for males are usually a few percentage points below their population proportion. If males constitute 48% of the eligible population, as they do in this example, they may represent between 42 and 46% of the final interviews. At the moment, let's not worry about adjusting the numbers in the table by guessing the cooperation rates. Let's use the numbers in the table as our best guess of the outcomes by subgroup. The question we need to ask is, "Are the number of interviews to be conducted with each of these subgroups adequate to meet our objectives?" In effect, can we live with the levels of precision the various sample sizes will produce?

Exhibit 7.2

1990 Population of Raleigh by Age, Sex, Race, and Hispanic Origin

Place and [in Selected States] County Subdivision [10,000 or More Persons]	Raleigh City							Reidsville City		
	All persons	White	Black	American Indian, Eskimo, or Aleut	Asian or Pacific Islander	Hispanic origin (of any race)	White, not of Hispanic origin	All persons	White	Black
All persons	**207951**	**143862**	**57354**	**584**	**5127**	**2940**	**142237**	**12183**	**7353**	**4745**
Under 5 years	12976	7590	4796	26	455	253	7453	792	391	385
Under 1 year	2361	1403	858	4	80	40	1381	143	66	73
1 year	2940	1737	1075	4	104	54	1706	153	79	69
2 years	2747	1599	1022	3	96	54	1571	176	85	88
3 years	2441	1393	932	7	82	59	1360	148	73	73
4 years	2487	1458	909	8	93	46	1435	172	88	82
5 to 9 years	11133	6773	3866	28	381	199	6666	707	363	336
5 years	2369	1415	834	5	93	55	1386	156	74	81
6 years	2218	1385	743	8	64	42	1361	125	67	56
7 years	2264	1374	784	6	79	42	1352	148	71	74
8 years	2126	1290	734	5	85	30	1275	139	76	61
9 years	2156	1309	771	4	60	30	1292	139	75	64
10 to 14 years	10540	6201	3939	29	313	168	6103	725	363	355
10 years	2229	1337	816	8	54	40	1313	143	76	66
11 years	2079	1212	782	7	64	34	1195	129	56	71
12 years	2125	1238	810	6	60	30	1222	159	70	86
13 years	2032	1194	752	4	75	30	1172	157	91	66
14 years	2075	1220	779	4	60	34	1201	137	70	66

(continued on next page)

Exhibit 7.2

1990 Population of Raleigh by Age, Sex, Race, and Hispanic Origin (continued)

Place and [in Selected States] County Subdivision [10,000 or More Persons]	Raleigh City							Reidsville City		
	All persons	White	Black	American Indian, Eskimo, or Aleut	Asian or Pacific Islander	Hispanic origin (of any race)	White, not of Hispanic origin	All persons	White	Black
15 to 19 years	15223	9617	5147	51	316	230	9520	850	421	420
15 years	2021	1207	753	2	50	29	1193	175	83	90
16 years	1969	1168	738	3	46	33	1153	177	88	87
17 years	2174	1333	750	3	72	32	1320	153	73	80
18 years	3440	2214	1124	17	66	54	2191	183	88	93
19 years	5619	3695	1782	26	82	82	3663	162	89	70
20 to 24 years	27427	19087	7502	91	575	479	18841	769	429	332
20 years	6062	4196	1705	21	113	96	4152	163	96	66
21 years	5646	3944	1526	24	122	93	3892	137	74	61
25 to 29 years	25508	17563	6884	87	770	447	17351	946	538	400
30 to 34 years	21377	14471	5906	82	790	367	14269	934	531	397
35 to 39 years	17799	12338	4833	73	497	236	12194	892	524	358
40 to 44 years	15108	10979	3691	33	356	185	10872	741	474	262
45 to 49 years	10767	8099	2365	27	252	101	8030	596	374	221
50 to 54 years	8039	6126	1735	20	141	74	6075	558	351	205
55 to 59 years	7015	5397	1481	10	115	52	5359	553	362	187
60 to 64 years	6707	5236	1395	7	64	39	5208	708	480	228
65 to 69 years	6252	4873	1320	9	44	39	4846	748	524	224
70 to 74 years	4549	3538	976	2	31	21	3520	606	439	167
75 to 79 years	3333	2619	698	2	14	28	2594	487	359	127

80 to 84 years	2384	1911	462	5	5	15	1897	367	271	96
85 years and over	1814	1444	358	2	8	7	1439	204	159	45
18 years and over	167138	119590	42512	493	3810	2226	118349	9454	5992	3412
62 years and over	22314	17484	4657	21	137	133	17378	2832	2044	787
65 years and over	18332	14385	3814	20	102	110	14296	2412	1752	659
Median age	30.2	31.6	27.4	28.8	28.6	26.4	31.7	36.9	41.1	31.8
Female	**107103**	**73556**	**30481**	**294**	**2354**	**1361**	**72743**	**6759**	**4051**	**2672**
Under 5 years	6475	3750	2452	12	198	151	3672	404	208	190
Under 1 year	1169	671	450	2	37	23	659	69	32	36
1 year	1471	861	549	2	46	34	842	83	50	32
2 years	1369	789	516	3	45	28	777	85	43	41
3 years	1231	734	451	1	30	37	713	80	42	36
4 years	1235	695	486	4	40	29	681	87	41	45
5 to 9 years	5517	3334	1945	13	190	83	3289	345	178	164
5 years	1145	678	412	3	43	23	666	76	40	36
6 years	1094	685	373	3	27	11	677	66	36	28
7 years	1132	675	402	3	43	20	665	75	30	44
8 years	1064	643	368	2	47	14	635	68	41	27
9 years	1082	653	390	2	30	15	646	60	31	29
10 to 14 years	5265	3099	1974	16	147	93	3040	356	172	181
10 years	1092	661	399	4	22	20	648	73	38	35
11 years	1059	618	398	4	34	16	608	61	29	32
12 years	1091	631	420	5	28	19	622	82	30	50
13 years	991	593	364	1	31	18	578	73	40	33
14 years	1032	596	393	2	32	20	584	67	35	31

(continued on next page)

Exhibit 7.2

1990 Population of Raleigh by Age, Sex, Race, and Hispanic Origin (continued)

Place and [in Selected States] County Subdivision [10,000 or More Persons]	Raleigh City							Reidsville City		
	All persons	White	Black	American Indian, Eskimo, or Aleut	Asian or Pacific Islander	Hispanic origin (of any race)	White, not of Hispanic origin	All persons	White	Black
15 to 19 years	8024	5066	2757	22	142	106	5018	432	224	204
15 years	1016	607	386	—	20	10	602	90	41	48
16 years	999	602	370	—	20	17	595	92	47	44
17 years	1131	687	397	2	37	21	678	73	35	38
18 years	1901	1219	636	10	29	23	1209	84	44	40
19 years	2977	1951	968	10	36	35	1934	93	57	34
20 to 24 years	13127	8953	3869	36	215	178	8846	417	215	198
20 years	2964	2040	864	8	42	36	2018	80	42	38
21 years	2598	1782	756	7	48	29	1763	74	36	37
25 to 29 years	12401	8298	3605	38	381	191	8195	477	258	217
30 to 34 years	10564	7089	3037	49	349	159	6988	492	262	227
35 to 39 years	9036	6145	2587	42	237	109	6079	490	273	212
40 to 44 years	7838	5672	1961	18	166	91	5612	388	246	139
45 to 49 years	5555	4184	1226	13	124	51	4148	336	200	135
50 to 54 years	4225	3189	951	13	62	37	3165	332	199	133
55 to 59 years	3742	2825	846	6	58	24	2808	299	194	103
60 to 64 years	3683	2840	808	3	29	17	2830	420	280	140
65 to 69 years	3547	2734	782	5	24	25	2716	425	294	131
70 to 74 years	2821	2188	616	2	13	13	2177	396	288	108
75 to 79 years	2193	1719	462	2	10	18	1702	328	243	85

80 to 84 years	1710	1371	332	3	3	10	1362	263	193	70
85 years and over	1380	1100	271	1	6	5	1096	159	124	35
18 years and over	86700	61477	22957	251	1742	986	60867	5399	3370	2007
62 years and over	13868	10822	2954	13	70	80	10757	1816	1307	509
65 years and over	11651	9112	2463	13	56	71	9053	1571	1142	429
Median age	31.1	32.9	28.0	31.3	29.0	26.6	32.9	39.6	44.7	34.0
Male	**100848**	**70306**	**26873**	**290**	**2773**	**1579**	**69494**	**5424**	**3302**	**2073**
Median age	29.4	30.5	26.8	27.0	28.3	26.3	30.5	34.2	37.6	29.0
Males per 100 females	94.2	95.6	88.2	98.6	117.8	116.0	95.5	80.2	81.5	77.6

Source: U.S. Bureau of the Census. (1992). *1990 Census of Population: General Population Characteristics—North Carolina.* Washington, DC: U.S. Government Printing Office. (1990 CP-1–35)

Exhibit 7.3

Estimates of the Number of Telephone Interviews for Selected Subgroup Characteristics for a Survey of 600 Adults in the City of Raleigh

	Population		Interview Estimate
	N	%	
Race			
White	119,590	71.5	429
Black	42,512	15.4	152
Other	5,036	3.1	19
	167,138	100.0	600
Gender			
Male	80,438	48.1	289
Female	86,700	51.9	311
Age			
18–39	101,170	60.5	363
40–64	47,636	28.5	171
65 and older	18,332	11.0	66
18–34	83,371	49.9	299
35–64	65,435	39.1	235
65 and older	18,332	11.0	66
18–34	83,371	49.9	299
35–59	58,728	35.1	211
60 and older	25,039	15.0	90
Race and Gender			
White males	58,113	34.8	209
White females	61,477	36.8	221
Black males	19,555	11.7	70
Black females	22,957	13.7	82

Let's do a few calculations and see. For males we expect about 289 interviews. If we set a 95% probability and we assume a .30/.70 variance, and solve for d, we get a result of ±5.3%. For what we are trying to do, a confidence interval (range) of 10.6% is reasonable.

Let's look at race. Our survey should yield 429 interviews with whites, 152 with blacks, and only 19 interviews with people of other races. There are two major inequities here. One, 19 interviews with any group is too few for any meaningful analysis. Our choices are to

(1) combine people of other races with whites or blacks; (2) screen other races out of the study by asking about the respondent's race at the start of the survey and treating people who are not white or black as ineligibles; or (3) interview all respondents and exclude other races from the analysis. The third strategy is best. To open the interview with a personal question about race in order to avoid 19 ineligible interviews is not worth the risk of offending potential respondents and increasing the overall refusal rate. The strategy of combining other races with the whites or blacks is also unacceptable. It is very likely, and the literature seems to support this, that the attitudes and smoking behaviors of people of Chinese, Japanese, Malaysian, and other descents might be very different from those who are white or black. Thus, the best compromise strategy is to exclude people of other races from the analysis.

The second inequity concerns the great difference in the number of interviews that will be conducted with white and black respondents. Our previous sample size examples have illustrated that, when the variances between groups are equal but the sample sizes are different, the size of the confidence interval will also be different. Ideally, when comparing groups, we want the confidence intervals to be equal. Using the sample size estimates in Exhibit 7.3 and the assumptions used for the other races, the confidence intervals would be ±4.3% for whites and ±7.3% for blacks. The size of the interval range is 8.6% for whites and 14.6% for blacks. For most social science variables these ranges may be adequate; for others, however, more precision may be needed. We must remember that these ranges are for a .30/.70 variable split. As the percentages move toward .50/.50, the size of these ranges will increase. One alternative is to oversample blacks. This means screening households for race which, as we mentioned earlier, may have negative consequences. Screening would also increase costs, reducing the number of interviews we could afford. The choices are not easy. In a situation like this, the researcher must look carefully at the key variables and the required degree of precision in making final design decisions.

Recall that each variable or combination of variables has its own variance. If we are interested in the attitudes and behavior of white males and females and black males and females, we need to do the same calculations. Exhibit 7.3 shows that we can expect a little over 200 interviews with each white gender group, but we will only have about 70–82 interviews with the black gender groups. We can get a rough idea of the confidence intervals for whites from our previous calculations, so let's see what it might be for black males, the smallest group. Using a .30/.70 variance estimate and a 95% probability level, a sample size of 70 gives a confidence interval of ±10.7% or a range of 21.4%. If our study found 30% of the black males to be smokers, the 95% confidence interval would provide a population estimate of 19.3–40.7% of the black males to be smokers. If this is a critical variable, we would want to consider the options for increasing this sample size. One additional comment. If we are interested in the behavior of young black males, we would get even fewer interviews and the sample size would be totally inadequate.

The age figures in Exhibit 7.3 illustrate another important point. Initially, we had an interest in three age groups: 18–39 (young), 40–64 (middle), and 65 and over (older). These groups are not equally distributed in the population. The bulk of the interviews will be with young adults, and the older adults have a smaller sample yield than even the black males. One additional option to better equalize the size of the confidence intervals is to change the definition of our age groups. We would do this only if it makes sense substantively. For example, we could define the young as 18–34 and the middle age group as 35–64. This better equalizes each group's confidence intervals but it does not change the situation for the older respondents. Another possibility is to redefine the middle age group as 35–59 and the older age as 60 and over. This change gives us a slightly better sample size for the older adults than the sample sizes that we will get for the black gender groups. Other definitions are also possible.

We conclude by emphasizing that data are available to assist the researcher in planning for the most effective study possible. Even with a good research idea, one should not blindly march ahead and begin collecting data without planning to achieve the best possible outcome. It is unpardonable, for example, to decide to study attitudes of Caucasians and African Americans, conduct the study, and then learn that African Americans comprise only 12% of the population and that the number of interviews with them is inadequate for data analysis. The elderly—those 65 and older—typically comprise a similar percentage of the total population. Before designing a study of the elderly, the researcher should know not only this proportion but also that the elderly usually have lower response rates than other segments of the population. Information is available from census data, existing studies of similar populations, textbooks, data archives, and other sources to help design and plan an effective study. Chapter 10 and the References also provide a number of sources that should be consulted in designing or implementing a study.

8   Selecting a Sample

Telephone and mail surveys are the two types of studies students are most likely to conduct. In this chapter we describe many of the decisions that must be made in selecting samples for a community telephone survey and how these procedures can be extended to select a national RDD sample. We then illustrate two examples of selecting samples from lists: (1) where the order of the individuals can be manipulated to take advantage of the benefits of stratifying a sample and (2) a sample of natural clusters such as classes of students.

Exhibit 8.1 outlines the major steps in the selection of a sample. The examples in this chapter illustrate these steps. Before you begin Example 1, you may want to read these steps so you can get a sense of how the discussion of the examples is organized.

Exhibit 8.1
Steps in Sample Selection

- Define the population
- Find and/or develop a frame
- Determine sample size
- Select sample
- Manage sample and resample
- Select respondents

Example 1: A Community Telephone Sample

Defining the Population

To begin, we review the early stages of a study. Assume we want to study attitudes of adults 18 and older in the Raleigh area about abortion. We have concluded that a telephone study is an acceptable method for collecting these data because this method has low response effects, and it fits our time schedule and budget. **Response effects** are the amounts of error in the answers to questions that are due to factors such as faulty memory, the respondent misunderstanding the question, or method of data collection (Sudman and Bradburn, 1982). We have also considered what proportion of households do not have telephones and we are willing to accept this potential bias. In Wake County the estimate is 3.4%, and in the city of Raleigh, it is 3.6% (U.S. Bureau of the Census, 1993a). Both estimates are below the national average.

Selecting a Frame

Our next task is to find an acceptable sampling frame and to assess its coverage and recency. The Raleigh telephone directory has a residence section that presumably contains only households, no businesses. The directory includes Raleigh (1990 population = 207,951), Cary (1990 population = 43,858), six smaller cities (1990 population = 28,836), and rural, unincorporated areas (1990 estimated population = 88,139). Approximately 85% of the county population is covered by the directory. Since liberal and conservative attitudes about abortion may be correlated with location of residence, and we wish to test this and other hypotheses, the coverage of the telephone directory suits our purposes.

As a frame, however, the telephone directory has one major drawback. It does not include people with unlisted telephone numbers. An estimate by Survey Sampling, Inc. (1994), indicates that 23% of the households in the Raleigh-Durham-Chapel Hill metropolitan statistical area are unlisted. This potential bias is too large to ignore; thus, our survey requires an RDD sample.

For a study that covers a small geographic area and is represented by one telephone directory, our preference is to use that book to select a directory-based RDD sample. (For statewide, regional, or national samples, we would use the Bellcore data file, which contains every area code and telephone prefix in the United States.) For the current sample, we will select numbers randomly from the telephone directory, drop the last two digits of the telephone number, and replace them with two randomly selected digits. Two assumptions underlie this method. One is that the telephone directory includes all existing telephone prefixes and that no new prefixes have been established since it was published. New prefixes could lead to potential bias because households that are assigned these numbers would not have a chance of being in the study. Let's assume the telephone directory is only a few months old, so this possibility is unlikely. However, when in doubt, we should call the telephone company and ask. A second assumption is that the unlisted telephone numbers are distributed proportionately among the listed numbers. If this assumption is not true and the unlisted numbers are clustered in a few prefixes, then the unlisted numbers would have a smaller probability of selection. Another concern is that in many geographic areas, prefixes are confined to specific geographic locations. If an area has a disproportionate percentage of unlisted numbers, it will be either overrepresented or underrepresented, which is likely to bias the final results. We do not know of any studies that have tested this assumption; researchers either assume proportional distribution or ignore the potential problem.

For this study, we will develop a systematic random sample, selected in stages. To do that, we need to estimate the total number of sample selections, compute a sampling interval, and select a sample starting point. This procedure is far simpler and more efficient than a simple random sample (srs). For example, the residential section of the Raleigh telephone directory is 440 pages long. Each page has four columns, and each column contains 104 lines. To select a simple random sample from this book, we would need to number every household telephone number on the 440 pages, a total of approximately 122,500; we would then select unique random numbers between 1 and 122,500. The hard part is the initial numbering. How long do you think it would take you to write the numbers between 1 and 122,500?[1]

Expression 8.1 is the formula for determining the number of sample selections needed for the proposed telephone study. Over the next few pages we are going to discuss Expression 8.1: (1) how to solve it, (2) the assumptions we are using, and (3) how we arrive at the numbers and percentages we will use to solve it. The expression, or parts of it, is used several times in this chapter so we will discuss it in detail. In words, the expression means that to determine the number of sample selections, divide the desired number of completed interviews by the product of the percentage of the eligible telephone numbers that occur at each stage of sample selection and the percentage of residential numbers that become completed interviews.

---

[1] The residential listings of some telephone directories are available for a fee as computer files from commercial organizations. Using a computer file would make it easy to select a simple random sample.

$$\begin{array}{l} \text{Number of} \\ \text{sample} \\ \text{selections} \end{array} = \dfrac{\text{Required number of completed interviews}}{\begin{pmatrix} \text{\% of residential} \\ \text{telephone \#s in} \\ \text{the phone book} \end{pmatrix} * \begin{pmatrix} \text{\% of RDD} \\ \text{telephone \#s} \\ \text{that are} \\ \text{households} \end{pmatrix} * \begin{pmatrix} \text{\% of residential} \\ \text{telephone \# s that} \\ \text{become completed} \\ \text{interviews} \end{pmatrix}} \qquad [8.1]$$

The three components in the denominator correspond to points in the sample selection and data collection processes where ineligibles or noninterviews occur. The sampling rate must compensate for ineligibles and noninterviews.

Solving for the Number of Sample Selections

To determine the requisite number of sample selections, we need to think through the entire sample selection process and estimate how well the interviewers will do. First, we need to decide on the desired number of completed interviews. Assume we want 500. Second, we need to think through the sample selection process. We are going to select residential phone numbers from a hypothetical telephone directory. We will drop the last two digits and replace them with two random digits. One question we must ask is how good our sampling frame is. Is every listing a residence? Does every listing have the same chance of selection? To answer these questions we need to check the frame.

Exhibit 8.2 is a facsimile of part of a telephone directory. Look at column 2—not every line of type ends in a telephone number. Note, for example, that B. Edward Smith's listing takes up three lines: One line lists the name, the second lists a business address and telephone number, and the third lists the residence address and telephone number. We can see that our frame is not "pure"—there are some businesses and, while most people are listed on one line, some people's listings are longer. The more lines a person has, the higher the probability of selection or the larger the chance of being in the sample. To equalize the probabilities of selection and to estimate the number of ineligible lines, we need a decision rule. Our decision rule will be to select the phone number only if the sampled line contains a residential telephone number. For example, if the line in the third column that lists the names of C. George and Margaret Ann Smith fell into our sample, we would consider that line blank and treat it as ineligible. However, two lines above, which gives the residence of C. Dallas Smith, would be eligible if it fell into the sample because it gives the residential telephone number.

Exhibit 8.2
A Facsimile of Part of a Telephone Directory Page

SMIT–SMITH	AREA CODE 101	RESIDENTIAL SECTION	378
SMIT Robert 231-0401	SMITH Brock 1775 Charles St 271-1661	SMITH C Allen 272 Lane St 271-0408	SMITH D A 452 W Lane St 463-3629
SMITE A J 276-1112	B Charles 784 Falls Rd 221-7743	C Bruce 248 Brooks Ave........... 271-7003	D Billy & Sally 172 Lane St 271-9103
	B Douglas High St Ashe 221-0909	C Dallas CPA 10 Main St 785-2838	D Carl 3334 Vernon 421-4746
SMITH—See Also Smythe	B Edward	Res RR 1 253-1180	Daryl D 4127 Shela Ln 483-1988
	Ofc 154 Flint St 826-1122	C F 7812-E Apple Blossom Ct. 482-6001	D Elvis 333 Drexel Ave 271-0369
A B 8403 Lawrence Rd 482-1364	Res 1225 Charles St 271-6665	C George & Margaret Ann	D Francis 6235 N Green St 785-1111
A Curt 113 Adam Ln Ashe ... 221-0123	B Frank 621 Beaver Ln 463-7723	5720 Benton Rd. 785-9902	D Glen 1534 Lakes Rd 482-4371
A Don 804 Monk Cir Mdvl ... 253-4444	B Greg & Michelle P	C Hal 421 Davis Rd 271-7801	D Hank 638 Lewis St 482-5300
A Ed 7821 Adam Ln Ashe 451-2233	6698 Prince Charles Rd ... 271-3434	C Ike 1013 Falls Lake Ashe 221-2311	D Islam 3947C Pepper St 281-4400
A Floyd 831 Woodley Rd 785-4131	B Harry 686 Round St Mdvl... 253-7246	C John 23 Wilber Hall 281-0028	D Justin 1221 Shellie Rd 482-2200
A Gilbert 7740 Lawrence Rd .. 482-9264	B Irv 9465-C Clarke Ln 785-5232	C Kurt Ofc 10 W Main St......... 271-6050	D Kirk 2604 W Green St 276-1662
A Helen 144 Wolfline Ashe 451-7203	B John 81 Mullen St 281-8552	486 Brentwood Mdvl 253-6112	D Linda 767 Sherron St 483-1933
A Irene 1113 Winslow Ln 281-4455	B Kelly 4653 Bryant Cir 482-0013	C Luke 333 Weaver Ln 785-2331	D Mark 1517 Burn St 271-0839
A Jess 4455 Hillcrest Rd 785-9999	B Lawrence	C Molly 2517 Country Club ... 463-4545	D Neil 516 Sanders Ct 271-5915
Anthony K 123 Lyons Rd 223-7845	243-B6 Apple Blossom Ct 482-0065	C Nick 6442 Clarke Ln 785-6668	D Opra 946 Harvey St. Ashe ... 221-0009
A Paul & Wanda	B Ryan 781 Main St Ashe 221-6251	C Quinton 510 Adam Ln Ashe 221-9155	D Phillip 2854 N Clark 783-5815
322 Adam Ln Ashe 451-6547	B Steve 200 Newport Ct........... 787-7831	C Rick 954 Bryant Cir 482-6835	D Raymond 1735 Harris St 751-0435
A Robert 742 Smallwood Ln .. 271-2801	B Thomas 154 Styles Rd 223-4654	C Scot 84 Prince Charles Rd 271-0003	D Yates 12 E Lane St 251-6666
. . .	. . .	. . .	. . .

Note: Names, addresses, and phone numbers are fictional.

We also need to estimate the proportion of business listings and blank lines. We do this by taking a sample from the directory. For this study twenty-five columns were randomly selected from the 440 pages and, in each column, the blank lines and businesses counted. The total was 231, or an estimate of 8.9% of the lines.[2] We will use this information shortly.

Once we create a new telephone number by substituting digits, we must think through what can happen to this number. There are three basic possibilities: the number can be an eligible household, it can be ineligible (e.g., a business), or its status can be unknown. Let's talk about the last two possibilities first.

When we create a new telephone number, it may be a business telephone number, a disconnected number, or a nonworking number, all of which would be classified as ineligible. It is necessary to estimate the proportion of selections that will be ineligible when calculating the number of sample selections. The best way to do this is to consult the results of previous surveys. However, if this is the first time this procedure is being used in the area, the pretest results can be used as a guide.

Also affecting the number of sample selections is the estimated frequency of unknown status numbers, which ring when called but which no one ever answers. Many researchers have interviewers ring a number at least seven times before hanging up. However, after repeated calls at different times of the day and on different days of the week, some numbers may still result in a "ring-no-answer." Groves and Kahn (1979) report making twelve contact attempts at this type of number, and they conclude that very few of these telephone numbers were eligible households.

In addition, not all eligible households can be interviewed. A number of things, such as refusals, or language problems, may preclude an interview. Or, the selected respondent may be ill or out of town or unavailable for other reasons. Nevertheless, the response rate, or the number of completed interviews from the total number of eligible households, must be estimated. Again, this is best done from previous surveys or from pretest results.

We now return to Expression 8.1 to determine the number of sample selections required to yield 500 completed interviews. We

---

[2]In chapter 7 we learned that the larger the sample size, the more confidence we can have in the sample estimate, all other things being equal. A sample of twenty-five is very small and has a large sampling error. The reader must keep in mind that when using small samples for planning purposes, the final results may differ significantly from the planning sample.

use the results of the sample of columns as the estimate of the first term in the denominator (1.00 − .089 = .91). In addition, let's assume we found that 28% of the RDD numbers in our pretest were ineligible and that our response rate was 70%. Putting these numbers in the expression gives the following result:

$$\text{Number of sample selections} = \frac{500}{.91 * .72 * .70} = \frac{500}{.45864} = 1{,}090$$

This means that we must select 1,090 lines from our hypothetical telephone directory to end up with enough telephone numbers to achieve 500 completed interviews. If our assumptions are correct, the results will be as follows:

Of the 1,090   telephone directory line selections,
          98   (9%) will be ineligible (i.e., blank lines or busi-
                nesses), giving us
_____
         992   (91%) residential telephone numbers.

We convert these 992 numbers into new telephone numbers by dropping the last two digits and replacing them with two random digits.

Of the   992   telephone numbers, we estimate that
         278   (28%) will be ineligible (i.e., businesses, discon-
                nected and nonworking numbers), and that
_____
         714   (72%) will be eligible households.

Of the   714   eligible households, we further assume that
         214   (30%) will result in noninterviews (i.e., refusals,
                unknown status, noncontacts, etc.) and that
_____
         500   (70%) will be interviews.

Selecting the Sample

Now let's focus on making the telephone directory selections. The hypothetical directory has 440 pages with four columns per page and 104 lines per column. We want to select a systematic random sample. The first thing to notice is that we need to make more selections than there are pages. In fact, we need to make more than two but less than three selections per page. How do we do this? Note that there are four columns per page or a total of 1,760 columns. Let's see how the total number of selections compares to the total number of columns:

1,090/1,760 = .619. According to this calculation, we should take one selection from 62% of the columns or one selection from every six out of ten columns. These are not easy intervals to work with. We want to make the selection process easier but still random. Notice that 62% is close to 66.7% or 2/3. One possibility is to take more selections than we need and then to randomly delete some of the selections. The remaining sample is still a random sample because a random sample of a random sample is a random sample.

The easiest way to select two of every three columns is probably to delete one of every three columns. We do this by selecting a random number between one and three. Then, we add three to this number until we exceed the number 1,760. Each of the columns selected in this manner is excluded from sample selection. Depending on the random number selected, this process would delete approximately 587 columns, leaving us a total of 1,173 columns from which to make a selection. To select from each of the 1,173 columns, we select a random number between one and 104 (number of lines in each column). Using a table of random numbers, we select the number 017. In each selected column, then, we examine the seventeenth line, using a template that measures the distance from the solid line at the top of the column to the seventeenth line. If it is a residential household, it falls into our sample; if it is a business or a blank line, we consider it ineligible and go on to the next selected column.

Refer to Exhibit 8.2 again. Assume that column 3 is deleted from the sample. Thus, we examine the seventeenth line in columns 1, 2, and 4. The seventeenth line in column 1 lists the residential telephone number of A. Paul and Wanda Smith, who live in Ashe. We select their telephone number, B. Steve Smith's telephone number from the second column, and D. Raymond Smith's phone number from column 4. For all the phone numbers selected, we drop the last two digits and substitute two random digits. From a table of random numbers we have selected the digits 07, 79, and 91. Replacing the last two digits of our selected phone numbers with these random digits yields the following new telephone numbers: 451-6507, 787-7879, and 751-0491. This is the procedure that we follow to select all the remaining numbers.

If our sample estimates are correct, we expect to encounter about 106 blank lines and businesses and 1,067 residential telephone numbers. If our other assumptions are correct, we can expect 28% of the new telephone numbers to be ineligible ($n = 299$) and we would end up with approximately 768 eligible households. If our survey **cooperation rate** is 70%, we would complete 538 interviews. If a completed interview costs about $30, these 38 additional interviews would add $1,140 to our survey costs. Not a trivial amount. Thus, our goal is to manage the sample so that the number of final interviews is close to 500. How to achieve this goal is illustrated later in the chapter.

It is extremely important to realize that the proportions we inserted in the denominator of Expression 8.1 are only *estimates* of what we expect will happen. As we go through the process of selecting numbers and attempting interviews, the outcome at any stage can be better or worse than we estimated. We could end up with fewer ineligible numbers and a better response rate than we expected. This would give us more sample numbers than we need. We could also get more ineligibles than we counted on and a poorer response rate, which would give us too few sample cases to achieve 500 interviews. Any number of combinations are likely outcomes and, therefore, it is important for the researcher to keep close watch on the process as it unfolds and to take corrective actions when necessary.

The following example illustrates how we can best achieve the desired number of completed interviews through the process of subsampling and monitoring. This process is illustrated in Exhibit 8.3.

Assume that our estimates of the proportion of blank lines and businesses are correct and the sample selection yields 1,067 RDD

Exhibit 8.3

Management of RDD Sample Numbers

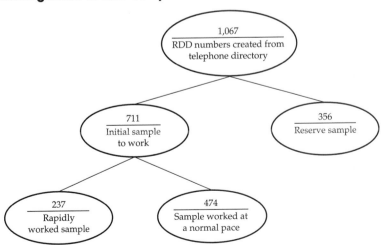

numbers. Each telephone number released to an interviewer must be thoroughly worked to maintain our random sample and minimize bias. Because our particular sample of numbers could yield fewer ineligibles and/or a higher response rate, we do not want to release all 1,067 numbers at once. We want to subsample the numbers, see what happens to those cases, and use that information to plan activities for the next week or few weeks. To do this, we try to anticipate the best possible outcome for our numbers. We can think of this as a sample distribution problem—that is, try to determine what outcomes might be three standard deviations on the positive side from our 72% estimate of eligible numbers and our 70% estimate of a response rate. Because we do not know this information, we need to make an educated guess. Let's use 85% for eligible numbers and 80% for a response rate. We can again use Expression 8.1, without the proportion for blank lines and businesses, because that phase has been completed. The result is:

$$\text{Number of sample selections} = \frac{500}{.85 * .80} = 735$$

We want to select a systematic random sample of 735 numbers from our sample of 1,067 numbers. To do this, we go through the same mechanics as we did earlier in the selection of columns from the telephone directory. We find that $735/1,067 = .689$, which is very close to .667 or 2/3. Even though $.667 \times 1,067 = 711$, or 24 fewer numbers, this is a reasonable number of cases to begin with. After selecting the 711 numbers, it would be a good strategy to split them into two samples. One sample would be worked thoroughly at a rapid pace to monitor our assumptions and to determine if additional sample cases are needed. The other sample would be worked concurrently, but at a more normal pace. The rapid sample might be a one-third subsample of the 711 cases, or 237 telephone numbers. We would want to contact each case a minimum of seven times over a 5- to 7-day period. This random subsample should give us a good indication of the number of ineligibles and interviews we can expect from the initial release of 711 numbers. As the data collection period progresses, we continue to monitor the results against our assumptions. In reserve, we have a random subsample of 356 numbers $(1,067 - 711 = 356)$. Random subsamples can be taken from this pool and released as required, or, if necessary, all numbers can be released at once.

Example 2: Other RDD Telephone Samples

There are a number of other ways to select an RDD sample. One method is to determine the telephone prefixes that cover the area and add four random digits. This makes the sampling tasks easier but the interviewing is more difficult than in the first example, as we will see shortly.

The front section of a telephone directory typically lists the residential telephone prefixes in the local calling area. Exhibit 8.4 lists the prefixes for Raleigh and selected nearby cities that we defined as the area of earlier interest. It is worth noting that the number of prefixes correlates with the size of the city. Raleigh, the largest city, has the greatest number of prefixes, followed by Cary and then Garner. Also, many, but not all, cities have unique prefixes. Note that Apex has its own set of prefixes but Morrisville has a subset of Cary's prefixes; Knightdale, Wendell, and Zebulon have some overlap; and Garner has a subset of the Raleigh prefixes. Unique prefixes allow the researcher to focus on a specific area if she or he so desires. If the prefixes overlap and the researcher is interested in only one city, screening questions about geographic residence are required at the start of the interview to eliminate the ineligible respondents.

Exhibit 8.4

Prefix Codes for Raleigh and Selected Nearby Cities

Location	Prefix Codes
Apex	303, 362, 387
Cary	319, 380, 460, 467, 469, 481, 677
Garner	662, 772, 779
Knightdale	217, 266
Morrisville	467, 469, 481
Raleigh	212, 231, 233, 250, 301, 302, 420, 501, 505, 508, 512, 515, 516, 518, 546, 571, 662, 664, 676, 713, 715, 733, 737, 740, 755, 772, 779, 781, 782, 783, 787, 790, 801, 821, 828, 829, 831, 832, 833, 834, 836, 839, 840, 846, 847, 848, 850, 851, 856, 859, 860, 870, 872, 876, 878, 880, 881, 890, 899, 954, 971, 976, 981
Wendell	266, 365
Zebulon	269, 365

There are seventy-seven unique prefixes in the geographic area. To develop the RDD telephone numbers, we simply add four random digits to the prefixes. But how many numbers do we need? We can use some of the assumptions in Expression 8.1. If we want 500 interviews, the numerator is the same. Since we are not selecting numbers from a telephone directory, we don't need to deal with blank lines and businesses. We also omit the percentage of residential numbers in the telephone directory because that does not apply here.

We do need to estimate the number of ineligible numbers and the response rate. We can assume a response rate of 70%, as we did earlier, so that leaves one unknown. Can we use 72% again as the proportion of eligible numbers? No, because we are using a much different procedure to generate telephone numbers. The major difference is that we are adding four random digits to a prefix rather than dropping two digits from an existing telephone number. This may not seem, on the surface, like much of a difference, but we will show shortly that it can be.

The four digits after the prefix are called a suffix. Each prefix can have 10,000 potential suffixes attached to it—from 0000 to 9999. When we select a phone number from the telephone directory and drop the last two digits, we know that the telephone company has assigned numbers using the first two digits of that suffix. Earlier, we selected the telephone number 787-7831. We know that for prefix 787 the telephone company is using the suffix 7_ _ _ and 78_ _. When we add four digits to a prefix, we don't usually know the suffixes that the telephone company is using until we call the numbers. Thus, using four-digit random suffixes leads to more nonworking telephone numbers.

We can estimate the proportion of ineligible telephone numbers when we add four random digits to a prefix by using census data and knowing the number of unique prefixes. In 1990, the Raleigh geographic area of interest had 144,621 occupied households (U.S. Census Bureau, 1992). Approximately 96.5%, or 139,559, of these households had telephones. In the 10-year period from 1980 to 1990, the urban population of Wake County increased by 49% and the rural component by 19%. Using this past decade as a guide, we assume there has been about a 14% growth since 1990, which translates to 159,098 households with telephones. Exhibit 8.4 shows seventy-seven unique prefixes in the area. Since each prefix can have 10,000 unique suffixes, there can be a total of 77 × 10,000 = 770,000 unique telephone numbers in our geographic area. The estimated number of eligible telephone numbers is 159,098 ÷ 770,000 = .2066. The number of four-digit random numbers we need to create is determined by using our new assumptions in Expression 8.1.[3]

$$\text{Number of sample selections} = \frac{500}{.2066 * .70} = \frac{500}{.1446} = 3{,}457$$

This result, much larger than the 992 numbers we needed from the directory-based method used in example 1, indicates that we need to call approximately seven numbers to get one completed interview. Many of the calls and much of the budget will be spent in eliminating nonworking numbers.

Continuing with our example, we have 77 prefixes and we estimate that we need 3,457 numbers to get 500 completed interviews. The number of four-digit random numbers we need to create for each prefix is 3,457/77 = 44.89 or 44.9. Rounding up to 45 changes the total by 8, an insignificant difference: 45 × 77 = 3,465. Thus, we select 45 unique four-digit random numbers for each prefix. We select the digits from a table of random numbers or generate four-digit random numbers by computer. Since our total of 3,465 is an estimate, we would create all the telephone numbers, take a systematic random subsample of the numbers, and call and monitor the subsample results as we did in example 1 and illustrated in Exhibit 8.3.

In this example, interviewers will spend a considerable amount of time eliminating nonworking numbers. However, there are aids to help cut down on the number of nonworking numbers. Haines & Co. of Middleburg Heights, Ohio, publishes criss-cross telephone directories for selected cities. Rather than listing patrons alphabetically, the directory lists them by street address and in ascending numerical order by prefix and suffix. This latter listing is helpful in finding suffixes that are not being used and can be eliminated in the selection process. For example, assume the two smallest prefix numbers are 212 and 217. Since the suffixes are listed in ascending order, we may note that the last listed telephone number in prefix 212 is 212-4356 and that the next listed telephone number is 217-0018. We might, then, conclude that in prefix 212 suffixes 5 _ _ _ , 6 _ _ _ , 7 _ _ _ , 8 _ _ _ , and 9 _ _ _ are not being used. If this is correct, we can exclude 5,000 nonworking numbers from our potential list of

[3]The terms for the percentage of blank lines and businesses are omitted from the expression because they are not applicable to this method of creating RDD numbers.

telephone numbers. We would make similar checks through our entire list.

In areas where criss-cross directories are not available, sometimes it is possible to scan a large sample of the telephone directory pages to create a pseudolisting in ascending order. This should be done cautiously, however, because when a suffix is excluded, respondents with those telephone numbers have no chance of selection. Finally, large blocks of numbers can be eliminated by checking to see whether the large employers in the area have been assigned their own prefix. In Raleigh, for example, North Carolina State University uses prefix 515, and the State of North Carolina uses prefixes 715 and 733. We could safely eliminate these 30,000 potential telephone numbers.

National RDD Sample

Many of the procedures discussed in the previous sections are also used to select a national RDD telephone sample. The differences are the use of a national sample frame and the selection of numbers in a two-step process. It would be possible, but not very efficient, to select a national sample from telephone directories. There are about 5,100 telephone directories published annually in the United States. These books come in different sizes, they are published at different times of the year, and they are the products of the more than 4,700 telephone companies. Obtaining copies and selecting a sample from these directories would be a very expensive and time-consuming task. Fortunately, there is a better method.

The Traffic Routing Administration of Bell Communications Research (Bellcore) produces an updated listing every month of every telephone area code and working prefix in the United States. In mid-1994, there were 122 area codes and more than 44,000 area code and prefix combinations. The cost to obtain this information on magnetic tape or floppy disk is $650.00.[4]

We would use the Bellcore data tape as the sampling frame for a national RDD survey. Selecting a sample of area codes and prefix combinations and then adding a four-digit random suffix, however, suffers from the same problem encountered in example 2: many nonworking numbers. Using this approach, Groves and Kahn (1979)

[4]The *Local Exchange Guide* can be ordered from Traffic Routing Administration, 290 W. Mount Pleasant Avenue, Room 1E 235, Livingston, New Jersey 07039-2798, (201) 740-7500.

found that only 23% of the sampled numbers were working residential numbers. To overcome this problem, Mitofsky and Waksberg (Waksberg, 1978) have proposed a method that is widely used by academic and government survey organizations; it is somewhat complex, but it greatly increases calling efficiency. The sample selection and interviewing are done in two stages. Initially, the researcher must decide the total number of interviews required, how many of these will be done with first-stage sampling units, and how many will be done with second-stage sampling units. Let's work through an example.

Assume we want 1,600 completed interviews in 400 geographic areas. (We will define geographic area shortly.) We create telephone numbers for first-stage interviews, conducted in all 400 geographic areas, by taking a systematic random sample of area codes and prefix combinations from the Bellcore data tape. How many of these area code–prefix combinations do we select? To determine this, we divide 400 by the proportion of eligible numbers found by Groves and Kahn. The result is:

$$\text{Number of first-stage sample selections} = \frac{400}{.23} = 1,739$$

Thus, we need to select a systematic random sample of 1,739 area code–prefix combinations from the Bellcore total of 44,129.[5] To the six-digit area code–prefix combinations, we add four-digit random numbers to create the telephone numbers. The 1,739 numbers should yield about 400 residential telephone numbers. However, we know that not all of these will be completed interviews. Having estimated a 70% response rate, we can expect about 280 interviews.

The sample is split into two stages because we know from our previous examples that once we find a residential telephone number, there are likely to be more such numbers in that area code and prefix combination. The second stage of the Mitofsky-Waksberg design is to keep the first eight digits of the numbers that are determined to be residences in the first stage—that is, the area code, the prefix, and the first two digits of the four-digit suffix. To this eight-digit number, we add two-digit random numbers until we contact a fixed number of additional residential telephone numbers using the eight-digit number. For example, assume that the number 919-387-7892 yields a residential telephone number. To create the second-stage telephone numbers, we drop the last two digits and keep substituting two other

[5] This was the number of combinations in December, 1993.

random digits until we identify a fixed number of additional residential telephone numbers.

To complete our example, how many other numbers must we create? In the first stage, the 1,739 numbers yielded 400 households and resulted in 280 interviews. We need to complete 1,600 − 280 = 1,320 more interviews using the 400 first-stage telephone numbers. This means an average of (1320/400 =) 3.3 interviews for each residential number identified in the first stage.[6] How many second-stage numbers do we select? Groves and Kahn (1979) found that 66% of the numbers at the second stage were households. If we use a 70% response rate, Expression 8.1 can be solved as follows:

$$\begin{array}{l}\text{Average number} \\ \text{of second-stage} \\ \text{sample selections} \end{array} = \frac{3.3}{.66 * .70} = 7.14$$

Creating an average of 7.14 telephone numbers per first-stage household number would result in calling approximately 2,856 (7.14 × 400) more numbers to obtain 1,320 interviews. The second-stage numbers are created by dropping the last two digits of the residential numbers identified in stage 1 and substituting groups of unique two-digit numbers until the fixed number of residences is identified.

The Mitofsky-Waksberg design is a two-stage cluster sample with the probabilities of selection being equal after the second stage. The probability of selection for a group of 100 numbers at the first stage of selection is proportional to the number of residential numbers in the group. Thus, the more residential numbers in the group, the higher the probability of selection. For this reason, a fixed number of residential units must be selected in the second stage to equalize the overall probabilities of selection.

We can illustrate this as follows. Assume telephone number A is in a group of 100 numbers that has 80 residential telephone numbers and telephone number B is in a group of 20 residential numbers. If one telephone number is selected from each group of 100 numbers, the probability of Group A being in the sample is 80/100 = .80 and for Group B it is 20/100 = .20. At this first stage of selection, the likelihood of Group A being in the sample is four times greater than that for Group B. At the second stage of selection, we want to identify four more residential numbers so that we call a total of five residen-

---

[6]We use 400 because it is the number of households identified in stage 1. This is the important number, not the number of completed interviews.

tial numbers in each group. The overall probability of selection of a number in each group is the product of these two probabilities. As we illustrate below, the probabilities are equal after stage 2.[7]

$$\text{Group A} = \frac{80}{100} \ * \ \frac{5}{80} = .8 \ * \ .0625 = .05$$

$$\text{Group B} = \frac{20}{100} \ * \ \frac{5}{20} = .2 \ * \ .2500 = .05$$

This type of design introduces a number of complexities that are not part of simple random samples. First, the formula used to compute the sample variances must take the two-stage design into consideration (Kalton, 1983). Second, because people who live in the same area tend to be more similar in attitudes and behaviors than the population as a whole, this type of sample tends to be more homogeneous than a random sample of the population, and it will underestimate the population variance. This results in a **design effect**—the ratio of the variance of a cluster sample to the variance of a simple random sample of the same size. A third complexity is that the sample must be worked sequentially and a great deal of monitoring is required to ensure that the fixed number of residential households is not exceeded within the clusters. Why then is this procedure used? Multistage cluster samples are the preferred choice when the design effects are small for the key variables and when sampling and data collection costs are significantly lower for a cluster sample than for a simple random sample.

Selecting Respondents within Households

A sample of telephone numbers is a sample of households. It is possible to collect fairly accurate information at the household level on activities such as the number of doctor visits by all household members in the past 2 weeks, the number of overnight hospital stays in the past 12 months, the number and types of durable goods purchased in the past 6 months, the number of automobiles owned and

---

[7] This example has been simplified and these are not, technically, the overall probabilities of selection. The sampling fraction at the first stage of selection must be multiplied by the probability .05. The final overall probability of selection, however, will be the same.

total miles driven in the past 12 months. In conducting such a survey, we call the telephone number and we tell the person who answers what the survey is about. We ask to speak to the person in the household who is most knowledgeable about these activities. This type of study seeks to interview the adult who can provide accurate information.

Many times, however, we want to generalize our results to, or estimate characteristics for, a population of individuals. If we were to interview the person who answers the telephone, we would end up with a disproportionate number of teenagers, women, people who are active in community affairs, and people who run a business from their home. To satisfy the ability to generalize to or estimate characteristics of individuals, we usually select randomly one individual per household and weight the interview data by the number of eligible respondents in the household. The weighting is required because households are clusters of eligible individuals. When we select one individual per household, people in households with two or more eligible respondents don't have the same probability of selection as do people in one-person households. The person in a one-person household has a 1.0 or 100% chance of selection because that individual is the only eligible respondent. People in a two-person household each have a .5 chance of selection; people in a three-person household each have a .33 chance of selection, and so on.

The classic within-household selection procedure was designed by Kish (1965) for face-to-face surveys and has been adapted for telephone surveys. In telephone surveys, after a brief introduction, the interviewer asks the respondent to list all the eligible household members by gender and age. The interviewer must then number each eligible household member starting with the males in descending order by age and then the females in the same manner. Using a table of preselected random numbers—in a two-person household the number is a 1 or 2—the interviewer selects the individual whose number corresponds to the preselected random number. While the Kish method is unbiased, it requires a significant amount of time at the beginning of the interview. Many respondents are suspicious of detailed household enumeration questions before survey legitimacy or rapport has been established. For that reason, many investigators believe this selection procedure leads to higher refusal rates.

Other procedures have been proposed by Troldahl and Carter (1964) and Bryant (1975) in an attempt to make household enumeration less invasive. In these procedures, the adult who answers the telephone is asked two questions:

1. How many persons 18 years or older live in your
   household, counting yourself?
2. How many of them are men (women)?

One of four or seven selection matrices is randomly assigned to each
sampled telephone number.[8] The selection matrices do not require a
listing of adults. Instead, the interviewer asks to speak with the "old-
est" or "youngest" man or woman, or simply a man or woman, depending on the household composition. In an experimental comparison of these methods, we did not find the Troldahl-Carter-Bryant
methods to be better than the Kish method (Czaja, Blair, and Sebestik,
1982). Our preference was the Kish procedure.

A more recent technique has been proposed by O'Rourke and
Blair (1983) and Salmon and Nichols (1983). These procedures do not
require household enumeration. Interviewers simply ask to speak to
the eligible member of the household who had the "last" or will have
"the next" birthday. The last-birthday methods works as follows:

Hello, I'm _____ calling from the University
of Maryland. We are doing a study to find out how
people in the Washington Metropolitan Area feel
about things that may concern them. Your household
was chosen at random to participate. For this
study, I need to speak with the adult living in
your household, who is 18 or older, and had the
most recent birthday. Who would that be?

   IF THE PERSON DOES NOT KNOW ALL THE BIRTHDAYS,
   ASK:

Of the ones you do know, who had the most recent
birthday? I need to speak with that person,
please.

Both methods seem to give each eligible member an equal chance of
selection. The last birthday method probably has less selection error
than the next birthday method because it may be easier to recall
a past event than to know an upcoming event, unless the future
event is much closer in time. Methodological studies are required to

[8]Selection matrices 5, 6, and 7 give higher probabilities of selection to males because
males have lower cooperation rates than females.

determine if this hypothesis is true and to better evaluate the reliability and validity of these selection procedures. Oldendick, Bishop, Sorenson, and Tuchfarber (1988) did a methodological study comparing the Kish and the last-birthday method. The authors compared refusal rates, demographic characteristics of the samples, and substantive responses to questions. They found very few statistically significant differences, and they concluded that the results did not differ by method. More such studies need to be conducted.

Example 3: A List Sample of Students

Studies of university students are frequently conducted by professors or by other students. We have already discussed one method for conducting such studies, a telephone survey.[9] For this example, however, let's assume that we have very little funding and time is not a major factor. Therefore, we have decided to do a mail survey using campus mail as much as possible. (In Example 4, we will discuss another possibility—selecting a sample of classes for a group-proctored survey.)

Selecting a Frame

The registrar's office has the most current information on enrolled students. We have found these offices to be cooperative when the survey has a serious academic focus and the collection of information can be useful to other campus groups. Almost all universities and colleges keep student information in computer files; these files are usually in alphabetical order. Let's assume we want to study undergraduates only and that our university has 20,000 undergraduate students: 8,000 freshmen, 6,000 sophomores, 3,000 juniors, and 3,000 seniors. We want to select a sample of 1,000. One method would be to ask the registrar's office to select a simple random sample of 1,000 undergraduate students from its computer file. With a sample of this size, we should get approximately 400 freshmen, 300 sophomores, 150 juniors, and 150 seniors, although there is no guarantee that the sample will be proportionate to the population by class year.

---

[9]A possible sampling frame would be the published university directory of students. A sample of names could be selected in the same manner in which we selected our directory-based RDD sample. In this example, however, we would not want to create random-digit telephone numbers.

Deciding on a Sampling Method

There is a better way to select the sample if key characteristics of sample members (e.g., year in school, gender) are likely to be related to important dependent variables. It is called **stratified sampling**. Sudman (1976) presents four reasons for stratifying a sample:

1. Groups are of interest for purposes of analysis
2. Variances differ by group
3. Costs to conduct interviews vary by group, and
4. Amount of prior information differs by group

In stratified sampling, we want to arrange the population into groups of similar individuals. We want the elements within groups to be homogeneous and the groups to be different from other groups, or heterogeneous. The grouping variable or variables must be related to the dependent variable, otherwise the effort involved in stratifying the list will be a waste of time.[10]

Implied stratification is one method of improving sampling efficiency by ensuring proportional distribution of the sample on specified variables. Returning to our example, let's assume that we believe the results for our key dependent variables will differ by year in school. Therefore, instead of selecting a simple random sample from a list arranged alphabetically, we would ask the registrar's office to rearrange the list by year in school. The first 8,000 students would be the freshmen, followed by the 6,000 sophomores, who would be followed by the juniors and then the seniors. We then select a systematic random sample from the list. Since the population size is 20,000 and the sample size is 1,000, our sampling interval will be 20. We select a random start between 1 and 20, begin with that number, and keep adding 20 to each selected number until we exhaust the list. This gives us a sample that is proportional to the population size. Using implied stratification in this way, we are assured that the sample will include about 400 freshmen, 300 sophomores, 150 juniors, and 150 seniors.

We could have the list sorted on multiple variables. For example, if we believe gender is also an important variable, we could arrange the list by year in school and by gender: the male freshmen might come first, then the female freshmen, followed by the male sophomores, then the female sophomores, and so on. Selecting a systematic

---

[10]In some situations, stratifying is counterproductive, but those situations are beyond the scope of this discussion.

random sample would assure proportional representation by gender and year in school.

We learned in chapter 7 that the optimum design for comparing groups is equal sample sizes in each group. In this example, the sample sizes by year are unequal. To select equal numbers of students within each year in school, we would divide the students into four groups representing the four school years. Within each group, we would select a systematic random sample of 250 based on a sampling interval of 1:32 for freshmen, 1:24 for sophomores, and 1:12 for juniors and seniors. This is a disproportionate stratified sample. While the sample sizes and the number of completed interviews may be equal for each group, the sampling ratios and probabilities of selection for students by year in school are different. When we analyze our data, we can report the results by year in school, for example the proportion of freshmen, sophomores, and so forth, that had more than three alcoholic drinks last week, but we cannot simply combine data from the four groups because the probabilities of selection are different. To do that, we must weight the data. The equal probability of selection sampling ratio for all students is 1:20. Because freshmen and sophomores are undersampled, they must be given a weight greater than one, and because juniors and seniors are oversampled, they must be given a weight less than one. Weighting the data in this manner would allow us to combine the information from all groups to report an estimate of the proportion of all undergraduates who had more than three alcoholic drinks last week.

Example 4: A Sample of University Classes

One very efficient method of sampling students is to select a sample of classes. This method takes advantage of natural clusters and captive audiences. If the average class size is twenty-four, then in the span of time that it takes to complete one questionnaire, we can obtain twenty-three more. The major obstacle to this method is obtaining the cooperation of the professors for the selected classes.

Defining the Population and Preparing the Frame

The process begins, as usual, by defining the population—for example, undergraduates—and then obtaining a suitable frame, such as a list of current classes. We need to ensure that classes that may be excluded from the list are included in the frame and that classes which have been canceled are excluded. Also, we need to eliminate duplication. Classes that have both a general lecture and affiliated labs or discussion sections need to be identified. If the lecture contains many students, say more than 100, and the labs are closer to the average class size, we want to keep the lab sections in the frame and exclude the large general lectures. The reason is that the large lectures will have large intraclass correlations that will increase the estimates of variance.

The schedule of courses at North Carolina State University lists classes alphabetically by department and, within departments, lists courses in ascending order from introductory courses to the most advanced. We will select classes with equal probabilities using a systematic random sample. An alphabetic listing provides no benefits for stratification. If we believe that attitudes or behaviors may differ by college, we would ask the registrar's office to run a new frame that lists the classes by college and, within each college, in ascending order from lower- to upper-level courses.

Solving for the Number of Sample Selections

Before selecting the classes, we need to determine the average number of students in the classes on the frame, the average number of classes taken by undergraduates, the anticipated cooperation rate of professors and students, and, finally, the required number of completed interviews. The average class size and the average number of classes taken can probably be obtained from the registrar's office. Only rough estimates are required. The most important piece of information is the average number of students per class, which, if unknown, can be estimated by multiplying the number of enrolled students by the average number of classes taken and dividing by the number of classes offered. This yields:

$$\text{Average class size} = \frac{20{,}000 * 4}{3{,}320} = 24.1$$

Assume we want 1,200 completed interviews. If the average class size is about twenty-four, we need to obtain interviews in fifty classes. We know by now, that not every professor approached will agree to let us administer the questionnaire in his or her class. Thus, we need to estimate a cooperation rate. Once again we look to similar past surveys or to the pretest. In a similar survey conducted at the University of Maryland, College Park Campus, 65% of the professors cooperated, as did 99% of the students in their selected classes. If we use a 65% cooperation rate, we would need to select 77 classes using systematic random sampling.

Maintaining the Design Integrity

While this design is very efficient and economical, the researcher must be aware of three additional considerations to maintain the integrity of the design. One, this procedure results in a probability sample of all enrolled students. However, the student probabilities of selection are not equal since students enrolled in more classes have a higher chance of selection than those enrolled in fewer. For this reason, proper analysis of the data requires that each student receive a weight. The weights can be adjusted relative to each other so that the total weighted sample size equals the total unweighted sample size. Since the average number of classes taken is four, we give those students who are enrolled in four classes a weight of one. Those enrolled in more than four classes would be given a weight of less than one, and those who are enrolled in fewer than four classes would be given a weight of greater than one.

Two, as we all know, all students do not attend every class, for a multitude of reasons. If there are differences between those present and those who are absent on the dependent variables, it will be important to include the nonattenders in the survey estimates or else the final results may be biased. Following up to obtain interviews from nonattenders is much more expensive than administering and collecting questionnaires in a classroom. The researcher will want to follow up a sample of nonattenders by mail or telephone depending on the time schedule or budget. Neyman (1934) has devised a method in which the researcher calculates the cost of a follow-up interview and the cost of a classroom interview, and the square root of the ratio of these costs determines the percentage of nonattenders who need to be followed up. In the analysis of the data, the subsample of nonattenders are weighted to reflect all nonattenders and, thus, the final sample estimates are unbiased.

Three, a random sample of clusters is not a random sample of elements. In a cluster sample, we would like the clusters to be made up of heterogeneous elements so that a sample of clusters would reflect a sample of the population. However, natural clusters typically reflect similarities in the population rather than diversity. In effect, students enrolled in introductory sociology are more likely to be freshmen and sophomores than to reflect a random sample of all enrolled students. The extent to which clusters are more similar in composition than a random sample of the population is what is referred to as the design effect of a cluster sample. This design effect causes a cluster sample to be less precise than a simple random sample (srs) of the same size.[11] The extent to which it is less efficient is determined by the ratio of the variance of the cluster sample divided by the variance of an srs of the same size. This calculation is beyond the scope of our discussion and interested students should consult Kalton (1983).

---

[11]The confidence intervals or sample standard errors are larger for cluster samples than for srs samples of the same size. Thus, the estimate of the population value for a variable is less precise.

9 Reducing Sources of Error in Sampling and Data Collection

In this chapter, we turn from the rather broad perspective of major design issues to a closer look at how particular aspects of the implementation of the survey design can affect the accuracy of our results. We begin with the general topic of survey error and introduce the concepts of bias and variance. This is followed by a detailed discussion of steps we can take to reduce the main sources of error in the sampling and data collection phases of the survey. In the discussion of sampling, we focus primarily on frame errors. Errors from the data collection process are potentially more numerous and are examined in detail. The chapter continues with a discussion of cost allocation to minimize sources of error.[1] Finally, we look briefly at the ethics of survey research

The Origins of Error

Imagine the perfect sample survey. The survey design and questionnaire satisfy all the research goals. A sampling frame is available that includes accurate information about every population member. The selected sample precisely mirrors all facets of the population and its myriad subgroups. Each question in the instrument is absolutely clear and captures the dimension of interest exactly. Every person selected into the sample is contacted and immediately agrees to participate in the study. The interviewers conduct the interview flawlessly, and never—by their behavior or even their mere presence—affect respondents' answers. The respondents understand every question exactly as the researcher intended, know all the requested information,

---

[1]The most comprehensive treatment of survey errors is R. Groves's *Survey Errors and Survey Costs*, 1989, John Wiley.

and always answer truthfully and completely. Their responses are faithfully recorded and entered, without error, into a computer file. The resulting data set is a model of validity and reliability.

Except for trivial examples, we cannot find such a paragon. Each step in conducting a survey has the potential to move us away from this ideal, sometimes a little, sometimes a great deal. Just as all the processes and players in our survey can contribute to obtaining accurate information about the target population, so can each reduce that accuracy. We speak of these potential reductions in accuracy as sources of **survey error**.[2] Every survey contains survey errors, most of which cannot be totally eliminated within the limits of our resources, and some cannot be eliminated even in principle in a *sample* survey.

The recognition that perfection is unrealistic brings us quickly to some practical questions:

- What are the potential sources of error in the survey we are planning?
- Which of these sources should most concern us?
- What reasonable steps can we take to reduce these main sources of error?

As in all other aspects of the design and conduct of the survey, decisions about how to handle sources of error must balance costs and other resources against the potential harm of not addressing an error source.

Some sources of error are more damaging than others. Before we can assess these sources competently for our particular study, we need to understand sources of survey errors in general. This understanding rests on two concepts: variance and bias. These two error sources, taken together, are used to assess total survey error. For our purposes, only a general understanding of these concepts is necessary, so we will approach them mainly by example.

Variance refers to the differences measured in repeated trials of a procedure. This is a useful concept, even though, in most surveys, we do not actually perform repeated trials. The most common example of variance, already introduced, is that of sampling variance. Recall that if we select a sample of size n and take a measurement on it (i.e., ask each respondent a question such as How old were you on

[2]Note that the term *survey error* is not particularly directed at mistakes per se, such as incorrectly keying in data from a questionnaire, but is broad enough to include these as well.

your last birthday?), we produce one sample estimate of a population parameter, in this case, average age[3]. Then, if with all other aspects of the survey unchanged, we select a second sample of size n and take the same measurement, we produce a second estimate of average age. If this process is continued, we would expect to see variation in our estimate of average age from one sample to another. In other replications of a survey, again holding all procedures constant, we might expect to see random variations in such things as the percentage of respondents who can be contacted for an interview or in the number of refusals to answer a question about personal income. In any particular trial, the magnitude of the variation may be higher or lower than the average direction across trials.

By contrast, **bias** occurs when a measurement tends to be consistently higher or lower than the true population value. In the example just cited, there might be a tendency for some respondents to report that they are older than they actually are, a consequence, for example, of ambiguous wording of the question. Assume we ask simply, How old are you? Most respondents will give their current age—that is, their age on their last birthday. But some others may decide, if they are approaching a birthday, that they should report the age they are about to become. Virtually no respondents will report their previous age, even if they just had a birthday. So any misreporting is not random in both directions. In this case, we would say that this measurement is upwardly biased.[4] Note that this source of error exists in addition to the variance.

More often than not, especially in small-scale research, we do not (or cannot, within our resources) produce empirical measures of the various sources of error in our particular survey, with the major exception of sampling error. Our design decisions concerning the other error sources are driven by the findings of other surveys and experiments where such measurements have been made. We use the more general (and hopefully robust) findings from such prior methodological research to guide us in rooting out the *likely* sources of error in our study.

---

[3]In itself, the process of taking a measurement is also subject to error. Such measurement errors are, of course, not restricted to surveys but are found in every physical and social science.

[4]Note that this has nothing to do with intending to elicit a false report, i.e., to induce people to report their age as younger or to answer some other question in a certain way. As opposed to everyday usage, bias in survey research indicates effect, not intent.

In a discussion of the state of survey research as a science, Groves (1987) identified the two approaches to the issue of survey error as *measurement* and *reduction*. That is, there are those "who try to build empirical estimates of survey error and [those] who try to eliminate survey error." Logically, it would seem that the researcher should be equally concerned with both measurement and reduction and that his efforts would be directed, based on empirical estimates, to reducing the main sources of error. This is generally not the case (for reasons not discussed here). Nevertheless, the discussion to follow focuses mainly on the reduction of error, providing guidelines for identifying the main sources of error in a particular study and suggesting steps to reduce their effect on the study's results.

Our approach to survey error will focus on two types of decisions, those related to design and those related to procedures for implementing that design. By design, we mean the selection of a data collection method, a sampling plan (including the frame and estimation procedures), finalization of the questionnaire, and the data collection plan (including callback and refusal-conversion efforts). These design decisions, while not irreversible, are, once made, relatively set. In the course of the study, we cannot easily switch from mail to telephone, choose a different sampling frame, append questions we have neglected to include, or add a special round of refusal conversion. These decisions, made at the outset, define the main features of our study; changing them will usually have serious cost consequences.

We define *procedures* as components of the study's conduct in which we can make changes after the study is underway and which require ongoing monitoring and microdecisions in the course of the study. These include such things as setting rules for dealing with sampling frame problems, managing problematic interviewer or respondent behaviors, handling certain problems with respondent or sample cases, and handling missing data, among others.

To some extent, the distinction between design and procedures is artificial. For example, is analysis a component of the former or the latter? Still, we think this division will provide a useful framework for separating the main design decisions that must be fixed fairly early from the ongoing microdecisions that occupy most of our attention while conducting the survey.

Since the major design issues are discussed in other chapters, the focus here is on key components of procedures and the types and sources of errors associated with sampling and data collection in particular circumstances. Finally, guidelines suggest both ways to allocate resources and procedures for reducing the amount of error at each stage of the study.[5]

As is true of all our decisions about a study, these procedural choices are made within the constraint of our budget; each option has some effect on cost, which is interpreted here in a broad sense, encompassing both money and other resources, such as available time of the researcher or unpaid (volunteer) assistants or classmates, and, in some instances, even computer time. Even if we have available to us certain "free" materials and services, they are rarely unlimited. For example, while a university faculty member conducting a survey may not have to pay for a secretary to type the questionnaire, the secretary's time is not devoted solely to the project. So a choice may have to be made as to whether the available time is best used in typing the questionnaire, preparing tables for a final report, handling advance letter mailing, or performing other tasks. Finally, as will be discussed, sometimes it is necessary to reallocate resources during the survey to address particular problems.

Sampling

Sampling is, as we have seen, one source of variance. How the sampling plan is implemented can also be a source of bias. This is particularly a concern with the sampling frame. In addition to selection procedures, we must also have a set of procedures for dealing with potential frame bias. Recall that by sampling frame we mean the set, or collection, of sample elements available for selection. This collection is most often in the form of a list, such as a list or directory of students enrolled at a university or the telephone directory for a city or region. However, sets of sample elements can take other forms as well. Sampling frames can be things, such as products on a production line (sampled to measure quality levels), plots of farmland, or visitors passing through a turnstile into a museum. Sampling frames may be purchased (directories of businesses or a professional association's membership list), constructed by the researcher before data

[5]The most comprehensive treatment of this topic is Groves's *Survey Errors and Survey Costs* (1989).

collection (lists of households on a block), or generated during data collection (list of members in a household).[6]

Two points related to sampling frames will concern us. First, it is almost always more feasible to purchase a frame than to develop our own. Second, many of the frames we use were constructed for reasons that have nothing to do with survey sampling. As discussed in chapter 7, this latter fact often requires the use of modestly inventive methods to select true probability samples. Our focus in this chapter is not on selection but on the quality of frames and their contribution to bias.[7]

Exhibit 9.1 shows the typical amounts of error from each of five problems for several commonly used frames: RDD selection based on altering numbers in a telephone directory; samples based on the Bellcore list of all active area-code exchange combinations; telephone directory (non-RDD) samples; professional association membership lists; and published directories of university students.

We begin with the matter of frame coverage—that is, how much of the defined population the sampling frame contains. Ideally, we would like the frame to list all the members of the population we have defined—and no others. This is rarely the case. When members of the defined population are missing from the frame, we say that **undercoverage** exists.

Some undercoverage may be random, but when it is not, serious bias can be introduced. That is, people who tend to be missing from the list may differ in substantive ways from those included. The omission of some population members will simply be the result of clerical error. Another type of omission occurs if people choose either not to be on a list (such as a telephone directory) or to have certain information about themselves suppressed (such as home telephone numbers in a university faculty directory). Still others could have entered the population after the list was issued. For example, people who move into an area shortly after publication of the local telephone directory have no chance of inclusion. Similarly, people who have recently joined a professional organization may not be in

---

[6]The alert reader will have noticed from these examples that more than one frame might be used in a particular survey. We might, for example, use a census list to select counties in a state, use telephone directories to select households in each county, then, in each sampled household, construct a list of individuals from which the respondent is chosen.

[7]For a more comprehensive treatment of sampling frame issues, see Lessler and Kalsbeek, 1992; Kish, 1965, 1987; Groves, 1989.

Exhibit 9.1

Main Sources and Relative Occurrence of Frame Error

	Sampling Frame				
	RDD Directory-based	RDD Bellcore	Non-RDD Directory-based	Member List	Student Directory
Overcoverage	Medium	High	Low	Low	Low
Undercoverage	Low	None	Medium	Low–Medium	Low
Multiplicity	Medium	High	Low	Low*	Low
Clustering	Medium	Medium	Medium	N/A	N/A
Inaccuracy	Low	Low	Medium	N/A	Low

*Multiplicity is generally not a serious problem for single-organization lists. If several lists are combined to improve coverage, it can become a serious problem.

its published directory; they may, however, be on a computerized mailing list, raising the possibility of alternative lists for the same population. The key point is that these new population members may differ from the old ones, and we want to do what we can to see that the new ones are proportionally represented in our sample.

In general, these types of omissions will be a function of the age of the list and the rate of population change. For example, if we compare telephone directories from two similar urban areas, we would generally expect the more recent directory to be more accurate. However, if we compare a rural directory to one from an inner city, the rural directory is likely to have better coverage because the population is less mobile. This difference is likely to hold even if the urban directory is more recent. Because of the huge variety of types of directories one might use for sampling, it is not possible to provide general guidelines that cover all of them. But, for telephone directories, professional membership lists, and university directories, printed versions that are more than 6–12 months old are generally suspect. If an alternative computerized list is available, it may be worth the extra time and some extra cost to obtain it or have a sample selected from it.

We should also recognize the reverse problem, **overcoverage**; that is, the list may contain people who are not members of our defined population. This can be a problem if we cannot identify the nonmembers without contacting them. This problem occurs quite frequently when only people with particular demographic characteristics constitute the defined population. So, if the target population is people age 18 to 49, and we use either a telephone directory or an RDD frame, both frames are said to have overcoverage. That is, they include many people who are not part of our target group. Although this problem does not contribute to bias, we have to design the questionnaire to include an item to ensure that the ineligible members are correctly screened out during data collection.

It is, of course, important that the information in the frame be reasonably accurate. If, for a telephone survey, we sample students from a directory that has many incorrect or missing phone numbers, we will have to spend additional time and money to reach our sample.

Another frame problem is **multiplicity**, which means that some population members occur more than once on a list. This can occur in various instances for single lists but is most common when lists are combined. For example, in an effort to improve coverage of a population such as professional computer scientists, one might combine membership lists from several professional associations. People who belong to more than one organization have higher chances of inclusion in the selected sample. If the list can be purged of such duplicates, the problem is solved. Often, this cannot be easily done.

An alternative solution is to select the sample as usual, then check each sample member against the frame and subsample those who occur multiple times. That is, delete from the sample half the members who occurred twice on the list, two-thirds of those who occurred three times and so on.[8] The remaining sample will be an equal-probability sample of the list members. The key point is that the groups targeted for subsampling do not have to have been *selected* into the sample multiple times. As we saw in the chapters on sampling, it is the different probabilities of selection that we must allow for. This simple procedure will handle multiplicity. Ignoring the problem can, once again, introduce bias into the selection process.

A **cluster** occurs when several individual population elements have only one entry in the sampling frame, such as is the case when the frame is a list of households (as in a telephone directory), but the population is individuals. Clearly, each entry represents varying numbers of population members. One solution to the clustering problem is to take the entire cluster. In this example, that would mean taking all individuals (who meet the population definition) in the selected households. An alternative (and more common) solution is to randomly sample within each cluster. In this case, we would select one person per household and apply a weight in the analysis of the data to adjust for the different probabilities of inclusion. The weight equals, simply, the number of eligible individuals in the household.

We have raised many concerns and questions about sampling frames. But how do we determine the quality and accuracy of the sampling frame we plan to use? Like many things we do in survey research, such a determination is often an estimate. For example, by contacting a small sample of frame members (say fifty) we might get a rough assessment of both the accuracy of listings and the percentage of nonpopulation members.

Another way of gaining information about a frame is to talk to the person who is responsible for constructing or maintaining the

---

[8]Another way to look at this is that the *retained* sample is chosen with a sampling fraction equal to the inverse of the number of appearances on the list. Sample members that appear twice on the list are retained in the sample at the rate of 1/2, those that appear three times on the list are retained at the rate of 1/3, those that appear four times are retained at the rate of 1/4, and so on.

list. This method can be especially helpful when computerized membership mailing lists are being used. The person who maintains such a list usually has a good idea of the rates of entry and exit from the population and the rates of incorrect addresses. We should also note that all information on a list may not be equally reliable. For example, there is an incentive to keep addresses accurate if a list is used for frequent mailings, but there may be no such incentive to keep telephone numbers up to date.

Still a third way of judging a frame quality is to check with other researchers who have used it, especially if it is a commercial list available for purchase.

With so many tasks at the outset of the study, it may seem distracting to spend time assessing frame quality, yet such effort can be crucial. This is especially the case if we are using a frame that has not been previously used for survey sampling.

Data Collection Sources of Error

Whether interviews are obtained by mail, group administration, telephone, or other means, the data collection process has many potential sources of error. Much of data collection requires routine tasks, such as mailing, dialing sample phone numbers, and tracking the sample results. Fairly simple procedures can be set up to ensure that these clerical tasks are done carefully and do not introduce more than trivial error into the survey. This component of the survey is largely a record-keeping task. We will want to think through the steps that must be carried out and, for each, develop a record-keeping form. This mundane procedure will ensure that we do not find ourselves in such situations as omitting follow-up mailings to some nonrespondents (or wasting resources mailing to those from whom we have already received questionnaires), not giving each phone number equal call attempts, or neglecting to rework soft refusals,[9] all of which can contribute to error and wasted resources. However, with moderate attention to such details, these sources of error can be reduced to triviality. The main claim on our resources during data collection will be activities that have the potential to reduce more serious survey error. We now turn to those.

---

[9]Some respondents who refuse to be interviewed are more adamant than others. The less adamant refusals are termed *soft*.

Missing Data: Unit and Item Nonresponse

Ideally, of course, we want to obtain answers to every questionnaire item from all selected respondents. Deviations from this objective occur at two levels, the unit, by which we mean a person or household (though it can also be an institution such as a business or school); and the item, which is an individual question in our questionnaire. Data that are missing at either the unit or item level pose potential problems for the quality of our survey estimates. If we fail to obtain any information from some respondents, and for others fail to obtain complete information, our estimates and other analyses may be distorted, sometimes quite seriously.

Data may be missing randomly; that is, any unit or item is as likely to be missing as any other. Randomly missing data may be due, for example to interviewer mistakes, lost mail, or coding errors. If the amount of randomly missing data is not too large, our results should not be greatly affected. Certainly, if either at the unit or item level, randomly missing data do not exceed, say, 1% we are not too concerned about its effects. In such a case we should not expend many resources to reduce or eliminate the problem.

Unfortunately, when data are missing, frequently the omissions are not random. There are often patterns of missing information. For example, suppose that in the crime survey, at the unit level, respondents who are male, or have less education, or are elderly living in suburban areas tend to be less likely to cooperate. If such respondents, on average, have different attitudes or experiences than survey cooperators, then our results—which purport to represent the state's *entire* adult population—will be affected. For example, men may be less willing than women to consider sentencing alternatives; people with less education may rate the job police are doing lower than other respondents; or the elderly may be more likely to avoid going certain places because of concerns about crime. Each of these possibilities is speculation, but such patterns are often found in survey results.[10] To the extent that opinions and behaviors differ by subgroups, their overrepresentation or underrepresentation will affect results.[11]

[10]This is one reason we standardly collect demographic information as part of the survey. It allows us to compare our sample's demographic distribution to that of all people in the survey area meeting the target population definition.

[11]There are weighting adjustments that can be made after the data are collected to address this problem to some extent. However, as we will see in chapter 10, weights bring to the survey analysis their own complications and increases in other error sources.

Reducing Unit Nonresponse

The options available to *prevent* unit nonresponse include designing interesting and nonburdensome questionnaires; using effective data collection procedures, such as advance letters and well-crafted introductions or cover letters; and, of critical importance, carefully training the interviewers. All these tactics are discussed in detail elsewhere in this book. The question is, what do we do if, after all these efforts, we still find that nonresponse is high?

First, since our resources to address the problem are limited, our efforts need to be focused where they will be most effective. We will want to check the data for patterns of nonresponse. For example, are we having particular difficulties in certain geographic areas (such as central cities of metropolitan areas) or with particular subgroups (such as young males)? By comparing our data to census distributions (for telephone households), we can get a very good idea of such disproportionate response. If we find such patterns for missing units, we may want to shift our efforts to those underrepresented groups, by either allocating more of the total interviewer hours to these groups or assigning interviewers with particular skills to make the contacts. If, for example, it appears to be more difficult to complete interviews in certain locations, we might increase the proportion of those case assignments given to the more experienced interviewers. If there is a higher refusal percentage among men, we might assign those cases to interviewers that are our better refusal-conversion specialists. Another pattern that can emerge is that particular interviewers are contributing disproportionately to unit nonresponse. If that is the case, retraining or reassignment may be necessary.[12]

Reaching the Sampled Respondents

The effort and care we have taken to design and draw a probability sample means little if many of the selected respondents are not contacted and interviewed. We have noted the potential problems resulting from missing data and touched on the contributions of interviewer and respondent behaviors to this problem. Now we turn to the use of callback procedures. Numerous studies have shown that repeated callbacks have a major effect on increasing responses from the selected sample regardless of the data collection method.

---

[12]In a survey conducted as part of a research class, this would mean moving those individuals to coding, monitoring, or other noninterview work.

Mail

In mail surveys, callbacks are accomplished through multiple mailings, spaced optimally over the data collection period, often using different types or classes of mail. Dillman (1978) recommends an initial first-class mailing that includes a questionnaire and cover letter, followed by a postcard reminder, a second mailing with a different cover letter, and a final third mailing, which may use special class services, such as overnight or special delivery.

Each mailing should include a copy of the questionnaire; one of the main reasons for nonreturns is simple misplacement, loss, or (perhaps inadvertent) discarding of the questionnaire (Dillman, 1978). The spacing of the follow-up mailings depends on the flow of returns from the prior mailout. Until returns dwindle to a trickle, there is little advantage (or economic sense) in sending out additional mailings. We must, therefore, keep track not only of how many returns we receive but also of how many we receive on each day after the initial mailing and each follow-up mailing.

Typically, regardless of the survey population, a few people will respond right away; then there is a period of relatively high returns, with about the same number each day. The reminder postcard will help to maintain this flow for a while, but then it will decrease. At some point during this decline, we should send out the second mailing, including a questionnaire. To illustrate this typical pattern, Exhibit 9.2 shows the return rate for a national survey of county officials on the subject of how county priorities are determined.

During a mail survey, it is useful to track the number of returns per day (or the percentage of the target sample received) as a way to spot response-rate problems. In Exhibit 9.2, we see that, after the initial mailing there is, of course, a lag before returns begin to come in. During this waiting period, a postcard reminder is sent to all sample members. There is a large first-wave response, which trails off after a couple of weeks. At that point the second mailing, with a questionnaire, is sent out, with a similar result. Later phone follow-ups to nonrespondents bring in a few more cases, which finally dwindle to the point that we end data collection.

If, after tracking the initial mailing, we conclude that the rate of return is not what we anticipated, what should we do? First, we should determine whether there are any patterns to the nonresponse. If some sample subgroups are less willing to cooperate than others, we may want to shift some resources to them. This may be done by planning an extra mailing to them or allocating them a larger share of the nonrespondent sample to whom we send a special mailing. If

Exhibit 9.2

Return Rate in a Mail Survey

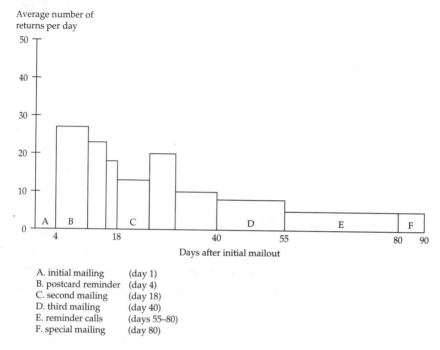

Average number of
returns per day

Days after initial mailout

A. initial mailing   (day 1)
B. postcard reminder   (day 4)
C. second mailing   (day 18)
D. third mailing   (day 40)
E. reminder calls   (days 55–80)
F. special mailing   (day 80)

monetary incentives are being used, some increased payment to such groups may help.

Second, it is almost always useful to try to determine reasons for nonresponse. If telephone numbers are available, a call to some nonrespondents to determine their reasons for not returning the questionnaires may help. If we find in the survey of county officers, for example, that the elected county board members are often not receiving the questionnaire promptly because many are only part-time on the board and spend most of their time at another job, we may want to channel some resources toward telephone calls to obtain these other addresses. Our second mailing would be redirected to the alternate addresses. Remember, in this case, it is the person, not the address, that is the sampling unit.

We might consider these kinds of issues on two other studies. First, we consider a regional survey of recreational boat owners about the problems of trash in public waterways; and second, a study of academic survey organizations about methods they use to develop questionnaires. If we should find that many of the recreational boat owners are concerned about the confidentiality of their answers to questions about trash disposal from their own boats (because they know some disposal practices are illegal), we may want to tailor the cover letter for the second mailing to address this issue. For the survey of survey organizations, we might find that there are delays because some requested information (e.g., the number of surveys that used particular pretest methods) is not readily available. A subsequent cover letter might acknowledge this likely problem but base its appeal on the need for the study to have a good response rate because the results will be reported at an industry conference. The organization's respondents, having often been in the same position themselves, may be motivated by this appeal to put in the extra required effort.

The options open to us during a study are limited, but sometimes a small adjustment can have enough of an effect to boost overall response rates or those of particular subgroups to the extent that we do not have to abandon plans for their separate analysis. The key point, with this and other procedural issues, is that if we see that things are not going well, we take what steps are available to us to improve the situation. Things sometimes turn around on their own, but a good researcher does not count on it.

Respondent Identification. A difficulty inherent in mail surveys is the lack of control over who actually answers the questionnaire. In telephone (or face-to-face) interviews, an interviewer can determine the appropriate respondent, whether by random selection or by stipulation of some other criterion, such as knowledge about a particular characteristic of a household or organization. In mail surveys, on the other hand, we depend on someone to read and follow the instructions about who should complete the questionnaire. In many instances, a mail survey is directed to a particular individual selected from a list, thus reducing the likelihood of error. However, even in these cases (especially in surveys of organizations), the respondent may delegate the completion of the questionnaire to someone else. What types of response error this leads to depends on the study. However, in the case of general population surveys, in which a random respondent is desired, we have much less faith that the correct respondent is selected. There is little evidence of how often this happens, but its potential is serious enough to render researchers leery of mail surveys of the general population.

Telephone

Whether the sampling frame is RDD, a list, or some combination, after the first round of calls, the sample is sorted into several groups. These groups include some interviews and identified nonhouseholds that need no further attention. There will also be some early refusals, telephone numbers whose status (household or not) we have not determined (ring-no-answer numbers), some households in which the respondent (or household informant) could not be interviewed (at least on the first attempt) because of problems such as difficulty hearing, illness, or languages other than English. In addition, we will have a large number of noncontacts, which include reaching answering machines and finding randomly selected respondents not at home or busy.

For each of these initial dispositions of the sample numbers, we must decide on a follow-up callback strategy. How well we do this has a major effect on our success in reaching and interviewing selected respondents and on the costs necessary to do so.

Unlike the situation in mail surveys, we have some information about the telephone numbers that did not result in an interview on the first call. Even if this information amounts to no more than when the call attempt was made, we can use it to fashion our callback strategy. But we have this information only if interviewers record it carefully.

Interviewers must be trained in the use of forms and procedures for recording, and aggregating, in sample status reports, the result of each call attempt.—that is, of each time a sample number is dialed. Regardless of the outcome, the interviewer codes what happened on the call. This kind of coding can be quite elaborate, but we recommend making it no more complex than is absolutely required by the study. The essential call results include: completed interview, initial refusal/partial interview, final refusal, noncontact, other nonrespondent problems. For each of these dispositions the date, time of day, and day of week should also be recorded.

The set of initial calls to each number in the sample determines how we will subsequently "work the sample," meaning whether and when we will schedule additional call attempts and, to some extent, which interviewers will make the calls. How well we do this has a major effect on both costs and nonsampling errors. Since each call to a sample number has a cost, the objective is to reach a disposition for each number with the minimum effort and to identify eligible sample members and complete interviews with as many of them as possible. Costs are affected because a large part of the total survey budget is for data collection, and calling the sample numbers represents—after the actual conduct of the interviews—the next major portion of data collection costs.

Exhibit 9.3 shows the distribution of initial call results (after one call to each number) and the actual final distribution for the University of Maryland Survey Research Center 1992 State Crime Survey. The first column is the equivalent of our first sample status report. A large number of nonhouseholds are identified after the one call, but more do turn up in the following calls. Initially, we are not sure whether a large group of telephone numbers are households or not. This category is greatly reduced (though not to zero) over the subsequent calls. In more than 60% (527/835) of the identified households, the selected respondent could not be interviewed on the first call attempt. However, by the end of the study, the noncontact rate is reduced to 5%.

Taking each disposition in turn, we consider what types of information we are likely to find out on the first (and subsequent) call attempts and how to use it. Some sample numbers almost immediately drop out because they are not part of the eligible household population: businesses, nonworking numbers, disconnected numbers, government offices, and so forth. However, even some of these numbers may require more than one call.

Exhibit 9.3

Maryland Crime Survey: Disposition of the Sample after 1 Call Attempt and after 20 Attempts

	After 1 Call		After 20 Calls	
Total sample	1,816		1,816	
Nonhouseholds	545		702	
Household status unknown	436		53	
Households	835	100%	1,061	100%
Interviews	181	22%	824	78%
Refusals	54	6%	164	15%
Noncontacts	527	63%	49	5%
Problem households (language, problems hearing, illness, etc.)	73	9%	24	2%

The second group that is quickly finalized are respondents who are easily contacted and agree immediately to the interview.[13] On average, these are respondents who are home frequently and who quickly comply with the request for an interview. Those at home more often are, as a group, more likely to be elderly, retired, unemployed, and, to a lesser extent, women. While all of these are eligible sample members, clearly they are not a random sample of the population. Using these samples would risk producing very biased population estimates. There are several tempting, but incorrect, procedures that would result in such poor samples. For example, we could draw a very large sample of phone numbers, begin calling and stop when we reached the target number of interviews, leaving the rest of the sample unworked. Or we could make one or two call attempts to each number in a selected sample. Both these approaches would skim off those respondents most available for interview, and both would result in overrepresentation of the demographic groups listed above.

Another factor that leads some respondents to immediately agree to do the interview is the survey topic. Respondents who are interested in the survey subject are less likely to put off the interviewer. In the Maryland crime survey, these respondents may be those who have been crime victims themselves or, for other reasons (for example, their profession or the experiences of friends) have strong feelings about crime issues. Once again, though they are eligible sample members, a survey that included only these types of respondents would probably provide misleading results. Both the easily reached and the quickly compliant require no further decisions or effort; both also illustrate the nonrandom nature of convenient subgroups of our sample. Now that it is clear that the transition from sampled household to completed interview is not a random process, we must decide how to direct our efforts (resources) to maximize the proportion of the sample that is interviewed and to weed out the ineligibles most efficiently.

The sample cases remaining after the first round of calls fall into two categories: households and household status unknown. As we

[13]The response rate is defined as interviews divided by eligible households. The cooperation rate is interviews divided by the sum of interviews, partial interviews, and refusals. At the end of the study, response rate is the main measure of data collection success. During data collection, the cooperation rate is a better indicator of how well interviewing is going. Why is this?

work the sample, these same patterns recur: some respondents are relatively easy to reach and interview; others require greater efforts either to contact or to persuade, or both.

As discussed in chapter 7 on sampling, we typically begin data collection by releasing a random subsample of numbers for calling. After estimating the interview completion rate (interviews divided by finalized sample) based on this subsample, we release additional random subsamples to attain the total number of interviews we want for the study. When these telephone numbers are released to the interviewers, the call-results pattern is usually similar though not identical.

Number of Contacts. The main factor in successfully contacting a high proportion of selected sample members is simply the number of contact attempts. Surveys that rely on a single contact attempt are likely, in almost all cases, to have serious nonresponse bias. For telephone surveys, the number of attempts typically ranges from about three to twenty, and for mail studies from two to four (Groves, 1989). We recommend no fewer than five attempts for general population telephone surveys and at least two mailings (each including a questionnaire and postage return envelope) for mail studies. If, during data collection, we realize that the planned level of effort is not producing the anticipated response rate, we may need to make some adjustments in our callback plan. Unfortunately, because of cost, we do not have the latitude to make many additional contacts. But adding one or two additional calls for all noncontacted sample members is often useful. This may be especially true if, by examining past call results on each number, we can focus those calls on days and times not yet covered.

Answering Machines. In recent years the ownership of home answering machines has greatly increased. Fortunately for survey researchers, early research (Oldendick and Link, 1994; Triplett, 1994) has shown that most of these households can be reached with proper scheduling. Weekend mornings are particularly effective times to contact these households, and they do not appear, once reached, to be any less cooperative than households without answering machines. In the crime survey, after one round of calls, about 13% of the identified households were dispositioned as answering machines. By the end of the survey, this number was reduced to about 2%.

Appointments. It is not uncommon for respondents to telephone surveys to request that they be recontacted at a more convenient time and are willing to set an appointment for the interview.[14] It is extremely important that the interviewing effort be organized to ensure that such appointments are kept. Missing them can easily turn a willing respondent into a noncooperator.

Call Scheduling. To properly and cost-effectively work the sample, interviewers must keep an accurate and complete record of the result of each call attempt. This is done through the use of a simple form that the interviewer completes immediately after calling each number. This record allows the interviewing staff manager to look for patterns as to when and when not to attempt additional call attempts for each household. If, for example, a particular household has never answered on weekday late afternoons, it makes sense to shift the next few attempts to later in the evening or to the weekend. Household informants, once reached, can often provide information about the best time to reach the randomly selected respondent. This information is recorded on the same form.

Identifying Bad Numbers. We will have difficulty determining the residential status for some telephone numbers even after several call attempts.[15] Due to technical features of the telephone system, a phone number that simply continues to ring each time it is called may or may not be a residence and may or may not be in service. Repeatedly calling a nonresidential number may not only be wasting effort and money but, in the case of the Mitofsky-Waksberg sample design (two-stage Rdd), would be costing us the opportunity to replace the number. There are three things we can try: first, schedule a few calls at earlier or later times than usual to try to catch people with, for example, odd work schedules. The few calls at odd times can be useful in bias reduction if the numbers turn out to be residences and an appointment for interview can be set up. Such respondents may be different, both demographically and substan-

---

[14]This is actually the rule, rather than the exception, for surveys of organizations. In planning that type of survey, allowance should be made for one or two calls simply to set up the appointment with the target respondent.

[15]For general population surveys, about 80–90% of calls should be made between about 6 and 9 P.M. on weekdays, Saturday and Sunday late mornings and afternoons, and Sunday evenings. Calls at other times are mainly to screen out business numbers and to reach respondents with unusual schedules.

tively, than those with more regular schedules. For example, people who work nights may, on the whole, have different responses to some of our questions on crime than do other respondents. Second, when possible, look up the number in a reverse directory.[16] Third, try the local phone company for information. Unfortunately, the usefulness of this last option varies greatly by the particular company's willingness to help. But it is an inexpensive option to try.

Reworking Refusals. A very important procedure for telephone surveys is refusal conversion. Respondents who refuse to be interviewed initially can often be "converted" on subsequent attempts. While there is little research on this phenomenon, we suspect that conversion is possible partly because the reason for many initial refusals has nothing to do with the survey itself. Keep in mind that while our survey is very important to us, it might mean little to the typical respondent. Some people, for example, caught at a bad time, will take a moment to set an appointment or just tell the interviewer to try some other time, while other respondents in the same circumstance will refuse. But, when recontacted, some will agree to the interview. Professional survey organizations can, using specially trained staff, typically convert 30–40% of initial refusers. While the nonprofessional will probably not achieve such rates, a nontrivial number of first refusals can likely still be turned into interviews. In addition to reducing the refusal rate, this procedure can also reduce bias if the initial refusers are generally different in some respects from the initial cooperators.[17]

Typically, we will want to let some time pass between the initial refusal and the attempt to convert. If the refusal was due to a "crisis" in the respondent's household, perhaps in several days it will be resolved. Also, many respondents will not even recall the original contact, so we may not want to even mention it, but, rather, start fresh. The approach we take for trying to convert a particular refusal depends, in part, on what happened the first time. For this reason, it is extremely important for the first interviewer to note the reason, as

[16]Reverse directories are telephone directories that are arranged in numerical order by telephone number, rather than alphabetically. Haines and R. H. Donnelley are the main publishers of these directories.

[17]In a study comparing respondents from converted refusals to others from several surveys, Blair and Chun (1992) found that there were some small differences in the number of "don't know" answers and item nonresponses between initial cooperators and those who were converted from refusals.

far as can be determined, for the refusal—the more detail, the better. The record should note the sex of the respondent and indicate, for example, that the person seemed very elderly. Keep in mind that the follow-up call might reach a different person in the household, if we had not gotten as far as random respondent selection on the first call.[18] Still, it is the circumstances of the first refusal that should be noted. If, for example, a person refused because she was about to leave for work, it would be foolish to make the conversion attempt at the same time of day as the first call, even though calling at that time increases the chances of reaching the respondent. Similarly, if a respondent refused initially because of a perceived sales purpose, the refusal converter should certainly be prepared to counter this perception quickly if it is raised in the follow-up call.

Problem Households. In some households, after reaching the randomly selected respondent, we find that the interview cannot be conducted. Some respondents do not speak English at all or not well enough to be interviewed. If we are doing the survey in an area with a large non–English speaking population, (e.g., Miami), we would risk serious coverage bias by not making provisions for interviewing in another language, in this case Spanish. However, in most small-scale research, we will not have this capability. Nevertheless, these households are still part of the defined population and must be counted as eligible households in our response rate calculations. Similarly, people who are too ill to be interviewed or have some physical or mental disability that prevent them from either hearing, understanding, or answering the questions are also lost to us.

Unfortunately, for mail surveys, such diverse tactics are not available. Rarely does a respondent send back a mailed questionnaire saying he refuses. So we cannot separate conscious decisions not to participate from nonreturn of questionnaires for other reasons. Thus, it is difficult if not impossible to tailor our follow-up efforts to the reasons for nonresponse. We are reduced to using general and multiple appeals. For example, a cover letter accompanying a follow-up mailing might mention things like the respondents' busy schedules or the possible misplacing of the first questionnaire. But the reason for the nonreturn may have nothing to do with either.

---

[18]Once a random respondent has been selected in a household, that person remains the target respondent for the survey regardless of what happens on subsequent call attempts.

One method we can make use of on mail studies is the special-delivery mailing and/or request for address correction. Both may be effective. The request for address correction should be done early to help ensure that subsequent mailings are sent to the correct address. Special delivery or other special methods, due to their cost, have to be focused on fewer cases later in the study. (See Dillman, 1978, for a full treatment of this issue in general population mail surveys.)

Reducing Item Nonresponse

Like unit nonresponse, unanswered questions (item nonresponse) frequently do not occur at random. Respondents may be reluctant to answer particular questions (for example, sensitive items such as whether or not they carry a weapon for protection) or may have difficulty answering others (such as how likely they think it is that in the coming year someone in their household will be a crime victim). Some items, like total household income from all sources, may be both somewhat sensitive and difficult for certain respondents. We should not forget the role of the interviewer in affecting the numbers of missing items. Because of their own feelings, interviewers may be averse to asking certain questions or unwilling to prod reluctant respondents to answer them.

A large part of our effort in questionnaire development is to reduce respondent error due to differing interpretations of questions or other response difficulties. This effort is undercut if respondents will not answer certain questions. In most surveys, item nonresponse is low. After agreeing to be interviewed, the typical respondent will answer all the questions. But interviewers must be prepared to handle reluctance. The interviewer has two main strategies for dealing with reluctance. First, let the respondent know why the question is necessary. Some respondents will want to know, for example, why some of the demographic questions (e.g., age, race, or income) are needed. Often, a simple response will suffice: "We want to compare our survey to the U.S. census to be sure it's representative." Second, remind respondents that all their answers are completely confidential and will never be linked to their name, address, or telephone number. If, after trying these approaches, the respondent still refuses an item, it is best to skip it and go on. Trying too hard to persuade the respondent to answer a particular question may lead to a breakoff and a lost case. Sometimes, if the item refusal happens early in the interview, it is possible to return to that question later, when the respondent may be more at ease with the interviewer and convinced of the legitimacy of the survey. Of course, these tactics are not available in mail surveys. There, again, the cover letter and an assurance of confidentiality at the top of the questionnaire must serve this function.

Interviewers as a Source of Error

Imagine that, for the crime survey, an interviewer contacts a household and selects, at random, an adult who says "I really don't have time for this. I was just going out. Why don't you talk to my wife. She keeps up with news and politics more than I do anyway." The interviewer responds with "Ok. She'll probably really like this survey." When the wife comes to the phone, the interviewer starts to read the introduction and the woman interrupts with "Why is the university doing a poll about crime?" "Well," the interviewer responds, "I'm not too sure, but it probably has something to do with the governor's reelection campaign. You know, to show he's serious about getting criminals off the street." Eventually, the interviewer gets to the question "In the past year, would you say that the VIOLENT crime situation in the STATE has gotten better, gotten worse, or stayed about the same?" The respondent says, "My daughter tells me she never goes out at night anymore since her next-door neighbor was mugged right outside his house." The interviewer responds with, "So I guess you really think crime's gotten worse."

Each of these interchanges shows how an interviewer can undo the careful design and procedures leading up to and including the interview. First, the random respondent selection procedure is abandoned for convenience; then, the introduction is cut short and a personal comment is interjected that may affect the respondent's reaction to later questions. Finally, instead of probing for a response that matches the answer categories, the interviewer infers the answer from the respondent's comment and puts words in the respondent's mouth. This not very farfetched example shows how easily, even naturally, interviewers can affect the quality of the survey.

We will spend a good deal of our resources in efforts to control interviewer behaviors through training, monitoring, and, most of all, showing them how inadvertent, well-intentioned, actions can be detrimental to the research effort. We must keep in mind that it is the interviewer we depend on to carry out crucial aspects of the survey design.

To that end, not only the training but also the selection of interviewers is important. Interviewing is a skill that requires good reading competence, personal interaction ability, and, often, no small amount of persuasive know-how. We ask interviewers to contact strangers, usually without advance notice, request their cooperation for the interview, explain the purpose of the study, answer their questions about the study or about particular survey items, administer the interview according to instructions, and accurately record the answers. All this must be done while maintaining a professional demeanor, sometimes in trying situations. Not everyone is suited to all the tasks that interviewing requires.

In some instances, the researcher has no role in interviewer selection—when, for example, the survey is a class project or a survey organization is hired to collect data. However, even in the case of a class project, it may be that not all the students need to or can properly conduct interviews. As we have noted, unlike other aspects of the survey process, interviewing requires not just an understanding of what happens in the interview process but the skills to carry it out as well. The best way to find out who has these skills is live practice, after some training. One approach is to have everyone participate in the pretest and then decide who should conduct interviews and who should instead do interview monitoring, data entry, or some other project task.

Whether we are actually recruiting or just making assignments from the interviewers available to us, there are a few guidelines to consider. First, it is useful to have the prospective interviewers go through a structured test. Four areas should be covered: reading and following instructions; gaining respondents' cooperation; reading questions properly; and recording answers accurately. How much skill we can expect in the last two areas depends on how much prior experience, if any, the prospective interviewer has had. But we will find that even novices will differ in how instinctively they react to respondents' reluctance or how naturally, after even a few tries, they can read survey questions. The simplest way to screen possible interviewers is to have a few study-specific instructions available, along with a draft of the questionnaire. We should explain to each interviewer the purpose of the study and what we are going to ask them to do. After allowing each interviewer a few minutes to read the relevant instructions and the questionnaire, then a supervisor (or another student) plays the role of respondent, at first going along easily with the request for an interview and answering the questions without incident. On subsequent rounds, the "respondent" varies his or her behavior from this ideal, creating progressively more difficult situations for the interviewer. An observer (or the class as a group) grades the performance. If this test can be set up so that the two parties are in separate rooms actually communicating by telephone, a more realistic assessment of the interviewer's skills, as well as his or her telephone voice can be made.[19]

The training session itself (or, more likely, sessions) should focus on skill-building practices. An effective training agenda will, at every opportunity, emphasize participatory exercises over lectures. We want constantly to point out behaviors, such as those illustrated at the beginning of this section, that seem natural in conversation and are well-intentioned but are inappropriate in an interview. Rather than simply laying down a series of rules—though we must do that too—we must show interviewers why such behaviors are detrimental to the project. This point and others are best conveyed through practice and example, not lecture. One aid to doing this is to require that the interviewers read background materials before each training session.

Training Interviewers in the Data Collection Process

The training of interviewers should cover both general interviewing skills and the specific requirements of the study at hand (Exhibit 9.4). The amount of general training required depends on the interviewers' prior experience; if possible, it should be conducted by an experienced trainer. The following discussion covers the most basic aspects of training; to supplement, a training manual from a professional survey organization should be followed closely.[20]

The two key training areas are gaining cooperation and conducting the interview. First, we focus on the reluctant respondent.

Gaining Cooperation

Many respondents will not immediately agree to the interview. Sometimes they want to know more about the survey than what is contained in the interview's introduction. The interviewer needs to

---

[19]If this type of training is to be conducted properly, a speakerphone should be placed in one or both rooms.

[20]The University of Michigan Survey Research Center's *General Interviewing Techniques* (Guensel, Berckmans, and Cannell, 1983) is an excellent source.

Exhibit 9.4

Key Subjects to Cover in the General Training of Interviewers

1. Gaining cooperation
   - Identifying or selecting the correct respondent
   - Explaining the purpose of the survey
   - Persuading reluctant respondents to cooperate

2. Administration of the interview
   - Getting started
   - Making the transition to the interview
   - Reading questions verbatim
   - Asking nondirective probes
   - Asking all questions and recording answers correctly
   - Following skip instructions
   - Recording answers correctly: open ends

be ready to provide this information quickly, concisely, and clearly. A common practice is to have a one page "info sheet" listing the study's sponsor, it's purpose, the length of a typical interview, and a thumbnail description of how the results will be used. If, in the course of the pretest or early interviews, other respondent questions or concerns frequently come up, these should be added to the info sheet and circulated to all the interviewers. It is also very useful to provide a phone number respondents can call to verify the legitimacy of the survey.[21] A few respondents will want to be reassured about the confidentiality of their answers. But, for most reluctant respondents, none of these will be the issue; they will simply not be interested enough to give their time.

The main appeal of a survey is its topic. The crime survey will, in general, be more interesting to a larger number of potential respondents than a study about the public libraries. But even with an interesting, newsworthy topic, many people will not immediately agree to the interview. The interviewer must be prepared for this reaction. In a telephone survey, the interviewer has very little time to gain cooperation. Remember, it is easy for a respondent to hang up.

---

[21]This should preferably be a 1-800 number if the survey is not local. In any case, it should be a number that is staffed during regular working hours.

Two tactics for responding to respondents' reluctance are: first, keep the respondent engaged and talking; second, address the specific reason the respondent does not want to do the interview. It is very important, therefore, that the interviewer listen closely to the respondent's reason for not wanting to do the interview, even though many times this will have nothing to do with the survey but simply with bad timing. If the respondent is about to leave for work, is in the middle of watching a ball game, or is dealing with a personal problem at home, the alert interviewer will quickly back off from requesting the interview and try to determine a better time to call back. This approach would seem to be dictated by simple common sense, but it is not unusual for overly aggressive interviewers to push on in such situations, turning reluctance into refusal.

Even though the interviewer has read an introduction giving the survey sponsor and topic, some respondents will still suspect it is a disguised sales call or some other solicitation. This is partly because some respondents do not really hear the introduction. Remember, they were not expecting the call, and also many marketing campaigns are disguised as surveys. The interviewer should be ready for this and quickly repeat the sponsor, especially if it is a university or recognizable government agency.

A large number of respondents will simply say that they are not interested or that they don't have time. Although these responses sound different, they often amount to the same thing, a stock response to end unwanted calls quickly. The main thing the interviewer must try to do is keep the person engaged to avoid the imminent hang-up. If the topic is a popular one, the interviewer should try to repeat it, still acknowledging that he or she listened to what the respondent said. For example, "Most people find they like giving their opinions about the crime problem once they get started. It won't take very long."

Some respondents will say they don't really know much about the issue, particularly if the topic sounds technical, like biotechnology or some aspects of the environment or the economy. The interviewer needs to assure such respondents that the interview is not a test of knowledge.[22] A response such as, "This is just about your *general* opinions. It doesn't require any special knowledge."

---

[22]It is important that surveys in general, and particularly those that might on their surface sound forbidding, not begin with knowledge questions. Remember, all respondents, but especially reluctant ones, still have the option to break off if the first few questions are difficult or make them uneasy.

Finally, in some situations, the reluctance is not from the actual respondent but from a household informant. When we contact a household, any adult can answer the questions used for random respondent selection. If the selected respondent is then someone other than the person on the phone, the interviewer asks to speak to the respondent. At this point, the situation may involve a **gatekeeper**— that is, a person who answers the phone and does not want to let the interviewer talk to the respondent. The reasons may include some already discussed as well as others. The interviewer strategies are essentially the same, with the added component of expressing the desire to describe the survey briefly to the respondent. If the informant is still reluctant, calling back at another time at least gives a chance to bypass the gatekeeper and reach the respondent directly. Exhibit 9.5 lists suggestions for handling reluctant-respondent situations.

Exhibit 9.5

The Reluctant Respondent: Typical Situations and Some Remedies

Bad Timing
- Don't try to push for the interview
- Show understanding of the bad timing
- Use judgment in deciding whether to even ask for a callback time.

Suspicion of Disguised Sales or Solicitation
- Repeat the sponsor and study purpose
- Assure the respondent that this is not a sales pitch or solicitation; offer an 800 number, if available, or request that the respondent call collect for verification

No Time/ Topic Not of Interest
- If survey topic is a popular one, focus on it; if not, focus on how quickly the interview goes.

Respondent Doesn't Know about Topic
- Focus on the opinion aspect of the survey; downplay any knowledge questions
- Let the respondent know we're interested in what all people think about the issue

Gatekeepers
- Ask that the respondent have a chance to hear what the survey is about.
- Call back to try to avoid the gatekeeper.

Conducting the Interview

A central component of all aspects of interviewer training is role playing, sometimes referred to as mock interviewing. As we have noted, successful survey interviewing requires not so much conceptual understanding (though, of course, a measure of that is essential) as execution of certain skills in gaining respondents' cooperation and properly administering the interview. Such skills are acquired only with practice. The less interviewing experience an interviewer brings to the task, in general, the more practice is necessary. It is also very important to realize that shortcuts on training are false savings. If the interviewers do not practice their skills in a training session, they will, of necessity, practice them with real respondents during the study. The preference is obvious.

In mock interviews, just as in the interviewer-screening process, interviewers take turns playing the role of interviewer and respondent. Each practice round is structured to address a particular set of skills. Practice continues in each area until the interviewer is comfortable, quick, and smooth in handling each situation. Remember, when a real respondent is on the line, there is no time to consult notes, hesitate, or back up and start over. Either an impatient respondent will end the interview or improperly administered questions will result in poor measures.

The exercises should follow the chronological order of interview administration, with at least one exercise to illustrate skill building for each stage of the interview. The number of exercises used and the amount of time devoted to each should be determined by the nature of the questionnaire, the interviewers' backgrounds, and how quickly they pick up the required skills. Whenever possible, after group instruction, having interviewers practice some of the exercises on the phone will lend realism to the training. The interviewers should know that the final step of the training will be to do a "live" interview with a real respondent. These practice cases should be selected from the study population but not from the actual survey sample. Of course, these final practice cases should be closely monitored.

The fundamental instructions to interviewers can be stated simply: Read each question and transition statement *exactly* as written, including all the response categories, without any deviation; ask all the questions, even if you think the answer has already been given; follow the questionnaire's skip patterns; and record answers carefully and, in the case of open-ends, verbatim. These rules are as easy to state as they are to break. This is particularly true of the maxim to read each question verbatim. Anyone who has conducted interviews has run into situations in which it seemed that adding a comment or changing a few words would "clarify" a question or "help" a respondent. The questions must stand on their own, without embellishments of any sort. While we cannot claim that every deviation from the exact wording of the question results in unreliable data, to open the door to invention completely undermines the foundation of uniform data collection. We must strive to develop questions that do not tempt interviewers to such circumvention.

One way to train for this skill is to have each interviewer, in turn, read a question or questions from the survey and have the others critique the reading for verbatim delivery and natural pacing, with proper pauses at punctuation marks and clear pronunciation. The interviewer's tone should be conversational and not sound like a reading from a book. Often, interviewers want to skip this practice, feeling that they are literate and can read well enough. It is quickly evident that even well-educated interviewers, on first practice with a new questionnaire, often misread questions, go too fast for many listeners, and make occasional mistakes in pronunciation. These errors seem trivial until there is an irritated or confused respondent on the line. Then these "trivial" errors often lead respondents to hang up or to misunderstand questions. Administering survey questions is not a reading skill but a performance skill.

After the survey introduction and respondent selection, the interview proper begins. We have tried to design the questionnaire so that the first questions ease respondents into the interview; and in most cases the interview will proceed smoothly and uneventfully. But, as we noted in the discussion of behavior coding, there can be some problematic interactions between interviewers and respondents. These have three sources: the questionnaire, the interviewer, and the respondent. We have tried, through the questionnaire design and the training of interviewers to read questions verbatim, to minimize the first two sources; we now turn to the third.

Handling Problematic Behaviors

There are three main behaviors of respondents that interviewers must be trained to handle (1) the respondent does not answer using one of the response categories; (2) instead of answering, the respondent himself asks a question; and (3) the respondent responds with a comment about the topic. The interviewer must deal with all of these carefully to avoid affecting the resulting data or having the respondent break off the interview.

For each of the problem situations, the interviewer must get the respondent to provide an appropriate answer, one that is codable into one of the given categories, yet maintain rapport. Remember the respondent is volunteering time and trying to be helpful. The interviewer knows that she needs an answer that fits a closed response category and that extraneous remarks cost time and money, but the respondent may view the interaction as something much more like a conversation, with digressions and asides. It is the interviewer's task to get the respondent on track and keep him there—but tactfully. In doing this, it is paramount that all interviewers handle similar respondent problems in the same way and in a manner that does not affect the respondent's answer choice. It is for these reasons that we instruct interviewers about what sorts of things to expect in the interview and impose strict guidelines on permissible behavior in each situation.

In the mock interviews, "respondents" should take turns deviating from being good respondents while the interviewer practices responding to each situation. After each round, the interviewer's performance should be critiqued by the group.

When interviewers do not receive acceptable responses, their main tool is the **probe,** a question designed to elicit an acceptable response. Interviewers must learn to recognize which answers are satisfactory and which are not and to use probes that are nondirective—that is, they do not suggest an answer to respondents.

Consider the first crime survey question:

```
In general, would you say that the crime problem
in YOUR NEIGHBORHOOD is very serious, somewhat se-
rious, not very serious or not at all serious?
     1 VERY SERIOUS
     2 SOMEWHAT SERIOUS
     3 NOT VERY SERIOUS
     4 NOT AT ALL SERIOUS
     8 DK
```

If, the respondent's answer is "serious," the interviewer should probe by repeating *all* the response categories. "Would that be . . . (read categories)?" The interviewer should not infer from earlier responses, even to very similar questions, which category to code. Nor should the interviewer's probe make such an inference, as in "So would that be 'very serious'? If the categories are such that a partial answer puts the respondent in one subset of response categories, then the probe can refer to that subset. For example, if the choices are "very satisfied," "somewhat satisfied," "somewhat dissatisfied," and "very dissatisfied," and the respondent simply says "satisfied," a proper probe would be "Would that be 'very satisfied' or 'somewhat satisfied'?" A bad probe would be one that did not repeat all the relevant categories. In each case, the respondent must always select the category. This practice should be followed even if the same problem occurs on several questions. Although most respondents will pick up quickly what is wanted, others have to be "trained" by the interviewer to be "good respondents," and the training must begin at the outset of the interview. Once the respondent is off track, returning is doubly hard.

In training sessions, interviewers should practice suggesting probes they would use in particular situations. It is also useful in practicing probes to note some tempting, but inappropriate, probes. For example, if a respondent answers "serious" to the question above, the interviewer should *not* say, "So, can I put you down as very serious?" Consider an open-ended question such as "What do you think is the most important problem facing Maryland?" Suppose the respondent answers, "Drugs." A poor (leading) probe would be "Why do you say 'drugs'? Is it because people on drugs commit so many crimes?" A better probe would be "Can you explain a little more fully what you mean?"

The second problem type has to do with questions asked by respondents. If the question is off the subject of the interview—for example, the respondent asks the interviewer how she likes doing interviews or what she thinks about a particular issue—the interviewer simply says that interviewers are not supposed to discuss their personal feelings during an interview. If the question is about the survey question, the interviewer must refrain from replying unless there are specific instructions on what to say. One never knows how a comment, even an offhand one, might affect an answer.

In response to the third problem—the respondent makes a comment about the topic—the interviewer should refrain from comment and lead the respondent back into the interview. As noted in an earlier example, when, in response to another crime survey question, the respondent mentioned that her daughter had been mugged, the interviewer should acknowledge hearing what the respondent said but avoid comment. A neutral filler, such as "I see" can serve this purpose.

Exhibit 9.6 provides examples of how to handle common interview problems. The same type of role-playing exercises can be used to practice these as well, mixing up the respondent behaviors, so each interviewer has to think and react quickly. Remember that in all of these situations, a quick—and correct—reaction may mean the difference between an interview and a break-off and refusal; between reliable, unbiased data and bad data.

As we have seen, the data collection process is fraught with potential sources of error. The most serious are generally unit nonresponse, respondent error, and interviewer effects. The number of these types of error, of course, is mainly a result of how well the various aspects of the study are designed and implemented. Still, experience has shown that the incidence of such errors is also

Exhibit 9.6

Conventions for Handling Problematic Respondent Behaviors

Respondent interrupts during the question text with an answer:
- The interviewer should read all of the question. However, if it is part of a series of identically structured items, the interviewer should use her judgment whether to accept the response or finish reading the text.

Respondent interrupts during the response categories with an answer:
- If the question is attitudinal, the interviewer should still read all the categories.
- If the question is factual, the interviewer should accept the response.

Respondent asks what a word or term means:
- The standard response is to tell the respondent "Whatever it means to you."
- For particular technical terms, all interviewers may have been provided a uniform definition.
- If the respondent says he or she cannot answer without knowing what is meant by a word or term, the interviewer should code it as a "don't know."

Respondent asks for more information or asks about conditions not in the question:
- The interviewer should say, "If your answer is based on just what I've told you, would you say . . . " and then repeat the response categories.
- If the respondent insists he cannot answer without knowing whether a particular condition applies, or without more information, the interviewer should code it as a "don't know."

Exhibit 9.7
Typical Levels of Error, by Data Collection Method

	Data Collection Method		
	Telephone	Mail	Group Administration
Unit nonresponse	Low	High	Low
Interviewer effects	Medium	N/A	N/A
Respondent errors	Low	Medium–High	Medium–High

closely associated with the data collection method. Exhibit 9.7 is a guide to the typical levels of these sources of error for three data collection methods.

Quality Control for Telephone Surveys

There are several routine procedures used to track the quality of tele phone survey implementation. Each is related to error sources we have noted as important in most telephone studies.

Monitoring and Verification

Three procedures are typically used to track interviewers' performance: monitoring, callback verification, and data checking. In **monitoring,** a small sample of each interviewer's cases are listened to during the interview, without the knowledge of either the interviewer or the respondent. This procedure, which requires a central telephone facility with appropriate equipment, allows a trained supervisor to evaluate interviewer behaviors on both a general level (e.g., professional interaction with respondents) and on a very specific level (e.g., verbatim reading of all the questions, proper probing of responses when necessary, and proper handling of respondents' questions or difficulties). The percentage of calls monitored depends on available staff time but should be about 10–20%. More frequent monitoring is advisable at the outset of the study to try to identify any problems as early as possible for new or less-experienced interviewers and for any interviewers who have had difficulty in either gaining respondents' cooperation or conducting the interview. A key aspect of monitoring is immediate feedback—both positive and negative—to interviewers.

Callback verification is sometimes used if monitoring facilities are not available. In this procedure, a sample of each interviewer's cases are recontacted to verify that the interview was done, to check its length, and to ask whether the respondent had any problems or questions and, if so, how the interviewer reacted to them. There is no set rule about how much verification should be done, but a 10% check is frequently used. Clearly, monitoring is more effective as a quality control procedure and should be considered essential to the conduct of a telephone survey.

Data checking is a procedure in which the collected data are tabulated and inspected during the data collection period. Data checks can uncover problems in questionnaire administration by interviewers as well as logic and question-design errors not found earlier. In data checking, frequency distributions are produced for each closed variable, and the verbatim responses to any open-ended items are also generated. These data are examined for such things as skip-pattern errors, patterns of missing items or excessive numbers of missing items, proper use of "other specify" categories (i.e., a check that answers are not being put under "other specify" if they should have been coded into one of the closed categories), consistency between related items, and the clarity of recorded responses to open-ended questions. Data checking is very valuable in spotting problems early enough in the data collection so that, if necessary, corrective actions can be taken.

CASIC: CAPI, CATI, and More

A major quality-control development in survey research has come from the extensive use of computer-assisted methodologies. The acronym CASIC, Computer Assisted Survey Information Collection, refers to the wide and expanding array of computer-driven technologies used to collect survey data.[23] The two major CASIC tools are Computer Assisted Telephone Interviewing (CATI) and Computer Assisted Personal Interviewing (CAPI). Both methods allow interviewers to enter survey responses into a computer file while conducting a interview. The main advantage of these systems is one of quality control. CATI and CAPI systems usually handle questionnaire skip patterns automatically, reducing interviewer error; limit

[23]In fact, though only recently introduced, the term has already been extended to include all aspects of survey computerization, such as data transmittal, processing, analysis, and dissemination.

the range of values that can be entered for some items—for example, requiring two-digit entries for age in a survey of adults; and check some answers against others for internal consistency—for example, alerting the interviewer if someone born in 1970 reports graduating from high school in 1980, an unlikely occurrence. The value of these technologies is that they perform these functions during the interview, rather than at a later, data cleaning stage, preventing costly recontacts of respondents. Many of these systems also automatically handle sample administration and scheduling of call attempts. Most professional and university survey organizations have some type of CATI system; CAPI is far less widespread.

If there is such a system available for our study, then the time and cost to learn how to use the system, including programming the questionnaire into it, must be added to our budget and project plan. For a one-time study, it is probably best to subcontract the programming rather than try to learn it.

Other new CASIC technologies include Touchtone Data Entry (TDE), allowing respondents to listen to a computerized voice and enter answers by pressing numbers on their telephone, and data collection over computer networks using e-mail transmission, among others. None of these methods have yet been widely used.

Quality Control for Mail Surveys

The procedures for quality control for mail surveys are fairly straightforward. Most have to do with handling missing or ambiguous data. When a mail questionnaire is received with unanswered items, there are three choices: ignore the items and code as "missing" in the data set; try to determine what the answer "should be," and insert that value into the data set; or recontact respondents to obtain the missing answers.

In making decisions about which options to choose, we must have a sense of which variables are crucial to our study. Obviously, all questions are valuable or we would not have included them, but there are priorities. For example, if the main analysis concerns racial differences, then missing race makes the case much less useful to the study. On the other hand, if differences by race are not central to the study purpose, we would be much less concerned if this item is missing.

If the amount of missing data is both very small (say, under 1%) and the items are not crucial variables, we want to select the options that use fewest, or no, resources. Either ignore it or see whether the answer can be determined from some combination of other answers in the questionnaire. For example, if gender is missing but elsewhere in the questionnaire the respondent reported having attended a Catholic high school known to be an all-girl institution, we can then confidently enter "female" for the missing item. Great care must be taken in using this process. Errors in such imputation can make the data worse, not better.

When it appears that data are missing because of a misunderstood "skip" instruction and the item is a key variable, it may make sense to recontact the respondent to obtain the information. This is especially appealing if the recontact can be done quickly by telephone. If the calls are long-distance, this cost must be factored in. It is useful to have a small amount of resources—funds and schedule time—set aside for such contingencies.

Finally, we want to consider samples of nonrespondents in situations in which unit nonresponse is high. Samples of nonrespondents are routinely used in mail surveys to assess differences between respondents and nonrespondents, as well as to increase the overall response rate. The method involves selecting a small number of sample members who did not return the mail questionnaire and trying to obtain the interview by another means, usually by telephone. We then compare their characteristics to those of the mail respondents to assess the direction and magnitude of possible bias in the mail sample. While a description of statistical adjustments based on such results is beyond the scope of this book, it is useful simply to know that these "reluctant respondents" are more often of a particular gender or background than the others, or that they tend to be more or less in favor of some proposal referred to in the questionnaire. Nonrespondent sampling is clearly a tactic that has to be planned in advance, as part of the overall design of the survey. But exactly how it is used procedurally can be determined after more is known about the nature of the nonresponse.

Costs and Contingencies: Expect the Unexpected

Now that we have examined both the general design issues and detailed procedures necessary to complete a survey, and we have some sense of what sorts of unexpected problems can arise, we return to a more detailed look at survey costs. We use the term costs in a broad sense to include materials or services (such as directories or telephone calls) that must be purchased, hourly labor costs (such as for telephone interviewers and data entry operators), and investments of time (such as an unpaid student researchers), even though no money has to be spent for it. We take as our example the Maryland crime telephone survey.

Budgeting is an inexact science (as anyone who has ever read a news story about government cost overruns knows), yet an essential one. Discovering, in the course of conducting a survey, that a major cost has been overlooked or underestimated can lead to such disasters as having to cut off data collection before obtaining the target sample size or not conducting the planned follow-ups to obtain a good response rate.

One simple way to approach survey budgeting is to list all the steps necessary to conduct the study and, for each one, to note what resources will be needed and whether there is a cost for them or not. Even if a task does not require payment, listing it will help guarantee realistic planning and, possibly, affect how we want to handle certain tasks. For example, the researcher may have planned to personally type all the questionnaire drafts, handling that part of pretesting for free. Listing the estimated hours needed to do this along with all the other "free" tasks, however, may lead to the decision that the researcher's time is best used elsewhere and that paying a secretary or typing service to handle the questionnaire drafts makes more sense.

By using a task/cost chart like the one in Exhibit 9.8, researchers can figure a budget fairly quickly, *if they know what things cost*. Finding exact costs for some items may be difficult or may require estimates (e.g., telephone charges). But following this procedure forces us to see where the uncertainties are in our budget and, perhaps, where contingencies need to be considered to allow some margin for error. It will also force us to assess realistically the time and cost of the survey. A very common error for the novice researcher is to underestimate the level of effort needed to conduct a first-rate survey.

We begin to construct the task list by listing the survey activities by three time periods: tasks that have to be completed prior to data collection; those that occur during data collection; and those done after data collection. A couple of iterations of the list may be necessary before it is complete, and in the course of making these lists and filling in the costs, some changes in resource allocation may occur, as in the example cited earlier of typing the questionnaire drafts.

Exhibit 9.8

Survey Tasks and Cost Projections: Maryland Crime Survey*

Task	Item	Cost
Pre–Data Collection		
Write outline of survey goals.	8 hrs., draft by researcher	free
Write topic outline of questionnaire.	24 hrs., draft by researcher	free
	16 hrs., review by colleague	free
Find example questions.	24 hrs., student assistant	$288
	4 hrs., review by researcher	free
Write new questions.	16 hrs., draft by researcher	free
	16 hrs., comment by student assistants	$192
Type draft questionnaire.	4 hrs., secretary	$38
Obtain sampling frame.	8 hrs., student assistant	$96
	2 hrs., secretary	$19
	purchase of computerized frame	$650
Select pretest sample.	2 hrs., researcher	free
	6 hrs., student assistant	$72
Prepare training materials.	16 hrs., researcher	free
	20 hrs., professional trainer	$360
	10 hrs., secretary	$95
	materials	$50
Train interviewers for pretest.	16 hrs., professional trainer	$288
	160 hrs., (10) interviewers	$1,280
	48 hrs., (3) interviewer supervisors	$480
	2 hrs., researcher	free
Conduct pretest and debriefing.	4 hrs., professional trainer	$72
	40 hrs., (10) interviewers	$320
	12 hrs., (3) supervisors	$120
	4 hrs., researcher	free
Review results.	6 hrs., researcher	free
	16 hrs., student assistant	$192
Revise and photocopy questionnaire.	16 hrs., researcher (photocopying)	free
	24 hrs., student assistant	$288
Select main sample.	8 hrs., student assistant	$96

*Estimates are based on 800 fifteen-minute telephone interviews in an RDD survey.

Exhibit 9.8

Survey Tasks and Cost Projections: Maryland Crime Survey
(continued)

Task	Item	Cost
Data Collection		
Train interviewers for main study.	16 hrs., professional trainer	$288
	160 hrs., (10) interviewers	$1,280
	48 hrs., (3) interviewer supervisors	$480
	2 hrs., researcher	free
Conduct 800 fifteen-minute interviews and monitor (5 weeks data collection).	700 hrs., (10) interviewers	$5,600
	200 hrs., (3) supervisors	$2,000
	telephone bill	$1,620
Do data checks.	25 hrs., student assistant	$300
Rework refusals.	20 hrs., interviewers	$240
	10 hrs., supervisors	$100
Post–Data Collection		
Enter data into computer file.	200 hrs., data entry operators	$1,300
	20 hrs., supervisor	$200
Complete data analysis runs.	20 hrs., researcher	free
	40 hrs., student assistant	$480
Write report.	20 hrs., researcher	free
	40 hrs., student assistant	$480
	30 hrs., secretary	$285
Total labor hours	2,155	
Total cost		$19,529

In terms of the sheer number of tasks to be done, the list quickly shows us that there is a lot of up-front work to be done to prepare for the study. Although most of the work hours are devoted to the telephone interviewing itself, many tasks precede that stage. It should also be noted that most of the cost by far for a telephone survey is for labor; only a small amount goes to materials and expenses. While this balance would shift in the less labor-intensive mail survey, the amount of up-front work still results in significant labor costs for that type of study as well. Looked at from this perspective, one can see that while mail surveys are less expensive than telephone studies, the development costs remain substantial.

While the numbers in Exhibit 9.8 are illustrative, they are approximately correct for surveys conducted by university survey organizations. Of course, if more time is "free"—if, for example, students do all the interviewing—the cost (but not the labor) is less. Often, for university surveys conducted in conjunction with a class, the interviewing is divided between the survey organization's staff and the class. In this way, a reasonable sample size can be achieved without filling all the class time with actual interviewing. As an exercise, you might compute what happens to costs under this and other scenarios of "free" versus paid labor.

Most of the costs and time to do tasks could be estimated or developed by talking with someone who has conducted a survey before (always a good idea during planning). One exception is the number of hours for the interviewing itself. One common way to estimate this is shown in the following calculation:

$$\text{Total interview hours} = \frac{\text{Interview length} \times \text{Sample size} \times \text{I.E.R.}}{60}$$

The only mystery here is the interviewer efficiency rate (I.E.R.), an estimate (based on past experience) of how much time is spent in ancillary activities (dialing nonproductive numbers, handling sample, taking breaks, etc.) for each minute of actual interviewing time. In this calculation, an I.E.R. of 3.5 was used, along with the target 800 fifteen-minute interviews to arrive at the 700 interviewing hours. That is, for every minute of actual interviewing, approximately 2.5 minutes of interviewer time are needed for other activities (such as contacting respondents, dealing with refusals, and so on). Since the I.E.R. is so crucial to a proper calculation of interviewer hours, we recommend seeking the advice of an experienced survey researcher.

The point of this detailed treatment of survey procedures to reduce sources of error is to show that, while there are myriad details one must attend to in properly conducting a survey, most are both conceptually and operationally simple. The key is careful planning, realistic allocation of resources and time, and a clear sense of priorities.

The Ethics of Survey Research

Our efforts have, to this point, been steadfastly focused on the obligation we have voluntarily assumed to conduct the best research possible within our means. But the responsibility of the serious researcher does not end with conducting the technical and theoretical aspects of the work. We also have obligations to the respondents who agree to participate in our study, to our fellow researchers, and to the users of our results. While an in-depth treatment of the origin and philosophy underlying these issues is beyond the scope of this book, it is essential that the beginning researcher at least be aware of them, if only on a general level.

Two concepts are central to our treatment of respondents: informed consent and protection of confidentiality. While we apply extensive efforts to obtain respondents' cooperation in the survey, the respondents' agreement must be reasonably informed. This means that we must not mislead respondents as to the nature and purpose of the research. We must honestly answer their questions about the project, including who is sponsoring it, its major purposes, the amount of time and effort that will be required of respondents, the general nature of the subject matter, and the use that will be made of the data. We must not badger or try to intimidate respondents either into participating or into answering particular questions after they agree to be interviewed.

Once respondents have agreed to be interviewed, we then assume an obligation to protect the confidentiality of their answers. This is true whether or not we have explicitly told respondents we will do so. Results or data sets that permit the identification of individual respondents should never be made available to others.

These ethical guidelines are recognized by the major professional organizations of survey researchers and are typically overseen by human subjects review committees at universities and other organizations that engage in population research.[24]

These obligations are no less applicable when a project is conducted by a class or a large team of researchers than when a single researcher is involved. In fact, perhaps additional cautions need to be observed in the former situation because there are additional

---

[24]See appendix C for the American Association for Public Opinion Research Code of Professional Ethics and Practices.

opportunities for inadvertent breaches of these ethical guidelines when many people are privy to the sample and the data.

Revealing or discussing an individual respondent's answers outside of the research group is inappropriate. Also, it is not proper to recontact survey respondents for purposes not related to the research for which they originally agreed to participate. The sample list used for a survey should not be made available to others (even other legitimate researchers) without the additional consent of the respondents. If the data are made available to another party, all identifiers that would permit linking answers to individuals should be removed.

Finally, as researchers, we make reasonable efforts to ensure the reliability and validity of our results both through the methods we employ and in our careful interpretation of the resultant data. It is incumbent on us to describe and disclose these methods in our reports and discussions of the survey. There are other reasons, as well, for a full and clear report of the survey methodology. This issue is taken up in detail in the final chapter.

10 The Methodology Report

We have sought to maximize the reliability and validity of the survey results by means of a series of design and implementation decisions. To assess the soundness of the survey findings, a reader (or user of the data set) must know what key decisions were made and something about the outcomes of the decisions. In their rush to analyze the substantive findings, researchers often omit this final phase of the survey or prepare a report that is incomplete. In this chapter, we show, through examples, that certain features of the survey methodology can have a crucial effect on the study's findings and their interpretation, and we discuss the key components of a typical methods report.

The Utility of the Methodology Report

The importance of describing the survey's methodological procedures and outcomes is difficult to formalize but can be illustrated quite simply. Consider the following hypothetical finding from the crime survey:

```
Within the past year, have you purchased a gun or
other weapon for protection?
                              Response distribution
        NO ................................. 66%
        YES ................................ 23%
        DK/Refused ........................ 11%
```

If it was simply reported that 23% of respondents answered "yes," we would have only part of the picture. How would our confidence in this sample estimate be affected if we knew the study had a 45% response rate? A 78% response rate? Certainly, we would intuitively trust the higher rate to lend more support to the finding. But, beyond intuition, the higher response rate is important because we would be less concerned that the nonrespondents, had they been interviewed, could have changed the result. Remember, we have a statistical basis for projecting from the *selected* probability sample to the target population. However, if we do not interview all the selected sample members, the *achieved* sample differs from the *selected* sample—and our ability to project to the population is weakened. Since surveys only rarely, and in special circumstances, have 100% response, the potential effect of nonresponse is virtually always an issue. So we have to ask ourselves how the nonrespondents might differ from the respondents. Of course, we do not know for sure, but our concern is proportional to the magnitude of the nonresponse.[1] If the nonresponse rate is low, then those people we were unable to interview would have to be very different from the respondents in order to change the results. On the other hand, if we failed to interview a large percentage of the sample, those people not interviewed could easily change the results.

The distribution of sample responses must also be taken into account in assessing the possible effects of nonresponse. If, on a yes/no item, we obtained a 93% yes/7% no sample estimate, we would be less concerned about the potential effect of nonresponse on our trust in the estimate than if the sample estimate were 55% yes/45% no. In the former case, even if the nonrespondents are very different from the respondents, it remains likely that the large majority of the population is in the "yes" category. This is not so with the close 55%/45% split, where a substantially different distribution among nonrespondents could substantially change the finding.

Consider two more examples of hypothetical outcomes for the same crime question. What if we knew that the sample was 64% women but that the adult population is only 53% female; or that 11% of respondents refused to answer this item? If women have generally bought weapons for protection more frequently than men have, we would reasonably want to know whether the data were weighted by sex (i.e., adjusted to match the population distribution), since an un-

---

[1]Sometimes *estimates* of this difference are possible from samples of nonrespondents. Typically, such samples are interviewed using an alternative data collection method which, while more expensive, achieves a higher response rate. The most common example is a phone survey follow-up of a sample of nonrespondents to a mail questionnaire.

weighted estimate would overestimate the proportion of the total population that has purchased a weapon for protection.

Last, on the issue of item refusals, we might expect that respondents who refused to answer the question are more likely to have purchased a weapon than those who responded. This is true for two reasons: First, many people may consider buying a weapon a private and somewhat sensitive matter and, therefore, may not want to answer; second, respondents who bought a weapon but did not get a permit or follow other legal requirements may be reluctant to admit the purchase. For both these reasons, we might be concerned that the 23% "yes" figure is an underestimate.

In the absence of such supplementary information, it is hard to know what to think about the 23% finding. We can now see how a sample statistic in itself can sometimes be quite uninformative outside of its methodological context.

In many instances, despite strenuous efforts, the distribution of our sample's demographic characteristics differs sufficiently from that of the population whose weights are used to make adjustments. This use of weighting is common enough—and has a large enough potential effect on results—to merit more detailed treatment.

Let us assume that of 800 statewide interviews, 560 (70%) are with urban respondents and 240 (30%) are with rural respondents. Assume further that on a different yes/no question, these urban respondents were split 40% "yes" and 60% "no"; while rural respondents answered 87% "yes" and 13% "no." The combined results, shown in Exhibit 10.1, give a statewide sample estimate of 54% "yes" and 46% "no."

Assume that we examine recent census data and find that 85% of the state's adult residents live in urban areas. We then have seriously underrepresented that part of the population in our survey and, consequently, overrepresented rural residents. This incorrect representation affects our state finding. We correct for this by applying a weight that adjusts the urban-rural split to match census data. We do this by counting each urban respondent slightly more than once and each rural respondent less than once. The weight, in this example, is simply the ratio of the census percentage to our sample percentage.[2] The weighted result is shown in the bottom half of Exhibit 10.1. We now have a weighted state sample estimate of 47% "yes" and 53% "no," almost the reverse of the unweighted figure!

[2] As an exercise, the reader should compute the weights from these percentages and regenerate the second half of Exhibit 10.1.

Exhibit 10.1

A Comparison of Unweighted and Weighted Data

	Unweighted Estimate		
	Urban	Rural	Total
Yes	224 (.4)	209 (.87)	433 (.54)
No	336 (.6)	31 (.13)	367 (.46)
Total	560	240	800
Percent	70%	30%	100%

	Weighted Estimate		
	Urban	Rural	Total
Yes	272 (.4)	104 (.87)	376 (.47)
No	408 (.6)	16 (.13)	424 (.53)
Total	680	120	800
Percent	85%	15%	100%

This extreme, but not wholly unrealistic, example suggests a few important points about weights that anyone writing a methods report (or analyzing survey data) should be aware of. First, weights can have nontrivial effects on the resulting estimates. They are often required by the sample design (as we have seen in the chapter on sampling) or, as in this example, to handle differential nonresponse. They are not optional niceties to be used or not according to the researcher's personal preferences, and they must be handled competently and carefully.[3]

Second, weights are effective in addressing nonresponse bias only if the respondents do not differ significantly from the nonrespondents. We applied a weight to urban respondents because they had a lower response rate than rural residents and so were underrepresented in the sample. That weight is wholly successful only if the urban respondents are similar on substantive items to the urban nonrespondents. The rather large weights used for purposes of illustration added 120 cases to the urban sample; this is, in effect, the 120

[3]The standard statistical packages, such as SPSS and SAS, allow for inclusion of weights to produce these estimates. Still, it is useful to do several calculations by hand to get a real sense of how weights affect results.

interviews we would have obtained had we achieved perfect urban-rural representation. In essence, we are saying that those "missing" respondents would have answered in the same manner as the ones we interviewed—that is, we kept the weighted yes/no distribution the same as the unweighted distribution.

In truth, we do not know how effective the weight is in addressing nonresponse bias. It is likely that it is at least partially effective. But, because of the uncertainty, we should include a careful discussion of differential nonresponse (particularly if it is as serious as in this example) in the methods report.

Last, we note that the weights have an effect on overall estimates only if there are differences between the groups being weighted. If the yes/no distribution for the urban and rural residents did not differ, the weights would have had no effect on the statewide result *for this particular item*. But, again, we must remember that the survey consists of many variables; some may be affected, others may not.

Another reason for providing a detailed methodological report is to aid comparison to other studies. If, for example, returning to the weapons question, two separate studies ask the same question but obtain different estimates that are greater than can be accounted for by sampling error, one would want to know why. If the Maryland crime survey, based on 800 interviews, found that 23% of respondents had purchased a weapon, that estimate would have a standard error of approximately 2.9% at the 95% confidence level. If the same question, asked of 700 respondents in Virginia, got a 40% "yes" result, it would be subject to a standard error of 3.6%, also at the 95% confidence level. The range, *based on sampling error alone,* for the Maryland result would be 20.1% to 25.9%; and for the Virginia result, 36.4% to 43.6%. Clearly, the highest estimate for Maryland is much lower than the lowest Virginia estimate.[4]

The different findings may, of course, reflect true differences between the states where the studies were done. It could simply be that more Virginia residents purchase weapons than do people in Maryland. But such dissimilar results may also be a by-product, or artifact, of the survey methodology.

In trying to understand these differences, we would look first at major aspects of the two surveys. If the method of data collection

---

[4]As an exercise, the reader should compute these standard errors at the 68%, 90%, and 99% confidence levels. Note that the calculations ignore the finite population correction and do not take a design effect into account. How might these two factors affect the sampling error estimates?

was not the same, that might account for the difference. Respondents may be more willing by mail to admit obtaining a weapon than they would in a telephone or face-to-face interview. Perhaps the position of the item in the questionnaire might have an effect. If one survey asked the item very early, before the survey's legitimacy or rapport with the respondent were solidly established, it might show lower rates of weapons purchase than a survey that asked the question later in the interview. Finally, if the two surveys were conducted by different organizations (or research teams) the difference might be due to a "house effect"—that is, something about the way interviewers are generally trained to conduct interviews, such as probing "don't know" responses or not, might affect the results. And, of course, the different findings might not be due to any single methodological difference but to some combination of them.

For example, such a combination might result if the question is asked earlier in the Maryland survey, leading to lower reporting. If the Virginia survey were done by mail instead of by phone, as it was in Maryland, this difference could add to the effect. In this instance, both effects are in the same direction—producing higher Virginia reporting. Such multiple effects could also pull in opposite directions, making our assessment even more complex. Finally, if Virginia has less stringent gun-purchase laws than Maryland,[5] more Virginia residents may have actually bought guns, *and* more Maryland respondents who bought guns may have done so illegally and thus have been reluctant to report the purchase. In this case, the different survey results could partly reflect true population differences and partly reflect a differential willingness to report the behavior. Clearly, trying to make comparisons between surveys may introduce enormous complications; but ignoring them may lead to conclusions that the survey results really do not support.

In all these examples, it is clear that the reader or data analyst must know the details of the survey methods in order to use the results appropriately. Therefore, the careful researcher is obliged to provide information about those aspects of the survey methodology that clearly or potentially bear on the survey's quality or on the interpretation of its findings. Some of this information, such as sampling errors, can be provided quantitatively, while other methodological points are typically descriptive. If we note all the kinds of

---

[5]And we assume guns are the main weapon people buy for protection.

methods decisions and their consequences, the list is quite long. Trying to address all of them would usually be prohibitively costly and time-consuming. Rather than providing all or nothing, we most often settle on some subset of methodological items.

What to Include in the Methodology Report

Exhibit 10.2 lists many of the survey characteristics that are often included in a methodology report, sometimes called an error profile or quality profile. We will give brief examples of what might be included in a methods report for each of these items and then note guidelines for deciding, in a particular survey, which issues are advisable or essential to report and which are less crucial.

Exhibit 10.2
Quality Profile

Sampling:
- sample design
- sampling errors
- frame problems: coverage

Data Collection:
- instrument development: pretesting special methods, cognitive procedures
- data collection: interviewer training, field period, callbacks, quality control/monitoring (verification)
- response bias: questionnaire problems
- unit nonresponse: response, refusal, and cooperation rates; screening
- special procedures: samples of nonrespondents, refusal conversion, incentives
- nonresponse bias: differential nonresponse by subgroups

Estimation:
- weights and estimation
- item nonresponse: edits and imputation
- data entry and coding: entry verification and entry errors, open-end coding

Sample Design

The methods report often begins with a discussion of the sampling design. This section provides a framework for the remainder of the report as well as a background for later discussion of frames, weighting, estimation, and other issues. It also begins to tell the reader whether the design was efficient in light of the study's primary objectives.

This section should, at a minimum, include the operational definition of the survey's target population and a general description of the main objectives and features of the sampling method—for example, whether stratification, clustering, or multistage selection was employed.

If stratification was used, was it proportional, disproportional, or some combination of the two? If disproportional stratification was used, the researcher should note whether the main reason was to provide sufficient cases for separate subgroup analysis, to compare subgroups, or something else. Within strata, were elements selected with equal probabilities or not? The definitions of the strata should, of course, be provided as well.

Sampling Errors

Sampling error is the most commonly reported measure of a survey's precision. It is often inadvisably reported in lieu of nonsampling errors. While this imbalance is inappropriate, every methodology report should still address the issue of sampling errors and, if at all possible, provide sampling errors for all or key variables or provide a generalized table that can be used for many of the study variables.[6] If the sample in our study is a simple random sample (or a systematic random sample), this task is simple. Statistical packages provide simple random sampling errors (often labeled standard errors[7]) routinely in their output. Unfortunately, in many cases, the

---

[6]Such a table is constructed by averaging the sampling errors for a wide range of study variables. These averages are then given in a table for splits on percentages of 90/10, 80/20, 70/30, 60/40, and 50/50. The table can then be used to find the *approximate* sampling errors for particular questions whose results can be expressed as percentage dichotomies. As an exercise, the reader should compute sampling errors at the 95% confidence level (assuming simple random sampling) for subsamples of 100, 200, 300, and 400.

[7]The standard error is the standard deviation divided by the square root of the sample size. Typically, one or two standard errors, corresponding to the 68% or 95% confidence levels, are given in methods reports.

sample design may be quite different from a simple random sample.[8] As we have seen, designs often involve stratification, clustering, or multiple stages of selection, frequently along with design, nonresponse, and post-stratification weights. In these cases, the simple random sampling errors will overstate (sometimes greatly) the precision of the measures.

What alternatives are available? For many designs, sampling errors can be computed by means of textbook mathematical formulas.[9] These calculations, however, are not necessarily simple, even for a moderate-size data set. The formulas need to be programmed and linked to the data.

A more realistic alternative is to use one of the software packages specifically designed for computing sampling errors (or design effects[10]) that take into account the specific sample design and weighting procedures. The most widely used package (for the IBM PC) for this purpose is SUDAAN (SUrvey DAta ANalysis) from Research Triangle Institute. The details of its implementation are beyond the scope of this book, but written manuals and short course instruction are available.

If even this cost (or level of programming expertise) is beyond our resources, then we may have to settle for a compromise guesstimate based on design effects noted in studies with designs similar to ours. This is a very risky approach, but one that, in many instances, is preferable either to reporting nothing or to reporting erroneous simple random sampling errors.[11]

Frame Problems: Undercoverage

The main sampling frame issue for the methods report is undercoverage, since presumably any other frame problems, such as

[8]It is very important to remember that an equal probability of selection method (epsem sample) is not at all the equivalent of a simple random sample. Many very complex designs may result in equal probabilities of selection, but their sampling errors are quite different from those of a simple random sample.

[9]See, for example, Kish, 1965.

[10]Design effect is the ratio of the variance of a complex design to that of a simple random sample of the same size (Kish, 1965). Once design effects are available, they can be used to convert simple random sampling standard errors to the correct complex ones (see chapter 7). These converted sampling errors are then used in the manner discussed above to generate a table of sampling errors appropriate to the particular sample design.

[11]If the methods description does not discuss this issue, the unsophisticated reader will sometimes assume that simple random sampling errors apply.

overcoverage and multiplicity, have been handled in the sampling, data collection, or estimation stages. The kinds of statements we can make are often fairly general, but they may still be informative—for example, "The telephone directories were 8 months old. Therefore, there were some omissions of new residents, but the percentage cannot be specified." Such a statement is useful if, on a particular set of variables, we note differences between long-term and newer residents. Even though the reader of our results cannot specify the bias in the estimates, at least something is known of its direction. Similarly, if we had to use a student directory as the frame at mid–academic year, we might note: "The directory did not contain students who enrolled in the spring semester. Based on past data from the university administration, about 10% of entering students enroll in the spring." The importance of including such statements depends on two things: the percentage of undercoverage and its likely relationship to our study variables. Admittedly, these are rough guidelines. Ideally, we would like to know both the direction and the magnitude of undercoverage bias. But if only one is known, that is much better than nothing at all.

When writing the methods report, we should not overlook the positive aspects of our study. It may be that we incorporated a full RDD design for which there is no frame undercoverage. Such design strengths should, here and elsewhere in the report, also be included.

Instrument Development: Pretesting and Special Methods

The methods report should briefly note the number and types of pretests conducted and whether this testing was confined to conventional pretesting or also included cognitive tests, behavior coding, focus groups, expert panels, or combinations of these methods.

If, even after pretesting, we suspect that some problematic questions remain, this should be discussed. Recall the following question from the student survey:

```
Most of the time you drank alcohol, on the
average, how many drinks did you have at
one time?
```

It could well be that, from conducting cognitive pretest interviews, we learned that respondents who drank alcohol on an irregular basis, say mainly at special social events, had difficulty coming up with an average. Even though we recognized this problem and could not completely eliminate it, the question was so central to our analysis that we decided to include it anyway. It is useful for the reader of our results to know that for these occasional drinkers, the results may be subject to somewhat more measurement error than for the respondent who, say, always has one drink with dinner or occasionally goes to "happy hour" on Friday afternoons. For these and other measurement problems, researchers are sometimes reluctant to mention such shortcomings. But as Sudman (1976) noted about discussions of sample-design biases, far from detracting from the value of the survey, these types of details make it much more useful by giving an indication of the study's limitations. Once again, how much of this type of information we choose to include depends on our judgment of the potential effect of such flaws on key variables—or on the readers' appreciation of the survey's strengths, weaknesses, and generalizability.

Data Collection: Interviewer Training, Data Collection Procedures, and Quality Control

The methods report should note when the data were collected. This is usually trivial, but it can be important if some variables may have seasonal effects (e.g., a survey asking about recreational activities), or if a public event occurred that might have affected some results (e.g., a widely reported heinous crime that occurred during our crime survey data collection could reduce people's willingness to consider alternative, nonjail sentencing).

A quick summary of the interviewer training should also be given, along with any especially important question-by-question instructions interviewers were given for handling particular problems or questions. For example, consider the question:

```
Suppose a [fill AGE]-year-old is convicted of
selling $[fill AMOUNT] worth of cocaine. He has
[fill NUMBER] prior convictions. Do you think he
should be sent to prison, required to report to a
probation officer once a month, required to report
daily, or monitored so his whereabouts are known
at ALL times?
            1 SENT TO PRISON
            2 REQUIRED TO REPORT ONCE A MONTH
            3 REQUIRED TO REPORT TO A PROBATION
              OFFICER DAILY
```

    4 MONITORED SO HIS WHEREABOUTS ARE KNOWN
      AT ALL TIMES?
    8 DK

Respondents might ask various questions such as, Do such monitoring devices really exist? or, What would happen if the person missed
reporting to the probation officer? If interviewers were instructed, in
the former case, to say that such devices do exist and, in the latter,
that the probation officer would decide what would happen, this
may be worth mentioning in the report. If there were many instances
of such special instructions, a report appendix that listed all instructions to interviewers might be advisable.

   The number of callbacks and the general rule for how they were
scheduled should be mentioned, as well as the percentage of calls
monitored or verified. Many surveys aim to monitor 10–15% of interviews, but it is our impression that this number usually includes
many interviews for which only portions were monitored.

Response Bias: Questionnaire Problems

If we have reason to believe, say from monitoring interviews in
progress or from interviewers' comments, that particular questions
caused problems for respondents, this should be mentioned as well.
It may be, for example, that many respondents expressed confusion
or resisted using the closed-response categories provided for a particular question. In most cases, we will have addressed such issues
during the development of the questionnaire. But if, even after these
efforts, problems appear to remain, it is the researcher's obligation to
report them.

Unit Nonresponse: Response, Refusal, and Cooperation Rates

Unlike some other indicators of survey quality, the survey rates are
never an optional report item. The issue is not whether to report, but
how. The terms *response, refusal, cooperation,* and *completion rates,*
among others, are used by different researchers to mean quite different things. While there have been recommendations (see CASRO report, 1982; Groves, 1989; and Hidiroglou, Drew, and Gray, 1993) for
the computation and presentation of these rates, they have not been
universally adopted. We propose a simple set of rates that are widely

accepted, but more importantly we urge that the researcher show exactly how the rates for the particular study were computed and what rules govern the sample dispositions that go into those rates.

In the general population telephone survey, recall that the major call results fall into three areas: nonhouseholds (or other ineligibles), households, and household (or other eligibility) status unknown. Nonhouseholds are fairly clear—numbers that are not working or are connected to businesses or other organizations, hotels, group quarters and so forth.[12] Within the household category, we will have interviews, refusals, and various types of noncontacts for identified (nonrefusal) households where the selected respondent, after the requisite number of contact attempts, was never contacted for a variety of reasons that last the length of the study, such as travel, vacation, an illness or injury, or constant use of an answering machine. In addition, some nonresponse will be due to households where only languages other than English are spoken. If these cases are eligible according to the study definition, then they must be included in the computation of rates. Finally, even after extensive callbacks, there will remain some (relatively small) number of telephone numbers whose household status cannot be determined. To count either all or none of these as eligible would be wrong; the most reasonable compromise is to consider a percentage of them as eligible households. The best guide we have for this is the household percentage for those numbers we were able to determine.

Returning to Exhibit 9.3, we note that of the 1,816 initial sample numbers, 702 were found to be nonhouseholds of various types, 1,061 were households, and 53 could not be determined after 20 calls. We recommend, as is common practice, using the 1,061 identified households as the lower bound on the denominator for computing the response rate and the refusal and noncontact rates, as shown in the exhibit.

To compute an upper bound, we note that 1,763 (1,061 + 702) telephone numbers were classified as households or not; of this total, about 60% (1,061/1,763) were households. If we apply this same percentage to the 53 undetermined cases, we would add 32 cases to the denominator, thus decreasing the response rate from 78% (824/1,061) to 75.4% (824/{1,061 + 32}). This procedure provides a range of

---

[12]For a complete definition of the types of dwelling units, see U.S. Bureau of the Census, *1990 Census of Population and Housing: Guide, Part A. Text* (Washington, DC: U.S. Government Printing Office, 1992).

response rates depending on the assumptions made about the telephone numbers whose household status is unknown.

A final rate that is often presented is the cooperation rate. This is computed as the number of interviews divided by the interviews plus the refusals and partial interviews. The value of this rate is to show how well the field operation did among those households that were actually contacted *and* included an eligible respondent. This rate is especially valuable in two situations. First, during data collection, we want to track the success of the field operation. While interviewing is going on there are a large number of noncontacts, so the response rate is naturally low and not a good indicator of how well things are going. Second, sometimes the data collection period is so short that few callbacks can be made. This might occur for reasons such as wanting to measure public reaction to a news event. Again, the result is a large number of noncontacts. In both situations the cooperation rate will be a better indicator of interviewing success than the response rate.

Special Procedures: Samples of Nonrespondents and Refusal Conversion

Any special procedures that were used as part of the data collection effort, such as refusal conversion or special follow-ups of samples of nonrespondents, should be described. The description should explain the procedure used and how successful (or not) the effort was. Additionally, if a large proportion of the cases (say, 15% or more) resulted from these efforts, it is useful to report whether these respondents differed on key variables (at statistically significant levels[13]) from the other sample respondents.

Nonresponse Bias: Patterns of Nonresponse and the Use of Weights

If unit nonresponse does not appear to be randomly distributed through the population, and especially if the pattern correlates with any substantive variables, a discussion should be included. If, in a statewide survey, for example, there is much poorer response in urban than in rural areas, this should be mentioned, even, perhaps especially, if weighting corrections have been made. If weights are

[13]Chi-square tests of crosstabulations would suffice for this comparison.

used to adjust for nonresponse, unequal selection probabilities, or poststratification, this should be reported, though the weights themselves may not be given in the methods report.

Estimation

In most small-scale surveys, the estimation procedures—that is, how we convert the sample estimates into estimates of the corresponding population parameters—are very simple, even self-evident. When this is not the case, then the mathematical form of the estimators should be included in the report. For most research done by the novice, this will not be necessary.

Item Nonresponse and Imputation

In most reports little, if anything, is said about item nonresponse. The guideline for inclusion in the report is whether there is anything unusual. For example, any items that exceed, say, 5% nonresponse should be mentioned. But, as is true for unit nonresponse, the distribution of the responses is an indicator of how important the nonresponse is for the findings. As we have noted, items are often not missing at random but follow a pattern; that pattern may affect our analysis.

Imputation is the substitution of constructed values for items that are either not answered or whose answers are not consistent with other responses in the same interview. These constructed values are most often based on *other* cases in the data set or on information from other variables in the *same* case. This is not a common practice in small-scale surveys, and we do not recommend it for the novice researcher. If the level of item nonresponse is sufficiently high that key analyses are jeopardized (say for particular subgroups), then imputation may be worth consideration. In such a case, the reader should consult Kalton (1981) for a discussion of alternative imputation procedures. Our main recommendation is to develop and test procedures to minimize item nonresponse problems beforehand, rather than trying to correct for them afterward.

Data Entry and Coding: Entry Error, Open-Ends

The error rate, or percentage of all key strokes estimated to be incorrect, for data entry is typically not reported unless there is some extraordinary general problem. A particular difficulty in coding certain items should be reported as well. If that does occur, it is usually for open-ended items. Such problems and their solutions should be discussed. In many instances, having monitored the pretest interviews closely and coded the pretest cases for practice researchers will avoid having to explain such problems in the methods report.

For Further Study: Suggested Readings

In this short book we have focused on the decisions and procedures that the novice researcher needs to address in conducting small-scale surveys. It is our hope that such a narrow focus is most appropriate to the many practical problems the first-time survey researcher confronts, but we realize that it may also give a distorted "cookbook" depiction of the field of survey research. That would be a disservice to both the discipline and to the reader with broader intellectual interests.

In recent years, building on the classic works of the field's pioneer researchers and practitioners, every area of survey research has witnessed high levels of methodological research and conceptual development. In questionnaire development, such seminal works of research and application as Payne's *The Art of Asking Questions* (1951), Schuman and Presser's *Questions and Answers in Attitude Surveys* (1981), and Sudman and Bradburn's *Asking Questions* (1982) have been built upon, most notably in the application of cognitive psychology to instrument design and data collection method. Beginning with Jabine, et al., *Cognitive Aspects of Survey Methodology* (1984), through Tanur's *Questions about Questions* (1992) and a series of books of collected papers from conferences organized by Schwarz, Sudman, and their colleagues,[14] this area has had explosive growth in the last ten years.

Much of the classic early work on sampling theory and methods such as Kish's *Survey Sampling* (1965) and Cochran's *Sampling Techniques* (1977), along with practical guides like Sudman's *Applied Sampling* (1976), has been carried on in books such as Sarndal et al., *Model-Assisted Survey Sampling* (1992). Even a brief list such as this

[14]Among these are Hippler et al. (eds.), *Social Information Processing and Survey Methodology* (1987); Schwarz and Sudman, *Autobiographical Memory and the Validity of Retrospective Reports* (1994); and Schwarz and Sudman, *Context Effects in Social and Psychological Research* (1992).

would be remiss if it omitted key works in data collection such as Dillman's *Mail and Telephone Surveys: The Total Design Method* (1978); in measurement error, Turner and Martin's *Surveying Subjective Phenomena* (2 Vols.) (1984); in general design issues, Kish's *Statistical Design for Research* (1987); and the wide-ranging Groves' *Survey Errors and Survey Costs* (1989). Finally, we should note that a series of conferences sponsored by the major survey research professional associations has produced several valuable books on particular areas of survey research. These include Groves et al., *Telephone Survey Methodology* (1988), Biemer et al., *Measurement Errors in Surveys* (1991), and Kasprzyk et al., *Panel Surveys* (1989). Finally, there are journal articles and conference proceedings too numerous to even attempt listing.

While a comprehensive reading of these sources would be of interest only to the professional researcher, we strongly recommend them—even for the relative novice—as references to each aspect of the survey process. True, they contain much theory, but they are also readable and give practical advice and explanations of fundamental concepts and concerns that can be found nowhere else. Even the student who devotes a few days to browsing through these works will be rewarded with useful insights from the best in the discipline as well as an overview of an exciting new research territory.

Appendix A
University of Maryland
Undergraduate Student Survey

Confidential. Do not sign your name.

For each question, unless otherwise instructed, please circle the number for the ONE response which best reflects your opinion.

The Book Center

1. How often have you shopped at the Book Center this semester, that is, since January?

    ```
    1. just once or twice
    2. less than once a week
    3. about once a week
    4. more than once a week
    5. or not at all ===> go to question 10
    ```

2. Have you shopped for *new textbooks* at the Book Center this semester?

    ```
    0. no ===> Go to question 4
    1. yes
    ```

3. How satisfied were you with the *new textbook's* quality, cost, and selection?

	VERY SATISFIED	SOMEWHAT SATISFIED	SOMEWHAT DISSATISFIED	VERY DISSATISFIED
a. Quality	1	2	3	4
b. Cost	1	2	3	4
c. Selection	1	2	3	4

4. Have you shopped for *general supplies* such as pens and paper at the Book Center this semester?

    ```
    0. no ===> Go to question 6
    1. yes
    ```

5. How satisfied were you with the general supplies' quality, cost, and selection?

	VERY SATISFIED	SOMEWHAT SATISFIED	SOMEWHAT DISSATISFIED	VERY DISSATISFIED
a. Quality	1	2	3	4
b. Cost	1	2	3	4
c. Selection	1	2	3	4

6. Have you used the Book Center this semester to *special order* books or other materials for your classes?

```
0. no ====> go to question 9
1. yes
```

7. How satisfied were you with the special order service?

```
1. very satisfied          3. somewhat dissatisfied
2. somewhat satisfied       4. very dissatisfied
        ⇓                            ⇓
```

7a. What was the MAIN reason for your satisfaction?

b. What was the MAIN reason for your dissatisfaction?

```
1. timeliness              1. timeliness
2. selection               2. selection
3. cost                    3. cost
4. service                 4. service
5. something else _____   5. something else _____
   (please specify)           (please specify)
```

8. What one thing can the Book Center do that would most improve the special order services?

_____

_____

9. In general how would you rate the Book Center staff's helpfulness, courtesy, and knowledge of products and services?

		GOOD	EXCELLENT	FAIR	POOR	NO EXPERIENCE/ NO OPINION
a.	Helpfulness	1	2	3	4	8
b.	Courtesy	1	2	3	4	8
c.	Knowledge of products & services	1	2	3	4	8

Academic Advising

10. Since you have been at UMCP, on average, how often have you met with an academic advisor?

    1. Never
    2. Less than once a semester
    3. Once a semester
    4. Twice a semester
    5. Three times a semester
    6. More than three times a semester

11. Is your current advisor:

    1. Professional advisor (full-time nonfaculty advisor)
    2. Peer (undergraduate student)
    3. Graduate Assistant
    4. Faculty
    5. Secretary
    8. Don't know
    9. No current advisor

12. What type of advisor do you prefer?

    1. Professional advisor (full-time nonfaculty advisor)
    2. Peer (undergraduate student)
    3. Graduate Assistant
    4. Faculty
    5. Secretary
    6. No preference

13. Have you ever had a peer advisor?

    Yes
    No ===> skip to question 14

13a. Do you think that a peer advisor should be at least the same class rank as the student, or does it not matter?

    1. Should be at least the same class rank
    2. Class rank does not matter

14. How important is it to you that your academic advisor provide:

	VERY IMPORTANT	SOMEWHAT IMPORTANT	NOT VERY IMPORTANT	NOT AT ALL IMPORTANT
a. Information on academic requirements for graduation?	1	2	3	4
b. Referrals to other campus services?	1	2	3	4
c. Walk-in advising sessions?	1	2	3	4
d. Help deciding which courses to take each semester?	1	2	3	4
e. Advice on planning your undergraduate program?	1	2	3	4

15. Since you have been at UMCP, how helpful to you has advising been in general?

    1. Very helpful
    2. Somewhat helpful
    3. Not too helpful
    4. Not at all helpful

16. How helpful has advising been in assisting you in selecting elective courses?

    1. Very helpful
    2. Somewhat helpful
    3. Not too helpful
    4. Not at all helpful
    5. No experience

17. How helpful has advising been to you in making decisions about academic goals?

    1. Very helpful
    2. Somewhat helpful
    3. Not too helpful
    4. Not at all helpful
    5. No experience

18. What is your current grade point average (GPA)?

```
1.  3.6-4.0
2.  3.0-3.5
3.  2.5-2.9
4.  2.4 or below
```

19. Compared with other students of your class rank, do you think your grade point average (GPA) is:

```
1.  a great deal above average
2.  somewhat above average
3.  average
4.  somewhat below average
5.  a great deal below average
```

20. Compared with students of your class rank and *your race,* do you think your grade point average (GPA) is:

```
1.  a great deal above average
2.  somewhat above average
3.  average
4.  somewhat below average
5.  a great deal below average
```

21. How frequently have each of the following happened to you?
[If you don't know (DK) or if you're not sure, circle 8.]

	OFTEN	SOMETIMES	RARELY	NEVER	DK
a. I have received unfair grades because of my race.	1	2	3	4	8
b. I have had teachers of my race who expect me to do better than students of other races.	1	2	3	4	8
c. I have had teachers of other races who expect me to do less well than students of their race.	1	2	3	4	8

Treatment of Black Students

This section is about how you think black students are treated by others.

22. How frequently have you observed the following anti-black behaviors on campus?

	OFTEN	SOMETIMES	RARELY	NEVER
a. Racist comments by students	1	2	3	4
b. Exclusion from social events because of race	1	2	3	4
c. Racist comments by faculty	1	2	3	4
d. Discrimination in awards and honors	1	2	3	4

23. What was the racial make-up of the high school from which you graduated?

1. About equally black and white
2. Predominantly black
3. Predominantly white

Alcohol and Drugs

24. What is the university's maximum penalty for the following violations:

	PROBATION	DRUG TESTING	LOSS OF HOUSING	SUSPENSION	EXPULSION	DON'T KNOW
a. Possession or use of illegal drugs	1	2	3	4	5	8
b. The underage possession of alcohol	1	2	3	4	5	8
c. Sale or distribution of illegal drugs	1	2	3	4	5	8
d. Providing alcohol to someone under 21	1	2	3	4	5	8
e. Drinking on campus	1	2	3	4	5	8

25. Overall, how familiar are you with the campus policies concerning . . .

	VERY FAMILIAR	FAMILIAR	NOT VERY FAMILIAR	UNFAMILIAR
a. Possession or use of illegal drugs	1	2	3	4
b. Sale or distribution of illegal drugs	1	2	3	4
c. Drug testing	1	2	3	4
d. The underage possession of alcohol	1	2	3	4
e. Providing alcohol to someone under 21	1	2	3	4
f. Drinking on campus	1	2	3	4

26. Depending on the circumstances of the case, some students found responsible for the possession and/or use of illegal drugs are given the option of random drug testing for a period of two years in lieu of actual suspension from the University.

How fair do you think this policy is? (circle one)

VERY FAIR	FAIR	UNFAIR	VERY UNFAIR	NO OPINION
1	2	3	4	8

27. How do you feel about . . .

	SUPPORT	STRONGLY SUPPORT	OPPOSE	STRONGLY OPPOSE	IT DEPENDS
a. Undercover investigation on campus	1	2	3	4	9
b. Mandatory expulsion	1	2	3	4	9
c. Random police patrols of residence halls	1	2	3	4	9
d. Laws against drinking alcohol during football games	1	2	3	4	9

28. Assuming you wanted to, how easy do you think it would be for you to get the following on campus?

		VERY EASY	EASY	DIFFICULT	VERY DIFFICULT	IMPOSSIBLE
a.	Marijuana/Hashish	1	2	3	4	5
b.	Cocaine/Crack	1	2	3	4	5
c.	LSD (Acid)	1	2	3	4	5
d.	Amphetamines (Speed)	1	2	3	4	5
e.	Alcohol	1	2	3	4	5

29. How often in the *last 12 months* have you used the following drugs?

		NEVER	1-2 TIMES	3-10 TIMES	MONTHLY	WEEKLY	DAILY
a.	Marijuana/Hashish	1	2	3	4	5	6
b.	Cocaine/Crack	1	2	3	4	5	6
c.	LSD (Acid)	1	2	3	4	5	6
d.	Amphetamines (Speed)	1	2	3	4	5	6
e.	Alcohol	1	2	3	4	5	6

30a. Most of the time you drank alcohol, on the average, how many drinks did you have at one time? _____

[One drink = a beer, a mixed drink, or a glass of wine]

☐ Have not drunk alcohol

30b. If you never used illegal drugs, or have not used them in the last year, what was your *main reason for NOT using them*? (Please circle *one*.)

1. It's against my beliefs
2. It's against the law
3. Others disapprove
4. Hard to get
5. Concerns about physical health
6. Did not get desired effect
7. Had bad experience with drugs
8. No desire
9. Other: _____

31. If you never used alcohol, or have not used it in the last year, what was your *main reason for NOT using it*?
(Please circle *one*.)

```
1.  It's against my beliefs
2.  It's against the law
3.  Others disapprove
4.  Hard to get
5.  Concerns about physical health
6.  Did not get desired effect
7.  Had bad experience with alcohol
8.  No desire
9.  Other
```

Demographic Information

D1. Are you:

```
1.  Male
2.  Female
```

D2. Are you:

```
1.  White, Non-Hispanic
2.  Black or African-American, Non-Hispanic
3.  Mexican American, Puerto Rican, or other Hispanic
4.  Asian American
5.  Native American, American Indian
6.  Other: _____
```

D3. Are you currently a:

```
1.  Freshman
2.  Sophomore
3.  Junior
4.  Senior
```

D4. How old were you on your last birthday? _____

D5. In what college are you currently enrolled? _____

D6. What type of institution did you attend just before coming to UMCP?

```
1.  High school
2.  Transferred from a 2-year college
3.  Transferred from a 4-year college
4.  Returning after an absence
```

THANK YOU FOR COMPLETING THIS QUESTIONNAIRE.

ALL YOUR ANSWERS ARE COMPLETELY CONFIDENTIAL.

PLEASE RETURN THE QUESTIONNAIRE IN THE ENCLOSED ENVELOPE.

Appendix B
Maryland Crime Survey

Hello, I'm calling from the University of Maryland. My name is
_____. We are doing a study for the state of Maryland's
Summit on Violent Street Crime. I need to speak with the adult in
your household, who is 18 or older and will have the NEXT birthday. Who would that be?

1. In general, would you say that the crime problem in YOUR
   NEIGHBORHOOD is very serious, somewhat serious, not very
   serious, or not at all serious?

   ```
   1 very serious
   2 somewhat serious
   3 not very serious
   4 not at all serious
   8 dk
   ```

2. In general, would you say that the crime problem in THE
   STATE is very serious, somewhat serious, not very serious or
   not at all serious?

   ```
   1 very serious
   2 somewhat serious
   3 not very serious
   4 not at all serious
   8 dk
   ```

3. In the past year, would you say that there is more VIOLENT
   crime in YOUR NEIGHBORHOOD, less, or about the same?

   ```
   1 more
   2 less
   3 about the same
   8 dk
   ```

4. In the past year, would you say that there was more VIOLENT crime in THE STATE, less, or about the same?

```
1 more
2 less
3 about the same
8 dk
```

5. In the past year, did anything happen to you or your property that you thought was a crime or an attempt at a crime?

```
0 no      [go to question 7]
1 yes
8 dk
```

6. Were you personally threatened or was force used against you?

```
0 no
1 yes
8 dk
```

7. In the past year, did anything happen to anyone (else) in your household that they thought was a crime or an attempt at a crime?

```
0 no      [go to question 9]
1 yes
8 dk
```

8. Were they personally threatened or was force used against them?

```
0 no
1 yes
8 dk
```

9. In the coming year, how likely it is that you, or someone in your household, will be robbed or mugged? Would you say:

```
1 very likely
2 somewhat likely
3 not too likely
4 not at all likely
8 dk
```

10. In the coming year, how likely is it that your home will be broken into? Would you say:

```
1 very likely
2 somewhat likely
3 not too likely
4 not at all likely
8 dk
```

11. Next I want to ask you about some things you may have done within the past year to protect yourself or your family against crime.

   Within the past year, have you joined a community crime-prevention program?

```
0 no
1 yes
8 dk
```

12. (Within the past year, have you) had extra locks put on doors or windows?

```
0 no
1 yes
8 dk
```

13. (Within the past year, have you) had a burglar alarm installed in your home?

```
0 no
1 yes
8 dk
```

14. (Within the past year, have you) taken self-defense training?

```
0 no
1 yes
8 dk
```

15. (Within the past year, have you) gotten a dog for protection?

```
0 no
1 yes
8 dk
```

16. (Within the past year, have you) purchased a gun or other weapon for protection?

```
0 no
1 yes
8 dk
```

17. When you are not at home, how often do you leave your lights on because of concerns about crime? Would you say:

```
1 always
2 frequently
3 seldom
4 or never
8 dk
```

18. When you are out, how often do you have neighbors watch your home because of concerns about crime? Would you say:

```
1 always
2 frequently
3 seldom
4 or never
8 dk
```

19. How often do you avoid certain areas that you'd like to go to because of concerns about crime? Would you say:

```
1 always
2 frequently
3 seldom
4 or never
8 dk
```

20. How often do you avoid going out alone because of concerns about crime? Would you say:

```
1 always
2 frequently
3 seldom
4 or never
8 dk
```

21. How often do you carry a weapon for protection because of concerns about crime? Would you say:

```
1 always
2 frequently
3 seldom
4 or never
8 dk
```

22. Three important parts of the criminal justice system are the police, the courts, and the prisons. I'd like to ask you about the job each is doing.

    Do you think that the police are doing an excellent, good, fair, or poor job?

```
1 excellent [go to 23]
2 good [go to 23]
3 fair
4 poor
8 dk [go to 23]
```

22a. Why is that? _____

23. How do you feel the courts are doing? (Are they doing an excellent, good, fair or poor job?)

```
1 excellent [go to 24]
2 good [go to 24]
3 fair
4 poor
8 dk [go to 24]
```

23a. Why is that? _____

24. (How about) the prisons? (Are they doing an excellent, good, fair, or poor job?)

```
1 excellent [go to 25]
2 good [go to 25]
3 fair
4 poor
8 dk [go to 25]
```

24a. Why is that? _____

25. Would you be willing to pay $100 a year in extra taxes to build more prisons in Maryland?

```
0  no
1  yes
8  dk
```

26. Not everyone convicted of a crime can be put in prison. Maryland prisons are seriously overcrowded. It costs $17,000 to keep someone in prison for a year.

As a result, many people are not sent to prison but sentenced to report to a probation officer ONCE A MONTH.

One alternative would be to require reporting on a DAILY basis.

Another alternative would be to monitor individuals so that their whereabouts are known at ALL times.

I'd like to ask you when you think these alternative sentences would be appropriate.

{AGE OF PERSON, VALUE OF COCAINE
AND CRIMINAL RECORD RANDOMIZED}

26a. Suppose a [fill AGE]-year-old is convicted of selling $[fill AMOUNT] worth of cocaine. He has [fill NUMBER] prior convictions.

Do you think he should be sent to prison, required to report to a probation officer ONCE A MONTH, required to report DAILY, or monitored so his whereabouts are known at ALL times?

```
1  sent to prison
2  required to report once a month [go to 27a]
3  required to report to a probation officer daily
   [go to 27a]
4  monitored so his whereabouts are known at all times
   [go to 27a]
8  dk
```

26w. Should he serve some prison time and then be released and monitored at ALL times for the rest of his sentence, OR should he spend all of his sentence in prison?

```
1 released and monitored
2 all in prison
8 dk
```

WEAPON ALSO RANDOMIZED

27a. Suppose a [fill AGE]-year-old is convicted of robbing someone of $100 on the street. He threatened the victim with a [fill TYPE OF WEAPON]. He has [fill NUMBER] prior convictions.

Do you think he should be sent to prison, required to report to a probation officer ONCE A MONTH, required to report DAILY, or monitored so his whereabouts are known at ALL times?

```
1 sent to prison
2 required to report once a month [go to 28a]
3 required to report to a probation officer daily
  [go to 28a]
4 monitored so his whereabouts are known at all times?
  [go to 28a]
8 dk
```

27w. Should he serve some prison time and then be released and monitored at ALL times for the rest of his sentence, OR should he spend all of his sentence in prison?

```
1 released and monitored
2 all in prison
8 dk
```

VALUE OF PROPERTY RANDOMIZED

28a. Suppose a [fill AGE]-year-old is convicted of breaking into a home and taking property worth $[fill VALUE]. He has [fill NUMBER] prior convictions.

Do you think he should be sent to prison, required to report to a probation officer ONCE A MONTH, required to report DAILY, or monitored so his whereabouts are known at ALL times?

```
1 sent to prison
2 required to report once a month [go to 29a]
3 required to report to a probation officer daily
  [go to 29a]
4 monitored so his whereabouts are known at all times
  [go to 29a]
8 dk
```

28w. Should he serve some prison time and then be released and monitored at ALL times for the rest of his sentence, OR should he spend all of his sentence in prison?

```
1 released and monitored
2 all in prison
8 dk
```

SERIOUSNESS OF INJURY VARIES

29a. Suppose a [fill AGE]-year-old is convicted of starting a fight with a stranger. The victim's injuries did [fill REQUIRE/NOT REQUIRE] treatment by a doctor. The offender has [fill NUM-BER] prior convictions.

Do you think he should be sent to prison, required to report to a probation officer ONCE A MONTH, required to report DAILY, or monitored so his whereabouts are known at ALL times?

```
1 sent to prison
2 required to report once a month [go to 30]
3 required to report to a probation officer daily
  [go to 30]
4 monitored so his whereabouts are known at all times
  [go to 30]
8 dk
```

29w. Should he serve some prison time and then be released and monitored at ALL times for the rest of his sentence, OR should he spend all of his sentence in prison?

```
1 released and monitored
2 all in prison
8 dk
```

30. What do you think is the MAIN cause of violent street crime in Maryland?
    ** RECORD ONLY ONE ANSWER

    _____

    _____

31. Other than building more prisons, if you could suggest two things to the governor or the legislature to deal with the crime problem, what would they be?

    1 _____

    2 _____

D1. Finally, I'd like to ask you some background questions.

    Including yourself, how many adults 18 years of age or older live in this household?

    ```
    01-10   record actual number
    11      more than 10
    99      na-ref
    ```

D2. How many children younger than 18 live in this household?

    ```
    0-7     record actual number
    8       more than 7
    99      na-ref
    ```

D3. In what year were you born?

    ```
    00      before 1900
    01-74   19__
    88      dk
    99      na-ref
    ```

D4. What is the last grade or year of school you completed?

```
0        none
1-7      some elementary
8        elementary school
9-11     some high school
12       high school grad
13-15    some college
16       college grad
17       some graduate school
18       graduate or professional degree
99       ref
```

D5a. Are you of Spanish or Hispanic origin or descent?

```
0 no
1 yes
```

D5b. Are you:

```
1 White
2 Black
3 Asian [do not ask if yes to D5a]
4 or some other race: (SPECIFY) _____
9 ref
```

D6. Do you own your home or do you rent it?

```
1 own
2 rent
3 other
9 ref
```

D7. Are you currently:

```
1 married
2 separated
3 divorced
4 widowed
5 or have you never been married
9 ref
```

D8. Are you currently:

```
1 employed full time
2 part-time
3 or not employed at all
9 na-ref
```

D9. All together, how many years have you lived at your present
address?

```
00      less than one year
01-50   record actual number
51      more than 50 years
88      dk
99      na-ref
```

D10. All together, how many different phone NUMBERS does your
household have for nonbusiness use?

```
1-6     record
7       7 or more
8       dk
9       ref
```

D11. If you added together all the yearly incomes, before taxes, of
all the members of your household for last year, 1991, would
the total be more than $30,000?

```
0 no [go to D11a]
1 yes [go to D11c]
9 ref
```

D11a. Was it more than $20,000?

```
0 no [go to D11b]
1 yes [go to D12]
9 ref
```

D11b. Was it more than $12,000?

```
0 no [go to D12]
1 yes [go to D12]
9 ref
```

D11c. Was it more than $50,000?

```
0 no [go to D12]
1 yes [go to D11d]
9 ref
```

D11d. Was it more than $75,000?

```
0 no [go to D12]
1 yes [go to D11e]
9 ref
```

D11e. Was it more than $100,000?

```
0 no
1 yes
9 ref
```

D12.   In what county do you live?

D13.   And, your phone number is [fill in SAMPLE TELEPHONE
       NUMBER]

```
0 no - what number have I reached? (Specify)
1 yes
9 ref
```

Those are all the questions I have. Thank you for your time.

Appendix C
American Association for Public Opinion Research Code of Professional Ethics and Practices

We, the members of the American Association for Public Opinion Research, subscribe to the principles expressed in the following code. Our goals are to support sound and ethical practice in the conduct of public opinion research and in the use of such research for policy and decision-making in the public and private sectors, as well as to improve public understanding of opinion research methods and the proper use of opinion research results.

We pledge ourselves to maintain high standards of scientific competence and integrity in conducting, analyzing, and reporting our work in our relations with survey respondents, with our clients, with those who eventually use the research for decision-making purposes, and with the general public. We further pledge ourselves to reject all tasks or assignments that would require activities inconsistent with the principles of this code.

The Code

I. Principles of Professional Practice in the Conduct of Our Work

    A. We shall exercise due care in developing research designs and survey instruments, and in collecting, processing, and analyzing data, taking all reasonable steps to assure the reliability and validity of results.

        1. We shall recommend and employ only those tools and methods of analysis which, in our professional judgment, are well suited to the research problem at hand.

        2. We shall not select research tools and methods of analysis because of their capacity to yield misleading conclusions.

3. We shall not knowingly make interpretations of research results, nor shall we tacitly permit interpretations, that are inconsistent with the data available.

4. We shall not knowingly imply that interpretations should be accorded greater confidence than the data actually warrant.

B. We shall describe our methods and findings accurately and in appropriate detail in all research reports, adhering to the standards for minimal disclosure specified in Section III.

C. If any of our work becomes the subject of a formal investigation of an alleged violation of this Code, undertaken with the approval of the AAPOR Executive Council, we shall provide additional information on the survey in such detail that a fellow survey practitioner would be able to conduct a professional evaluation of the survey.

II. Principles of Professional Responsibility in Our Dealings with People

A. The Public:

1. If we become aware of the appearance in public of serious distortions of our research, we shall publicly disclose what is required to correct these distortions, including, as appropriate, a statement to the public media, legislative body, regulatory agency, or other appropriate group, in or before which the distorted findings were presented.

B. Clients or Sponsors:

1. When undertaking work for a private client, we shall hold confidential all proprietary information obtained about the client and about the conduct and findings of the research undertaken for the client, except when the dissemination of the information is expressly authorized by the client, or when disclosure becomes necessary under terms of Section I-C or II-A of this Code.[1]

2. We shall be mindful of the limitations of our techniques and capabilities and shall accept only those research as-

---

[1]Author's note: State universities and other public institutions typically can undertake only those studies whose results may be made public after a specified time period.

signments which we can reasonably expect to accomplish within these limitations.

C. The Profession:

1. We recognize our responsibility to contribute to the science of public opinion research and to disseminate as freely as possible the ideas and findings which emerge from our research.

2. We shall not cite our membership in the Association as evidence of professional competence, since the Association does not so certify any persons or organizations.

D. The Respondent:

1. We shall strive to avoid the use of practices or methods that may harm, humiliate, or seriously mislead survey respondents.

2. Unless the respondent waives confidentiality for specified uses, we shall hold as privileged and confidential all information that might identify a respondent with his or her responses. We shall also not disclose or use the names of respondents for non-research purposes unless the respondents grant us permission to do so.

III. Standard for Minimal Disclosure

Good professional practice imposes the obligation upon all public opinion researchers to include, in any report of research results, or to make available when that report is released, certain essential information about how the research was conducted. At a minimum, the following items should be disclosed:

1. Who sponsored the survey, and who conducted it.

2. The exact wording of questions asked, including the text of any preceding instruction or explanation to the interviewer or respondents that might reasonably be expected to affect the response.

3. A definition of the population under study, and a description of the sampling frame used to identify this population.

4. A description of the sample selection procedure, giving a clear indication of the method by which the respondents

were selected by the researcher, or whether the respondents were entirely self-selected.

5. Size of samples and, if applicable, completion rates and information on eligibility criteria and screening procedures.

6. A discussion of the precision of the findings, including, if appropriate, estimates of sampling error, and a description of any weighting or estimating procedures used.

7. Which results are based on parts of the sample, rather than on the total sample.

8. Method, location, and dates of data collection.

March 1986

References

Aday, L. A. (1989). *Designing and Conducting Health Surveys: A Comprehensive Guide*. San Francisco: Jossey-Bass.

Aneshensel, C. S., Frerichs, R. R., Clark, V. A., and Yokopenic, P. A. (1982). "Measuring Depression in the Community: A Comparison of Telephone and Personal Interviews." *Public Opinion Quarterly*, 46:110–121.

Belson, W. A. (1981). *The Design and Understanding of Survey Questions*. Brookfield, VT: Gower.

Biemer, P. P., Groves, R. M., Lyberg, L. E., Mathiowetz, N. A., and Sudman, S. (Eds.). (1991). *Measurement Errors in Surveys*. New York: Wiley.

Binson, D., Murphy, P. A., and Keer, D. (1987, May). "Threatening Questions for the Public in a Survey About AIDS." Paper presented at annual meeting of American Association for Public Opinion Research. Hershey, PA.

Bischoping, K. (1989). "An Evaluation of Interviewer Debriefing in Survey Pretests." In C. Cannell, L. Oksenberg, F. Fowler, G. Kalton, and K. Bischoping, *New Techniques for Pretesting Survey Questions*. (Final Report for Grant HS05616, National Center for Health Services Research). Ann Arbor, MI, University of Michigan, unpublished report.

Blair, J., and Chun, Y. (1992). *Quality of Data from Converted Refusals in Telephone Surveys*. Paper presented at the American Association for Public Opinion Research Conference, St. Petersburg, FL.

Blair, J., Menon, G., and Bickart, B. 1991. "Measurement Effects in Self vs. Proxy Response to Survey Questions: An Information-Processing Perspective." In P. P. Biemer, R. M. Groves, L. E. Lyberg, N. A. Mathiowetz, and S. Sudman (Eds.), *Measurement Errors in Surveys* (pp. 145–166). New York: Wiley.

Bradburn, N. M., and Miles, C. (1979). "Vague Quantifiers." *Public Opinion Quarterly*, 43 (1):92–101.

Bradburn. N. M., Sudman, S., and Associates. (1979). *Improving Interview Method and Questionnaire Design: Response Effects to Threatening Questions in Survey Research*. San Francisco: Jossey-Bass.

Bryant, B. E. (1975). "Respondent Selection in a Time of Changing Household Composition." *Journal of Marketing Research*, 12:129–135.

Campanelli, P. C., Rothgeb, J. M., Esposito, J. L., and Polivka, A. E. (1991). *Methodologies for Evaluating Survey Questions: An Illustration from a CPS CATI/RDD Test.* Paper presented at the annual meeting of the American Association for Public Opinion Research, Phoenix, AZ.

Campbell, B. A. (1981). "Race-of-Interviewer Effects Among Southern Adolescents." *Public Opinion Quarterly* 45:231–244.

Cannell, C. F., Fowler, P. J., and Marquis, K. H. (1968). "The Influence of Interviewer and Respondent Psychological and Behavioral Variables on the Reporting in Household Interviews." *Vital and Health Statistics*, Series 2, No. 26, Washington, DC: U.S. Government Printing Office.

Cannell, C., Oksenberg, L., Fowler, F., Kalton, G., and Bischoping, K. (1989). *New Techniques for Pretesting Survey Questions.* (Final Report for Grant HS05616, National Center for Health Services Research). Ann Arbor, MI, University of Michigan, unpublished report.

Caron, J. (1989). *An Introduction to Psycholinguistics.* Toronto, Canada: University of Toronto Press.

Caron, J. (1992). *An Introduction to Psycholinguistics* (T. Pownall, Trans.). New York: Harvester Wheatsheaf. (Original work published 1989)

CASRO (Council of American Survey Research Organizations). (1982). *Report of the CASRO Completion Rates Task Force.* New York, Audits and Surveys, Inc. Unpublished report.

Cochran, W. G. (1977). *Sampling Techniques* (3rd ed.). New York: Wiley.

Cohen, J. (1988). *Statistical Power Analysis for the Behavioral Sciences* (2nd ed.). Hillsdale, NJ: Lawrence Erlbaum.

Converse, J. M., and Presser, S. (1986). *Survey Questions: Handcrafting the Standardized Questionnaire.* Newbury Park, CA: Sage.

Czaja, R. F. (1987-88). "Asking Sensitive Behavioral Questions in Telephone Interviews." *International Quarterly of Community Health Education* 8:23–31.

Czaja, R. F., Blair, J., and Sebestik, J. P. (1982). "Respondent Selection in a Telephone Survey: A Comparison of Three Techniques." *Journal of Marketing Research* 21:381–385.

Davis, J. A., and Smith, T. W. (1991). *General Social Surveys, 1972–1991: Cumulative Codebook.* Chicago: National Opinion Research Center.

Davis, J. A., and Smith, T. W. (1993). *General Social Surveys, 1972–1993: Cumulative Codebook.* Chicago: National Opinion Research Center.

Demaio, T. J. (1983). "Approaches to Developing Questions." (Statistical Policy Working Paper 10). Washington, DC: Statistical Policy Office, U.S. Office of Management and Budget.

Dillman, D. A. (1978). *Mail and Telephone Surveys: The Total Design Method.* New York: Wiley.

Ericsson, K. A., and Simon, H. A. (1993). *Protocol Analysis: Verbal Reports as Data, Revised Edition.* Cambridge, MA: The MIT Press.

Fleiss, J. L. (1981). *Statistical Methods for Rates and Proportions* (2nd ed.). New York: Wiley.

Fowler, F. J. (1984). *Survey Research Methods*. Newbury Park, CA: Sage.

Fowler, F. J. (1989). "Coding Behavior in Pretests to Identify Unclear Questions." In F. J. Fowler (Ed.), *Conference Proceedings, Health Survey Research Methods* (pp. 9–12). Washington, DC: National Center for Health Services Research.

Fowler, F. J., and Mangione, T. W. (1990). *Standardized Survey Interviewing*. Newbury Park, CA: Sage.

Frey, J. H. (1989). *Survey Research by Telephone*. Newbury Park, CA: Sage.

Groves, R. M. (1987). "Research on Survey Data Quality." *Public Opinion Quarterly, 51*: 5156–5172.

Groves, R. M. (1989). *Survey Errors and Survey Costs*. New York: Wiley.

Groves, R. M., Biemer, P. P., Lyberg,L. E., Massey, J. T., Nicholls, II, W. L.,and Waksberg, J. (Eds.). (1988). *Telephone Survey Methodology*. New York: Wiley.

Groves, R. M., Cialdini, R. B., and Couper, M. P. (1992). "Survey Participation." *Public Opinion Quarterly* (Winter): 475–495.

Groves, R. M., and Kahn, R. L. (1979). *Surveys by Telephone: A National Comparison with Personal Interviews*. Orlando, FL: Academic Press.

Guensel, P. J., Berckmans, T. R., and Cannell, C. F. (1983). *General Interviewing Techniques*. Ann Arbor, MI: Survey Research Center.

Hatchett, S., and Schuman, H. (1975–76). "White Respondents and Race-of-Interviewer Effects." *Public Opinion Quarterly, 39*:523–528.

Hidiroglou, M. A., Drew, J. D., and Gray, G. B. (1993). "A Framework for Measuring and Reducing Nonresponse in Surveys." *Survey Methodology, 19* (1):81–94.

Hochstim, J. R. (1967). "A Critical Comparison of Three Strategies of Collecting Data from Households." *Journal of the American Statistical Association, 62*:976–989.

Jabine, T. B., Straf, M. L., Tanur, J. M., and Tourangeau, R. (Eds.). (1984). *Cognitive Aspects of Survey Methodology: Building a Bridge Between Disciplines: Report of the Advanced Research Seminar on Cognitive Aspects of Survey Methodology*. Washington, DC: National Academy Press.

Kalton, G. (1981). *Compensating for Missing Survey Data*. (Report for Department of Health and Human Services Contract HEW-100-79-0127, Survey Research Center, Institute for Social Research). Ann Arbor, MI: The University of Michigan.

Kalton, G. (1983). *Introduction to Survey Sampling*. Newbury Park, CA: Sage.

Kanninen, B. J., Chapman, D. J., and Hanemann, W. M. (1992). "Survey Data Collection: Detecting and Correcting for Biases in Responses to Mail and Telephone Surveys." In *Conference Proceedings, Census Bureau 1992 Annual Research Conference* (pp. 507–522). Arlington, VA: U.S. Department of Commerce.

Kasprzyk, D., Duncan, G., Kalton, G., and Singh, M. P. (Eds.). (1989). *Panel Surveys*. New York: Wiley.

Kish, L. (1965). *Survey Sampling*. New York: Wiley.

Kish, L. (1987). *Statistical Design for Research*. New York: Wiley.

Lessler, J. T., and Kalsbeek, W. D. (1992). *Nonsampling Error in Surveys*. New York: Wiley.

Locander, W., Sudman, S., and Bradburn, N. M. (1976) "An Investigation of Interview Method, Threat, and Response Distortion." *Journal of the American Statistical Association, 71*:269–75.

Marsden, P. V. (Ed.). (1994). *Sociological Methodology* (Vol. 24). Cambridge, MA: Blackwell.

Moser, C. A., and Kalton, G. (1972). *Survey Methods in Social Investigation* (2nd ed.). New York: Basic Books.

Neyman, J. (1934). "On the Two Different Aspects of the Representative Method: The Method of Stratified Sampling and the Method of Purposive Selection." *Journal of the Royal Statistical Society, 97*:558–606.

Oldendick, R. W., Bishop, G. F., Sorenson, S. B., and Tuchfarber, A. J. (1988). "A Comparison of the Kish and Last-Birthday Methods of Respondent Selection in Telephone Surveys." *Journal of Official Statistics, 4* (4): 307–318.

Oldendick, R. W., Link, M. W. (1994). "The Answering Machine Generation: Who Are They and What Problem Do They Pose for Survey Research?" *Public Opinion Quarterly, 58* (2):264–273.

O'Rourke, D., and Blair, J. (1983). "Improving Random Respondent Selection in Telephone Surveys." *Journal of Marketing Research, 20*:428–432.

Payne, S. L. (1951). *The Art of Asking Questions*. Princeton, NJ: Princeton University Press.

Presser, S., and Blair, J. (1994). "Survey Pretesting: Do Different Methods Produce Different Results?" *Sociological Methodology, 24*: 73–104.

Royston, P. N. (1989). "Using Intensive Interviews to Evaluate Questions." In F. J. Fowler (Ed.), *Conference Proceedings, Health Survey Research Methods* (pp. 3–8). Washington, DC: National Center for Health Services Research.

Salmon, C. T., and Nichols, J. S. (1983). "The Next-Birthday Method of Respondent Selection." *Public Opinion Quarterly, 47*:270–276.

Sarndal, C.-E., Swensson, B., and Wretman, J. (1992). *Model-Assisted Survey Sampling*. New York: Springer-Verlag.

Schuman, H., and Presser, S. (1981). *Questions and Answers in Attitude Surveys: Experiments on Question Form, Wording, and Context*. Orlando, FL: Academic Press.

Sudman, S. (1967). *Reducing the Cost of Surveys*. Chicago: Aldine.

Sudman, S. (1976). *Applied Sampling*. New York: Academic Press.

Sudman, S., and Bradburn, N. M. (1982). *Asking Questions: A Practical Guide to Questionnaire Design*. San Francisco: Jossey-Bass.

Survey Sampling, Inc. (1994). *Unlisted Rates of the Top 100 MSAs for 1993*. Fairfield, CT: Survey Sampling.

Tanur, J. M. (1992). *Questions about Questions: Inquiries into the Cognitive Bases of Surveys*. New York: Russell Sage Foundation.

Thornberry, Jr., O. T., and Massey, J. T. (1988). "Trends in United States Telephone Coverage Across Time and Subgroups." In R. M. Groves, P. P. Biemer, L. E. Lyberg, J. T. Massey, W. L. Nicholls, II, and J. Waksberg (Eds.), *Telephone Survey Methodology* (pp. 25–49). New York: Wiley.

Tourangeau, R., and Rasinski, K. A. (1988). "Cognitive Processes Underlying Context Effects in Attitude Measurement." *Psychological Bulletin,* 103:299–314.

Tripplet, T. (1994, May). "What Is Gained from Additional Call Attempts and Refusal Conversion and What Are the Cost Implications?" Paper presented at the International Field Directors and Field Technicians Conference, Boston.

Troldahl, V. C., and Carter, Jr., R. E. (1964). "Random Selection of Respondents within Households in Phone Surveys." *Journal of Marketing Research, 1* (2):71–76.

Turner, C. F., and Martin E. (Eds.). (1984). *Surveying Subjective Phenomena* (Vol 1). New York: Russell Sage Foundation.

U.S. Bureau of the Census. (1989). *Bicentennial Census Facts: 1990 Decennial Census.* Washington, DC: U.S. Government Printing Office.

U.S. Bureau of the Census. (1992) *1990 Census of Population: General Population Characteristics—North Carolina.* Washington, DC: U.S. Government Printing Office. (1990 CP-1-35).

U.S. Bureau of the Census. (1993a). *1990 Census of Housing: Detailed Housing Characteristics—North Carolina.* Washington, DC: U.S. Government Printing Office. (1990 CH-2-35).

U.S. Bureau of the Census. (1993b). *1990 Census of Population and Housing: Population and Housing Unit Counts—North Carolina.* Washington, DC: U.S. Government Printing Office. (1990 CPH-2-35).

U.S. Bureau of the Census. (1993c). *1990 Census of Population and Housing: Population and Housing Unit Counts—United States.* Washington, DC: U.S. Government Printing Office. (1990 CPH-2-1).

Waksberg, J. (1978). "Sampling Methods for Random Digit Dialing." *Journal of the American Statistical Association, 73* (361):40–46.

Wiseman, F. (1972). "Methodological Bias in Public Opinion Surveys." *Public Opinion Quarterly, 36* (1):105–108.

Glossary/Index

mates; often called total survey error, 7, 171-174

Survey rates, 24-25
- completion rate, 189
- cooperation rate, 34, 45, 136, 153, 167-168
- ineligible, 121-122, 125, 143, 148, 150-160
- noncontact, 24, 25, 32, 36, 42, 150-151, 189
- refusal, 24, 25, 32, 36, 42, 150-151, 164, 191
- response, 23-24, 32, 35, 36, 39, 41-42, 45, 49, 118, 150-151, 153, 156-157, 159, 182-185, 198-199, 226-229

T

Think aloud a one-on-one session between interviewer and respondent in which the respondent is asked to recount his or her thoughts when responding to survey questions; a questionnaire development practice, 22, 27-28, 100. *See also* Cognitive interview

U

Undeclared pretest a pretest in which respondents do not know they are participating in a survey development procedure, 99

Undercoverage the noninclusion in a sampling frame of some members of a defined population; can also result from the data collection method or errors in the interview procedures, 176, 223-224

Underreporting respondents stating they have less of something than they actually have or that they have done some activity or behavior less often than they actually have, 77

U.S. Bureau of the Census, 38, 108, 113, 115, 131, 135-136, 156

V

Validity, 20, 30, 94, 164, 172

Variance reflects the degree of spread or variation in a sample or population; the differences manifested in repeated trials of a procedure, 126-133, 142-144, 117, 161, 165, 167, 169, 172

Verification of interviews, 12, 206

W

Weighting procedure to correct for unequal probabilities of selection of sample members, unequal survey completion rates by demographic subgroups, or other factors related to producing unbiased estimates, 48, 119, 124, 125, 162, 166, 168, 217-219, 228